THE CHANGING ERA OF E-BANKING

THE CHANGING ERA OF E-BANKING

Dr. A. Vijayakumar
Reader in Commerce
Erode Arts College
Erode, TamilNadu
Email: sudvijay@sancharnet.in

MANGLAM

MANGLAM PUBLICATIONS
DELHI-110053 (INDIA)

Published by :
MANGLAM PUBLICATIONS
L-21/1, Street No. 5, Shivaji Marg, Near Kali Mandir,
J.P. Nagar, Kartar Nagar, West Ghonda, Delhi-110053
Phone : 011-22945677, (M.) 9968367559, 9868572512
E-mail: manglam.books2007@rediffmail.com
manglam.publications2007@rediffmail.com

The Changing Era of E-Banking

First Edition 2010

ISBN 978-93-80013-31-2

PRINTED IN INDIA

Published by Ravindra Kumar Yadav for Manglam Publications, Delhi-110053 Laser Typeset by Amandeep Singh Bansal, (Graphic Era), Delhi- 92, Printed at Sachin Printers, Moujpur Delhi- 53

Preface

For the Indian banking system, changes have been quite constant for the last two decades to achieve efficiency and customer friendliness amidst rising competition. Today, banks no longer restrict themselves to traditional banking activities, but are explore newer avenues to increase business and capture new markets. Either as a part of reform process, which, in a larger context is linked to the ongoing economic reforms or in an efforts to adopt the best international banking practices, the banking industry has been radical transformation in the areas of business portfolio restructuring, hiring strategies, domestic and overseas expansion plans, treasury portfolios and creation of a technological platform. With a strong regulatory regime pushed forward by the RBI, the new initiatives include strengthening the prudential norms in line with international best practices, improving credit delivery, planning sophisticated products, strengthening corporate governance practices and promoting financial inclusion, strengthening the urban co-operative banking sector while improving overall customer service.

The use of technology combined with some other initiatives helped to improve the customer services by banks, branch expansion, installation and use of ATMs also helped banks expand their reach. The banking system has made efforts to be more customer-friendly by facilitating doorstep banking. With the entry of new generation private sectors banks and foreign banks into the country, existing banks have introduced services such as phone banking, mobile banking and net banking. An interesting development was the setting up of credit information bureaus to obtain and share data on borrowers in a systematic manner for sound credit decisions by the banks. A big change in the Indian banking space in the last decade is that banking services in the country have become accessible to the customers. Alternate banking channels have gained immense popularity in the last 10 years.

This book is based on thought provoking empirical research articles, relevant to the field, that help the reader to understand the subject better and to strengthen the fundamentals of the subject. I am confident of the view point that the series of students pursuing research in the field would acquire balanced knowledge about the subject and it is surely going to stand in a good stead for those aiming for developing command over the latest developments in the field and would help them to explore the research areas beyond the given contents of the book. This book has been designed to meet the requirements of academicians, students and research scholars in their pursuit in the area of banking and the like.

I ventured to bring this publication containing 25 research papers focusing on trends and prospects of Indian Banking penned with an in-depth analysis, by academics and research scholars and duly edited by me, as a useful compendium on the Indian Banking for the benefit of all. In this book an attempt has been made to highlight the challenges and responses that have been taken place in the Indian banking system during post - liberalization. The research papers prepared by the ardent research scholars and academics drawn from different parts of the country have been classified in such a manner to facilitate a proper and fuller understanding of the fast changing role of Indian banking in developing the national economy.

This is truly a product of collaborative efforts. I wish to express my sincere gratitude to all the contributors who responded generously to my request, without their response this volume would not have taken in its present shape. The co-operation and support of all the contributors has been a great source of encouragement to this academic venture. It is hoped that volume would be welcomed by the academic community and found useful by researchers, policy makers and institution builders concerned with working and performance of Indian Banking.

I also extend my profound thanks to Mr. D.P. Yadav Director of Manglam Publications, New Delhi, for giving shape to my idea by publishing this book in a record time. I am solely responsible for any omission and inconsistencies in the book and look forward for constructive suggestions from readers. This is only a humble beginning of a great event contemplated for a wider understanding of the emerging trends and the changing role of Indian banking, thus, benefiting the community to a greater extent.

A. Vijaya Kumar

List of Contributors

1. **R.Vijayalakshmi** Lecturer-SG, Department of Commerce, PSGR Krishnammal College for women, Coimbatore.
   Pa. Keerthi Lecturer, Department of B.Com (CA), PSGR Krishnammal College for women, Coimbatore
2. **S. Sivasankaran** Senior lecturer in Commerce, S. T. Hindu College, Nagercoil.
   Dr. M. Nazer, Reader & Research Adviser in Commerce, Khadir Mohideen College, Adirampattinam.
3. **V. Sudhakar,** Professor and Head, Department of Commerce, Sri Kaliswari College, Sivakasi
4. **Dr.A.Selvaraj,** Reader in Commerce, Gobi Arts and Science College, Gobi.
   K.R.Vijaysanthi, Project Associate, Department of Commerce, Gobi Arts and Science College, Gobi.
5. **R.Maniganda durai,** Lecturer in Commerce, Maharaja Arts & Science College, Nelambur.
6. **P. Pirakatheeswari,** Lecturer in Commerce, Sri Sarada College for Women (Autonomous), Salem.
7. **P. Janaki,** Lecturer in Commerce, Vellalar College for Women, Thindal, Erode.

8. **Dr.A.Jayakumar**, Department of Commerce, Periyar University, Salem
N.Kanimozhi, Project Fellowship, Periyar University, Salem.

9. **Dr. Ayub Khan Dawood,** Reader in Commerce, Department of Commerce, Quaide Milleth College, Chennai.
Prof. Devamaidhan, Dept of Management Studies, University of Madras

10. **Dr.N.Piramela**, HOD of Commerce, Dhanalakshmi Srinivasan College of Arts and Science for Women, Perambalur.

11. **Dr.V.Murugan,** Dept of Corporate Secretaryship, Maharaja College for Women, Perundurai

12. **B. SeethaDevi**, HOD of commerce, Bharathiyar Arts & Science Collage for Women, Deviyakurchi, Attur, Salem.

13. **K. Nagarajan,** Lecturer in Commerce, Department of Commerce, K.S.R. College of Arts and Science, Tiruchengode.
RST.Kiruthika, Lecturer in Commerce, Department of Commerce, A.V.S College of Arts and Science, Ramalingapuram, Salem.

14. **Dr.N.Shaik Mohamed,** Reader in Commerce, Jamal Mohamed College, Trichy.
Kavitha Shanmugam, Senior Lecturer, MBA Department, SRM University, Chennai.
Dr.Jamaludeen, Reader in Commerce, Urmu Dhanalakshmi College, Trichy.

15. **R.P.Ramesh,** Senior Lecturer in Commerce, Dept. of Commerce, PRIST University, Thanjavur.
T. Anuja, Lecturer in Commerce, Dept. of commerce, PRIST University, Thanjavur.
K.Devanadhen, Lecturer in Commerce, Directorate of Distance Education, Annamalai University, Annamalai Nagar.

16. **P.Sridevi,** Lecturer of Commerce, Dhanalakshmi Srinivasan College of Arts & Science for Women, Perambalur.

R.Manjula, Lecturer of Commerce, Dhanalakshmi Srinivasan College of Arts & Science for Women, Perambalur.

17. **K.Murali Selvam,** Lecturer in Commerce, Selvamm Arts & Science College, Namakkal
18. **Dr.Palaniappan,** Head of the Department of Economics, Erode Arts College (Autonomous), Erode.
19. **V.Gunasekaran,** Lecturer in Dept of Commerce, The New College, Chennai.
20. **C.Sangeetha,** Lecturers, Department of Commerce with Computer Applications, Vellalar College For Women, Erode.

    P.Latha, Lecturers, Department of Commerce with Computer Applications, Vellalar College For Women, Erode.
21. **M. Mahalakshmi** , Lecturer, Department of commerce, KSR College of Arts and Science, Thiruchengode.
22. **G. Thamizh Chelvan,** Lecturer in Commerce, Dr. G.R. Damodaran College of Science, Coimbatore.
23. **Dr.L.Lakshmi**, Reader in Commerce, Sri Sarada College for Women (Autonomous) Salem.
24. **S.Palaniammal,** Lecturer in Commerce, Anbu Arts and Science College, Komarapalayam,
25. **M.N.Sivabalan,** H.O.D of Commerce, Kurinji College of Arts and Science, Trichy.

    B.Narayanan, Lecturer in Commerce, Kurinji College of Arts and Science, Trichy.
26. **Dr. T. Duraipandi**, Reader in Commerce, Kongu Arts and Science College, Erode

Contents

Contents

1

An Empirical Study on the Service Quality of ICICI Prudential

*Mrs. R.Vijayalakshmi & Miss. Pa. Keerthi

Insurance is a risk transfer mechanism where a known cost (a premium) is exchanged for an unknown cost (a loss) for a specified period. It is one of the important instruments designed to deal with risk through sharing. The main function of insurance is to provide financial cover against the possible chances of generating losses. It eliminates worries and miseries of losses at destruction of property and death. Further, it provides capital to the national economy by investing its accumulated funds in productive heads. Indeed, all the industries, business, and individuals are considerately benefited by the services of the insurance organisations. In line with the global trend of deregulation and the economic reforms in India and based on the recommendations of

* Lecturer-SG, Department of Commerce, PSGR Krishnammal College for Women, Coimbatore.

* Lecturer, Department of B.Com (CA), PSGR Krishnammal College for Women, Coimbatore

Malhotra Committee, the government of India passed the Insurance Regulatory and Development Authority Act in 1999. This Act paved the way for the birth of the Insurance Regulatory and Development Authority (IRDA) to open up the Indian insurance sector for private participation with foreign equity investment up to 26% of the total paid up capital. Currently, the industry holds 19 private players offering new, differentiated products and services at the customers reach.

Statement of the Problem

In today's liberalized environment, insurance companies operate in a market place that is extremely competitive. New entrants focus on improving customer service and increase the coverage of the insurance industry. The degree of competition among the private and public insurance companies has been increasing in the past years. The areas of challenges for the private insurance companies are increasing customer expectations, new products, greater mobility, faster development of new services, increasing customer relationship, offering quality services to the customers in the competitive environment and up gradation of technology to cope up with ever changing environment for meeting perceived satisfaction of the customers. Among the private insurers ICICI prudential stands first with respect to market share and premium collection and hence this survey is oriented to quantify the service quality of ICICI prudential.

ICICI Prudential

ICICI Prudential Life Insurance Company is a joint venture between ICICI Bank, a premier financial powerhouse and Prudential plc, a leading international financial services group headquartered in United Kingdom. It has sustained the No.1 position for the past seven years with a premium collection of Rs. 5162.13 cr. for the year 2006-2007 with the trust of 7 million policyholders. It is also the only private life insurer in India to receive a National Insurer Financial Strength rating of AAA (Ind) from Fitch ratings. The AAA (Ind) rating is the highest rating, and is a clear assurance of ICICI Prudential's ability to meet its obligations to customers at the time of maturity or claims and proving in providing quality service to its customers.

Objectives of the Study

- To measure the significant difference between the expectations and perceptions towards various aspects of service quality in ICICI prudential.
- To offer suggestions on the basis of the study.

Methodology

The study is restricted to Coimbatore city. Random sampling technique was administered in the study.100 interview schedules were distributed to the policyholders of ICICI prudential, of which only 96 were usable. The questionnaire was constructed based on the SERVQUAL technique designed by Parasuraman, et.al, to record various factors relating to service quality. It consists of 21 questions relating to expectations and perceptions of the customers. The responses are measured on a seven point Likert scale. With one indicating complete disagreement and seven indicating complete agreement. The collected data was analysed using SPSS software package. The following statistical tools were applied in tune with the objectives: Percentage analysis and Gap Analysis (Z Test). All tests were carried out at 5% level of significance.

Results of the Study

Demographic profile of the respondents

Majority of the respondents are male 68.7%. Of the total respondents 72.9% fall under the category of less than 30yrs of age. 67%of the respondents are unmarried.64 % of them are post graduates and 62.5% of the respondents' monthly income ranges between Rs.10,000 – Rs.20,000. 63% of the respondents are employed in various private organisations.

Results of Percentage Analysis

Percentage analysis was calculated for all the variables in a seven point scale on which 7 indicates complete agreeability and 1 indicates complete disagreeability. In general the expectations of the policyholders on the life insurance companies were very high on all the factors relating to services delivery. Perceptions are those services that are experienced by the policy holders. The perception levels are high on most of the aspects that are considered to determine the quality in services offered by ICICI prudential. With respect to modern / updated equipments it has scored 71.9%, physical facilities 81%, 65.6% in appealing pamphlets and statements, 60% in safe transactions and 50% in the knowledge of the employees to answer the queries of the policyholders.

Gap Analysis

The Gap Analysis is a technique used to identify the Gap - the difference between the level of perception and level of expectation on the various issues relating to the services, problems, infrastructure, staff / employees of the insurance companies. For this analysis Z test is employed to find if the Gap obtained is significant or not.

Hypothesis

There is no significant difference in the mean scores between the level of perception and the level of expectation (GAP) on the various factors considered in ICICI prudential.

Results: Table1

As per the results of gap analysis, It is found from the table that the hypothesis is accepted (not significant) in most the cases except in appealing physical facilities, appearance of the employees, the employees willingness to help customers, the knowledge of the employees to answer and individual attention given to the customers.

Suggestions

Though ICICI prudential stands number one in market share and premium collection, it can customize its service delivery operations so that it can hold strong trust in the minds of its policy holders. Frequent orientations can be conducted to its employees and agents to excel in service delivery. As the awareness of insurance products is less it can focus on creating life insurance awareness among the various strata of the country. ICICI prudential can focus on rural masses and customize products as per their needs so that it can extent its market share.

Conclusion

The study revealed that the insurance arena is more competitive with every player pacing to grab their share.. As insurance is a service industry, the main focus is on the effective and efficient delivery of services to its policy holders. Delivering excellent service is the mantra of every player to sustain in this liberalized environment so as to make their customers loyal and increase new customers. It's the trust and confidence of the policy holders are the two wheels on which the insurance industry runs and hence ICICI prudential can focus on these aspects by offering quality service to its policy holders.

Reference

Books Reference

1. Anand Ganguly, "Insurance Management", 2002, New age International (p) Limited, Publishers, New Delhi.
2. Arthur Williams .C, Michael L.Smith and Peter C. Young, "Risk Management and Insurance", Eight Edition, 1998, Irwin MCgraw – Hill, Singapore.

3. Christopher lovelock, Jochen Wirtz and Jayanta Chatterjee, "Services Marketing People, Technology, Strategy", 2006, Pearson Education, New Delhi.
4. Jha S.M, "Services Marketing", Sixth revised Edition, 2007, Himalya Publishing House, Mumbai.
5. Rajendra Nargundkar, "Services Marketing Text and cases", Second Edition, 2006, TaTa MCgraw – Hill Publishing Company Limited, New Delhi.
6. Ravi Shanker, "Services Marketing the Indian Perspective" 2002, Excel Book , New Delhi.

Journal Reference

1. Appi Reddy. V and Narasimha murthy.G, "Customer services in LIC – A case study", Indian Journal of Marketing, Feb-march 1996, Vol.XXV, No.2-3, pp. 18-22.
2. Shainesh. G and Mukul Mathur, "Service Quality Measurement: the Case of Railway Freight Services", Vikalpa, July- Sep2000, Vol.25, No.3, pp.15-22.
3. Ajay K.Raja and Mukesh Dhunna, "Liberalisation of Insurance sector: Social implications, Indian Management Studies Journal, 2002, Vol.6, No.1, pp. 109-117.
4. Arunajatesan.S, "Insurance in India and its future prospects", Management Matters, Sep 2002, pp. 53-56.
5. Ashok Thampy and Sitharaman.S, "Life insurance potential in India: A Economic Approach", VISION: The Journal of Business Perspective, July – Dec 2002, pp.11-18.
6. Parasuraman .A, Valarie A.Zeithaml, Leonard LBerry, "A conceptual model of service quality and its implications for future research", Journal of Marketing, fall 1985, Vol.49, pp.41-50.
7. Parasuraman .A, Valarie A.Zeithaml, Leonard LBerry, "SERVQUAL: A multiple – item scale for measuring consumer perceptions of service quality", Journal of Retailing, spring 1988, Vol.64, No.1, pp.12-36.

Table: 1 *Results of Gap Analysis – ICICI prudential*

Factors	Gap	t-values	p-values	S/NS
ICICI has up-to-date equipments	0.31	1.717	0.096	NS
ICICI physical facilities are visually appealing.	0.5	2.43	0.021	S
ICICI's employees appear professionally dressed.	0.81	2.919	0.006	S
ICICI's materials associated with the service (such as pamphlets and statements) are visually appealing.	0.34	1.938	0.062	NS
When ICICI promises to do something by a certain time, it does so.	-0.28	-1.555	0.130	NS
When you have problems, ICICI shows a sincere interest in solving it.	-0.13	-0.892	0.379	NS
ICICI gets things right the first time.	-0.25	-1.277	0.211	NS
ICICI provides its services at the time it promise to do so	-9.38E-02	-0.475	0.638	NS
The employees in ICICI tell you exactly when services will be performed.	0.13	0.626	0.536	NS
Employees in ICICI give you prompt service.	0.13	0.502	0.619	NS
Employees of ICICI are always willing to help you	-0.31	-2.154	0.039	S
Employees of ICICI are never be too busy to respond to your requests.	0.19	1.063	0.296	NS

Factors	Gap	t-values	p-values	S/NS
The behaviour of employees in ICICI instills confidence in you.	0.16	0.818	0.420	NS
You feel safe in your transactions with ICICI.	0.19	1.099	0.280	NS
Employees in ICICI are consistently courteous you.	-3.13E-02	-0.144	0.887	NS
Employees in ICICI have the knowledge to answer your questions.	-0.38	-2.104	0.044	S
ICICI gives you individual attention.	-0.44	-2.301	0.028	S
ICICI has operating hours convenient to all its customers	-3.13E-02	-0.162	0.872	NS
ICICI has employees who give you personal attention.	-0.13	-0.643	0.525	NS
ICICI has your best interests at heart	-0.22	-1.097	0.281	NS
The employees of ICICI understand your specific needs.	-0.41	-2.523	0.017	S
S : p-value ≤ 0.5; NS : p-value ≥ 0.5	S – Significant, NS – Not Significant			

2

Banking in the Cyber World: Some Challenges and Ways to Overcome

*S. Sivasankaran and Dr. M. Nazer

This paper attempts to highlight some of the challenges of cyber bank customers of modern age and also recommendations to overcome it. The present cyber banking system comes out with umpteen numbers of opportunities and one may not escape from hidden evils also, thanks to sophisticated technology being used very widely. Also the contributors of this paper try to out bring some information to investor in general, what are new products and services in modern competitive bourse market and information to customer.

IDENTITY THEFT

FRAUDSTERS commit identity theft by stealing your personal information. Often this is done by picking up

* Senior lecturer in Commerce, S. T. Hindu College, Nagercoil.

* Reader in Commerce, Khadir Mohideen College, Adirampattinam.

documents that you have carelessly thrown away, or by making contact with you and pretending to be from a legitimate organization. Identity theft can result in frauds affecting your personal financial standing. They also cost financial organizations huge losses every year. If your identity is stolen, you may have difficulty getting loans, credit cards, personal loans and home loans until the matter is sorted out.

How do you help yourself from being a victim?

1. Keep your personal information secure
   - Your identity and personal information are valuable assets. Keep them secure.
   - Be-extra careful with packets received in post/ courier. Other people should not have access to them.
   - If you change your residence, inform your bank, card issuer and all other organizations that you deal with immediately.
2. Keep all your plastic cards safe
   - If your debit/credit cards are lost or stolen, cancel them immediately. Keep a note of the emergency numbers you should call.
   - When giving your card details or personal information over the phone, Internet or in a shop, make sure other people cannot hear or see your personal information.
   - Never carry documents or plastic cards unnecessarily. When not in use keep them in a safe place.
3. Keep your documents safe
   - Keep your personal documents in a safe place, preferably in a lockable drawer or cabinet at home. Consider storing valuable documents such as property documents, fixed deposit receipts, will, etc. with your bank in a locker.
   - If your passport or driving license has been lost or stolen contact the issuing organization immediately.

- Don't throw away entire bills, receipts, credit or debit card slips, bank statements or even unwanted post in your name. Tear them into small pieces, preferably by using a shredder.
- Check statements as soon as they arrive. If any unfamiliar transactions are listed, contact the company concerned immediately.

4. Keep your passwords and PINs safe
   - Never give personal or account details to anyone who contacts you unexpectedly. Be suspicious even if they claim to be from your bank or the police. Ask for their phone number, check it is genuine and if so, call them back. Be aware that a bank will never ask for your PIN or password. Keep them secure.
   - Don't use the same password for more than one account and never use banking passwords for any other websites. Using different passwords increases security and makes it less likely that someone could access any other accounts.
   - If you cannot commit them to memory and have to write them down, keep your passwords safe and never record or store them in a manner which leaves them open to theft, such as in your purse or wallet.
   - If you receive a suspicious e-mail purporting to be from a bona fide institution which requests personal details, please do not part with the information.

BEWARE! YOU COULD BECOME A "MONEY MULE"

WHAT is a "Money Mule"?

Just as a mule carries the burden, and also gets whipped in the bargain, fraudster in the globalized world have started appointing "Money Mules". They are the unfortunate and often unaware victims, invariably job-seekers and easy money makers. They are lured by fraudsters posing as coming from companies with websites, to gain legitimacy in the eyes of the victims. Typically in such operations, a job is offered – that of an 'Agent' in the garb of Financial Manager, Admin manager, etc. Tempting as it is, the victims fall prey and get appointed to the job. Then they are told to open an account, where the fictitious company (the fraudster, now the 'employer' of the agent) would 'phish' funds and dump into the agent's account. The agents are sure to be caught sooner or later as the duped victims of 'phishing' alert banks, and law & order machinery, banks and the regulators start trailing the activities. That's when the whipping starts: the agents' accounts are not only frozen but the agents are charged with the serious financial crime of money laundering. They could end up in jail for many, many year.

Mode of appointment as a Money Mule:

Money Mules are recruited by a variety of methods, including spam e-mails, adverts on genuine recruitment web sites, approaching people who have their CVs available online, instant messaging and adverts in newspapers.

How it works?

- ❑ Fraudster contact prospective victims with "job vacancy" as a financial manager and suggest that no special knowledge is required.
- ❑ The fraudsters convince the victims to come and work for their fake "company". Some fraudsters even ask mules to sign official-looking contracts of employment.
- ❑ Once recruited, money mules will receive funds into their accounts. These funds would have been siphoned-off by the fraudsters from gullible victims through phishing.
- ❑ Mules are then asked to transfer these funds to the accounts indicated by the fraudsters.

How to avoid becoming a Money Mule?

- ❑ Convince yourself that easy money in today's cut-throat competitive world is impossible.
- ❑ If the job on offer is to receive and transfer funds, be alerted that you have been actually appointed as Money Mule.

- Verify the company's credentials before accepting a job offer.
- If you know that you have fallen a victim, at the earlier opportunity, share the details with the right law enforcement agency. This would help authorities take a lenient view of your "involvement" in the crime. Else, when caught, you would be charged under the Prevention of Money Laundering Act.

If you see an opportunity to make some easy money and offer seems too good to be true, then it probably is.

VISHING

"VISHING" is a combination of "Voice" and "Phishing" that uses Voice over Internet Protocol (VOIP) technology where fraudsters feigning to represent real companies such as banks attempt to trick unsuspecting customers into providing their personal and financial details over the phone.

Tips to protect your self from wishing

- Never call a telephone number provided in a phone call or an e-mail regarding possible security issues with any of your credit card or bank accounts.
- Only the phone number on the reverse of your credit card or on your bank statement should be called to report such an attempt.
- If anyone purporting to be a credit card provider calls and asks for the three-digit CVV of your credit card, hang up immediately, call the phone number on the reverse of your credit card and report the attempt.

SMISHING: ANOTHER FORM OF PHISHING

SMISHING is similar to Phishing. In Phishing, fraudsters use the cyber medium to fish out sensitive information from you. In Smishing, they use your mobile phones to do that, by sending an SMS. Though the medium is different, the aim remains the same - to collect sensitive information from you. This is how it happens:-

- The fraudster sends an SMS to you with a message reading "you will be charged amount "X" per day if you do not cancel the order at "www.xyz.com".
- If you are a gullible and ignorant customer, you would panic and log on to the site.
- The site would then download/tempt you to download a software which is in fact a SPYWARE / MALWARE / TROJAN.
- Once this software is downloaded on your computer then all the critical personal information –such as your Banking user ID, Passwords, Debit/Credit Card numbers, PIN - that you enter can be captured by the fraudster and misused.

SAFEGUARDS AGAINST SMISHING

- Never respond to unsolicited SMS, especially if it comes from the people or companies that you do not know or you have not contacted for any service.
- Keep a record of service that you sign up for, if you receive a Smishing message for a service you don't think you signed up for you probably didn't. Disregard the message.
- When it doubts does not respond to the message.
- If you happen to download by mistake, then don't use the banking site till the time you have not deleted such downloads from your computer.
- If you receive multiple messages, bring it to the attention of your Bank at once and help them to uncover the fraud.

SKIMMING

All plastic cards viz. ATM, debit and credit cards have on their reverse a prominent black stripe, about one cm wide, running across the length of the card. This is the magnetic stripe, which store the essential information of the card holder.

Skimming is unauthorized copying of information from the magnetic stripe of a credit/debit / ATM card. A device called skimmer is employed to copy the information contained in the magnetic stripe. The copied information is then used by the fraudsters to clone the card(s) or is traded for similar cloning. The fraudster can then create a card(s) with the same characteristics and freely use it / them for all purposes that you can do –till identified or caught.

Where can it happen?

Generally at petrol stations, restaurants, hotels, and such outlets where the swipe terminal is not in your sight.

Warning signs:

- ❑ A shop assistant takes your card out of your sight in order to process your transaction.
- ❑ You are asked to swipe your card through more than one machine.
- ❑ You notice something suspicious about the card slot on an ATM (e.g. an attached device).
- ❑ You notice any unusual or unauthorized transaction in your account.

How to protect yourself from Skimming?

- ❑ If you are using an ATM, take the time to check that there is no gadget attached to the machine.
- ❑ If the shop assistant appears to be taking your card out of the sight, and if you suspect something, offer to go with that person or change your mode of payment to cash, if possible.
- ❑ If the shop assistant wants to swipe your card on the second machine, you should ask for your card back immediately.
- ❑ If you notice such incidents, immediately contact your card issuing authority.
- ❑ Many card issuers provide the transaction alert service via SMS on your mobile phone. Do register for it. You will be alerted just in case your card is misused after skimming despite all precautions.

419 ADVANCE FEE FRAUD SCAMS

419 Advance Fee Fraud Scams are those where you receive an e-mail informing you of some windfall gain and asking you to deposit service charges in a certain bank account in order to claim the money. Beware and remember to recognize them. Here are some of them:

- ❑ Lottery scam
- ❑ Counterfeit postal draft scam
- ❑ Over-invoiced contract scam
- ❑ eBay check (over) payment and refund scam
- ❑ Unclaimed inheritance scam
- ❑ Counterfeit cheques scam
- ❑ Dating-romance scam
- ❑ Black (defaced) currency scam
- ❑ Gold dust scam
- ❑ Diamond scam
- ❑ Fake-bank scam
- ❑ Housing scam
- ❑ Anti-terrorist certificate scam
- ❑ Disaster-relief fund scam
- ❑ Financial representative in your country scam
- ❑ Work permit scam
- ❑ Payment for art scam
- ❑ Deceased next of kin scam
- ❑ Construction sub-contractor scam
- ❑ Lower priced crude oil scam
- ❑ SWIFT transfer scam
- ❑ Antique export payment scam
- ❑ University study place scam
- ❑ Money from former ruler scam
- ❑ Relative of holocaust victim scam
- ❑ Identity theft
- ❑ Jobs for professionals scam
- ❑ Dead millionaire funds for charities or disaster relief scam
- ❑ Very low interest loans for relatively small advance fees scam

- Hotel bookings and refund
- United Nations loan approval scam
- Death threat scam

Tips for prevention

Never reply or deposit any money against any of these scam e-mails. Instead, report it to your bank immediately for advice.

PLASTIC MONEY-CAUTION AND PRECAUTIONS

Convenience is no longer a luxury but a necessity. Both Credit and Debit Cards have made any transaction in which money is involved so easy that it is difficult to imagine what life would be like, without plastic! In fact not possessing either a Credit or Debit Card could be a serious handicap in several routine sceneries.

However convenience comes with a cost. Hence, exercising caution while using cards and taking necessary pre-cautions is imperative. According to senior police official, the card frauds have grown by 500% over the last few years. This implies that you have to be vigilant towards usage of cards. Here are some cautions and precautions:

- **Card Safety**: Keep the card in a prominent place in your wallet. You will be able to notice if it is missing. If you happen to lose it, inform the issuer immediately.
- **PIN Safety**: On receiving the PIN mailer, destroy it after changing the PIN at the ATM. Do not write it in seemingly obscure places.
- **Keep an Eye on the Card**: In a restaurant, hotel or a petrol pump, always ensure your card is swiped in your presence. This will ensure your card details are not copied for misuse.
- **Subscribe to Mobile Alerts**: Most card issuers provide transaction alert service via SMS on your mobile phone (for free). So, do register for such a service. You will be alerted – even if your card misused.

- **Online Safety**: If you have ensured the above, take care while being online by adhering to the following:
  - o Do sign up for the VBV or Master Secure feature provided by the issuer.
  - o When shopping on a website, make sure that the website is secured by SSL encryption so that your card information is protected when you make a purchase.
  - o Make sure that the latest version of anti-spy-ware or anti Trojan programmes are installed on your computer and are regularly updated. As far as possible, avoid using public computers (like the ones in the cyber cafes) for online banking transactions. The computers may have spy-ware.
- **Vishing**: It involves a phone call form a fraudster disguised as representative of bank/issuer. They call claiming to verify, enhance credit limit, up-grade the card which could make you feel that the individual is authorized to deal with you. They some times even ask you to dial a particular number and leave your card data there, which is equally risky. As a card user always remember that you can call your bank on the number given by the bank (usually printed on the reverse of the card) but never entertain people claiming to represent the bank.
- **Disposal**: If your card has been put out of use, cut the card diagonally while making sure that the magnetic strip has been damaged, so that no data can be retrieved.
- **Disguised Fraudsters**: Do not seek assistance from any one, certainly not from a stranger, with the transactions at an ATM. If there is a Customer Care facility at the ATM, do use it to resolve your issue.

TIPS TO PREVENT CHEQUE FRAUDS

- Fraudsters invariably keep pace with technological advances. Tec-savvy criminals see far greater opportunity in silently siphoning-off millions, than in wielding a gun and risk being jailed for a pittance. Fraudsters today can defraud you and your financial institution(s) quiet easily with a blank cheque taken from your cheque book, a cancelled cheque found in your garbage, or a cheque you mailed to pay a bill. Therefore it is extremely important to accord them the importance they deserve than threat them like any other ordinary booklet.

- Always cross your cheque. This helps in preventing encashment over the counter. Avoid issuing bearer cheques as far as possible.
- Always store your cheques, deposit slips, bank statements and cancelled cheques under at a safe place. Keep it locked.
- Reconcile your bank statement within 30days of receipt in order to detect any irregularities. Otherwise, you may become liable for any losses due to fraud.
- Never give your account number to people you do not know, especially over the phone. Beware of unsolicited phone calls.
- Unless needed, destroy old cancelled cheques, ATM receipts. The information on these would help some one to impersonate you and do a fraud.
- When you receive your cheque book, make sure all the cheques are there, and none of them are missing.
- If you have ordered for a cheque book and you have not got it in time, alert your bank. Cheques could have been lost in transit or stolen.
- In case your house is burgled, among other things, immediately check for your cheque books and also for any missing cheques. Instruct the bank to stop payment for such missing instruments.
- Limit the personal information on the reverse of cheques. For example, do not write your date of birth, address, etc.

TIPS TO PROTECT YOUR-SELF AGAINST FRAUDS/ SCAMS/ IDENTITY THEFT

- Don't give out any confidential information. Always avoid giving any confidential information to strangers. Never give out your account number, credit card number etc., on the phone or online. No bank will ever ask any detail through its website/ e-mail/ phone.
- Store new and cancelled cheques credit card statements or any thing with confidential information, in a safe place and shred them when it is not required.
- Protect your Personal Identification Numbers (PINs) for your ATM and credit cards, and don't write on or keep your PINs with your cards.
- Be creative in selecting Personal Identification Numbers for your ATM and credit cards, and passwords that enable you to access other accounts. Don't use birth dates, driver's license number address or children's or spouse's names. Always remember that if someone has stolen your identity, he or she probably has some or all of this information.
- Use a separate e-mail address when you post messages to any public forum, such as newsgroups and mailing lists. Never use your personal e-mail address for this purpose you will be flooded with spam.
- Report lost or stolen cheques immediately. The bank can block payment on the cheque numbers that are missing. Also, review new cheque book you receive, to make sure none has been stolen in transit.
- Reconcile your bank statement with in 30 days of receipt in order to detect any irregularities. Otherwise you may become liable for any losses due to fraud.
- Set up filters in your e-mail programme to filter all spam e-mail messages.
- Most banks provide transaction alert service via SMS on your mobile phone (for free). So, do register for such a service. You will be alerted - even if your credit/debit card/account misused.

- Be extra careful with packets received in post/courier. Other people should not have access to them.
- If you change your residence, inform your bank card issuer and all other organizations that you deal with immediately.
- Never carry documents or plastic cards unnecessarily. When not in use keep them in a safe place.
- Keep your personal documents in a safe place, preferably in lockable drawer or cabinet at home. Consider storing valuable documents such as property documents, fixed deposit, receipts, will, etc., with your bank in a locker.

BE-AWARE-COMPUTER VIRUS

A computer virus is deigned to spread from one computer to another quickly. It's a program or piece of code that is loaded onto your computer without your knowledge and runs against your wishes. Viruses can also replicate themselves. The various types of viruses re as explained below-

- **Worms** are self-propagating computer viruses. They are programs that replicate themselves over a computer network and usually perform malicious actions, such as using up the computer's resources and possibly shutting the system down.
- **Trojan Horses** –a Trojan horse performs some undesired –yet intended – action while, or in addition to pretending to do something else. A common example is a fake login program, which collects account information and passwords by asking for this information just like a normal login program does. One of the most insidious types of Trojan horse is a program that claims to rid your computer of viruses but instead introduces viruses on to your computer.
- **Spyware** – is a soft ware that tracks your actions and/or your internet use. It can capture what you type on your key word, including passwords and send it to the spyware creator. It is a soft ware that covertly gathers user information through the user's internet connection

without his or her knowledge, usually for advertising purposes. Once installed the spyware monitors user activity on the internet and transmits that information in the background to someone else.

- **Adware** – is a form of spyware that collects information about the user in order to display advertisements in the web browser based on the user's browsing patterns.
- **Scumware** – Changes how you view websites you visit. It replaces the actual content of sites with ads from scumware advertisers and generates traffic for the scumware advertisers.

Tips for prevention:

- Use and antivirus program to regularly scan your hard drive.
- Update your antivirus program regularly.
- Be incredibly careful with the e-mails you receive and the attachment and links that you open.
- Install a good anti-spyware programme.
- Avoid using cyber café for internet Banking transactions.

3

Consolidation in Banking Industry - Due to Banking Sector Reforms

V. Sudhakar*

INTRODUCTION

Consolidation means a combination of players operating in similar sectors with the result begin stronger than the parent entities. The importance of consolidation in financial sector assumes importance since a healthy financial sector is necessary if economies are to be equipped to meet the challenges of globalization. Banks and banking products are getting more and more commoditized. All banks, irrespective of whether they are nationalized, private or foreign, have developed a very customer centric approach. Each bank is optimizing the cross selling opportunities by targeting existing relationships and ensuring customer loyalty. The target is the entire customer wallet; therefore it becomes imperative for banks to be ale to offer all products needed by the customer at a

* Head, Department of Commerce, Sri Kaliswari College, Sivakasi

competitive price. Banking in modern economies is all about risk management.

Indian businesses are rapidly using Mergers and Acquisitions to expand internationally. M & As in the industrial and services sector have brought new life to the style of doing business in today's world. Globalization, technological changes, market deregulation and liberalization have driven the M&A wave across the world. The 1980's is often referred to as a decade of merger mania with approximately 55,000 M&As in the U.S.

While Indian manufacturers have adopted M&A as their business strategy for growth, the Indian banking industry has not been moving in tune with Indian businesses and has been slower to respond to the huge growth opportunities in the market. The ultimate goals of a bank are to increase its market power, become more diversified, reduce the risk of entering a new business and redefine the competitive edge though acquiring different streams of businesses. Consolidation will provide banks with new capabilities, technologies and products, help to overcome entry barriers, ensure immediate entry into new markets and lower operating costs through consolidation of resources. In order to attain the economies of scale and also to combat the unhealthy competition within the sector; the consolidation of Indian banking sector through mergers and acquisitions on commercial considerations and business strategies is the essential pre-requisite. Indian banks need to improve their skills and practices in a way compatible to International standards and they must look and behave like global banks in terms of their physical comfort, work processes, response time and operational and administrative efficiency etc. The consolidation exercise obviously intents to gain competitive advantage which may result in economics of scale through effective geographic coverage, gaining superiority in certain business segments etc.

M&A in Indian banking is not new and Dates back from Imperial Bank of India which was formed by the amalgamation of the three presidency banks- the Bank of Bengal, the Bank of Bombay and the Bank of Madras in 1921. Few mergers have taken place thereafter to protect the interests of depositors of weak private banks. (The State Bank of India taking over Bank of Cochin and Kashinath Seth Bank is an example) However, the Times Bank merger with HDFC Bank a few years ago and Bank of Madurai with ICICI Bank is a new wave of consolidation in the Indian banking industry for mutual benefit. With the opening up of the banking sector, Indian banks will face stiffer competition as large international banks with varies market experience enter the Indian Banking arena. To keep pace with these changing realities size is a critical element in the chase for avenues to profit. Two important factors that differentiate the profitability of operations of public sector banks vis-à-vis private sector banks are higher operating expenses and lower income generation. Public sector banks have sought to prune operating expenses through the twin measures of employee rationalization under the voluntary retirement scheme and simultaneous computerization. As banks focus on technology and customer service to increase scale and profit, the banking industry in India will see a wave of consolidation - perhaps mergers - which is necessary to contend with fierce local competition and achieve global power. In India, the State Bank and its seven associates have about 13,700 branches. It is the only bank in India which is ranked among the top 100 best banks in the world. After consolidation we will be having 3-4 banks of international level or standard. Size is a great competitive advantage for banks. Further, significant overhead infrastructure is essential for a wide variety of retail products that are demanded in today's customer-driven banking environment. Such large infrastructure can be effectively sustained only by large sized banks. A continuous capital infusion is an essential ingredient for growth in the banking industry.

Consolidation in many ways is a natural response in our rapidly changing banking environment and it will facilitate financial strength. Basel - II due to be implemented by 2007, will require increased capital commitments from all banks. As well as increased transparency and accountability to both regulators and the market. Geographic expansion allows banks to diversify risks by exploring more avenues for profitable business in the global market consolidation in banking industry by mergers and acquisitions is the need of the hour and cannot be avoided. Consolidation would also benefit employees in the banking system since it would lead to retraining and rejuvenate the existing skills of the work force enabling personal growth. The Indian banking industry expects consolidation to set in motion several future benefits arising out of synergies between businesses. Technology enables the banks to share customer and produce information, thereby increasing the share of the customer wallet, lowering the cost of serving a customer and increased profitability of even smaller branches. The key argument for consolidation within the banking sector is that it will result in increasing the balance sheet size of the banks, which in turn, would help them to compete internationally.

The main driver for the consolidation of the Banking Sector among others includes:

- Revenue growth from a larger customer base
- Efficiencies in operation
- The desire to become one stops Shop for all financial products/services
- Diversification of income from both products and geographic area
- Spread fixed costs over a larger customer base.
- Minimize transaction cost and reduce the cost of regulatory compliance in the context of Basel II norms.
- Optimal deployment of excess capital
- Ensuring maximum utilization of available resources

Huge amount of investments required for putting in place IT in infrastructure like Core banking Solutions, implementing Customer Relationship Management package and high end skills required for Modern Day Banking are some other reasons to consider consolidation among Indian Public Sector Banks.

Important Bank Mergers and Acquisitions since Nationalization

YEAR	BANK	MERGED WITH
1969	Bank of Bihar	State Bank of India
1970	National Bank of Lahore	State bank of India
1976	Belgaum Bank	Union Bank
1984-85	Bank of Cochin	State bank of India
1989-90	Bank of Tamilnad	Indian Overseas Bank
1989-90	Bank of Tanjavur	Indian Bank
1989-90	Parur Central Bank	Bank of India
1995-96	Kashinath Seth Bank	State Bank of India
1997	Punjab Co-operative Bank	Oriental Bank of Commerce
1999	British Bank of Middle East	HSBC
1999	Sikkim Bank Ltd	Union Bank of India
2001	Bank of Madura	ICICI
2002	Banaras State Bank	Bank of Baroda
2003	Nedungadi Bank	Punjab National Bank
2004	South Gujarat Local Area Bank	Bank of Baroda
2004	Global Trust Bank	Oriental Bank of Commerce
Source: V. Sridhar, "The Merger mantra", Frontline, Vol 21, Issue 21, Oct.9-22, 2004		

It can be seen that the tempo of mergers/amalgamation, by and large, appears to be picking up in the recent past.

HUMAN RESOURCE MANAGEMENT THROUGH CONSOLIDATION

Different persons have different qualities. Some are expert in marketing, some in table work whereas some in field work. Some others are expert in making policies. Some develop specific skills which others do not have. Maximum productivity can be achieved by optimizing capacity utilization azs well as efficiency utilization of each individual and by putting right person on the rightjob. If a person is a vgiven of his choice or expertise, he starts loving his job profile. Then the job becomes playing a game or singing a song for him. Thus the human resources will be managed in a better way after consolidation. Itr will also provide more career opportunities to employees.

Consolidation of banks will be a win-win situation for all the parties as under

Banks	Sound financial position Large business Large asset Benefit of Core banking solution Networking and the state of the art Technology Large profits Improved investor confidence
Customers	Better and competitive pricing of products Better services and Upgraded technology
Government of India and The Reserve bank of India	Better monitoring Interaction with less number of CEOs Easy implementation of policies Higher dividends
Rating agencies	Better of improved rating of Indian Banks
Foreign Institutions/Investors/NRIs	Ultimate safety of funds Better investment opportunities Negotiable environment
All other entities dealing with the Indian Banks	Sound and large Indian banks No risk in performance of the contracts and obligations Safer investments and higher dividends Better deal

Basically merger involves a marriage of two or more banks. It is generally accepted that mergers promote synergies. The basic idea is that the combined bank will create more value than the individual banks operating independently.

The future of Indian agriculture in general and small farmer in particular depends on how soon they become globally competitive. The benefits of consolidation and emergence of financially strong and globally competitive new entities in

Indian Banking will retain the local feel and render much more effective rural lending ensuring that the banking benefits reach out to the rural masses in our Indian sub-continent.

BANKING SECTOR REFORMS

The banking sector reforms undertaken in India from 1992 onwards were basically aimed at ensuring the safety and soundness of financial institutions and at the same time at making the banking system strong, efficient, functionally diverse and competitive. Their form is included measures for arresting the decline in productivity of the banking sector. Furthermore, it was recognized that the Indian banking system should be in tune with international standa4rds of capital adequacy, prudential reforms and accounting and disclosure standards. Financial soundness and consistent supervisory practices, as evident in our level of compliance with the Basel committee's core principles for effective banking supervision, have made our banking System resilient to global shocks.

FORCES FOR CHANGE

India has not faced any major economic/financial crises, though in 1990-91, there was some pressure on the external sector with the current account deficit and external debt servicing reaching large proportions. How ever, due to prudent macroeconomic policies, it was possible to return the country to a sustainable growth path. As well as the long history of regulation and supervision, Indian banks have limited exposure to sensitive sectors such as real estate, equity etc, and strict control over off-balance sheet activities. Larger holding of Government bonds (Which helps limit credit risk), relatively well diversified credit portfolios, statutory restrictions on connected lending, adequate control over currency and maturity mismatches, etc, which has isolated them from the adverse impact of financial crisis and contagion, Banks in India have played a significant role in the development of the Indian economy. However, with the structural reforms initiated in the real economy, from the early 1990's, it was imperative that a vibrant and competitive financial system should be put in place to sustain the ongoing process of reforms in the real sector.

In India, foreign banks account for only around 8% of the total assets of the banking system. Further, domestic households are not allowed to place deposits abroad. Similarly, conditions of accessing overseas capital market by domestic corporate have been stringent, in terms of size, maturity, pricing, etc. The impact of the entry of foreign banks on domestic banks is likely to depend on various factors such as the structure, strength and competitiveness of domestic banks, the share of foreign banks, and the regulatory/supervisory framework. While the entry of foreign banks could definitely improve the competitive environment, they are not likely to weaken domestic banks. With better technology and expertise in offering specialized banking products such as derivatives, advisory services, trade finance, etc, the entry of foreign banks can enhance healthy.

Competition and has a positive spillover effect on the domestic banks. The domestic banks would be under pressure to improve operational efficiency. It needs, however, to be recognized that the banking system in India is quite competitive with the presence of public private and foreign banks.

Thus, the major forces for change in the Indian context have been the following:

- Consistent and strong regulatory and supervisory frame work;
- Structural reforms in the real and financial sectors;
- Commitment to adopt and refine regulatory and supervisory standards on a par with international best practices; and
- Competition from foreign banks and new generation private sector banks.
- Privatization of State Banks

From 1990, however, it was recognized that steps were needed to improve the financial health of banks to make them visible, efficient and competitive to serve the emerging needs behave the efficiency of the real sector. While the role of the large state banks has not undergone any structural changes and they continue to serve the varying needs of economy, what ahs changed significantly, as a result of the reform process, is the focus on their consolidation, efficiency, resilience, productivity, asset quality and profitability through liberalization, deregulation and adoption of prudential standards in line with international best practices.

As a part of financial sector reforms and with a view to giving the state banks operational flexibility and functional autonomy, partial privatization has been authorized as a first step, enabling them to dilute the stake of the Indian government of 51%. The Government further proposed, in the Union Budget for financial year 2000-01, to reduce its holding in nationalized banks to minimum of 33 on a case by case basis. The major problems for gradual privatization are likely to be resistance from staff to rationalization of the branch network and emphasis on higher staff productivity.

DOMESTIC MERGERS

Under the banking Regulation Act, Banking companies cannot merge without the approval of the Reserve Bank of Indian. The government and the Reserve bank do not play a proactive role in either encouraging or discouraging mergers. It is our endeavor that the Government and the RBI should only provide the enabling environment through an appropriate fiscal, regulatory and supervisory framework for the consolidation and convergence of financial institutions, at the same time ensuring that a few large institutions do not create an oligopoly structure in the market. Mergers should be based on the need to attain a meaningful balance sheet size and market share in the face of heightened competition and driven by synergies, location and business-specific complementarities. While there is no regulatory deterrence to bank mergers, their incidence has not been significant and hence no problems have occurred in India;

Mergers of banks help to reduce the gestation period for launching promoting new places of business, strengthen product portfolios, minimize duplication, gain competitive advantage, etc. They are also recognized as a good strategy for enhancing efficiency. Ideally, mergers ought to be aimed at exploiting synergies, reducing overlap in operations.

ISSUES IN BANKS'S MERGERS WITH NON-BANKS

It has been our endeavour to preserve the integrity and identity of banks. The activities that the banks and their subsidiaries can undertake are restrictive, to ensure that the interests of existing and future depositors are fully protected. Banks are also not allowed to undertake trading in commodities. In pursuit of these objectives, the merger of a bank with a non-bank is generally not favoured. However, the merger of a non-bank financial company with a bank is allowed subject to the prior approval of the Reserve Bank of Indian and compliance with all the regulatory and supervisory standards applicable to banks. The issues that may arise in such mergers would be the bank's ability to comply with statutory and regulatory requirements in respect of liabilities and assets taken over by it from the non-bank.

RECOMMENDATIONS OF NARASIMHAM COMMITTEE ON BANKING SECTOR REFORMS

Globally, the banking and financial systems have adopted information and communications technology. This phenomenon has largely by passed the Indian banking system, and the committee feels that requisite success needs to be achieved in the following areas:

- Bank automation
- Planning, standardization of electronic payment systems
- Telecom infrastructure
- Data warehousing network

Mergers between banks and DFIs and NBFCs need to be based on synergies and should make a sound commercial sense.

Committee also opines that mergers between strong Banks/ FIs would make for greater economic and commercial since and would be a case where the whole is greater than the sum of its parts and have a "force multiplier effect". It also opined that mergers should not be seen as a means of bailing out weak banks.

A weak bank could be nurtured into healthy units. Merger could also be a solution to a weak bank, but the Committee suggests it only after cleaning up their balance sheets. It also says, if there is no voluntary response to a takeover of such banks, a restructuring commission for such PSB's can consider other options such as restructuring, merger amalgamation, or if not closure.

The committee also opines that, while licensing new private sector banks, the initial capital requirements need to be reviewed. It also emphasized on a transparent mechanism for deciding the ability of promoters to professionally manage the banks. The committee also feels that a minimum threshold capital for old private banks also deserves attention and mergers could be one of the options available for reaching the required threshold capitals. The committee also opined that a promoter group couldn't hold more than 40 per cent of the equity of a bank.

The bank pioneered in taking initiatives and providing one-stop financial solutions to customers with speed and quality, In a way to reach customers, it has used multiple delivery channels including conventional branch outlets, ATM's telephone call-centers and also through Internet. The bank also ventured into a number of B2B and B2C initiatives in the last year to maintain its leadership in India. The B2B solution provided by the bank is aimed at facilitating on-line supply chain management for its corporate clients by linking them with their suppliers and dealers in a closed business loop. The bank is always ahead in advanced IT and used as a competitive tool to lure new customers.

In February 2000, ICICI bank was one of the first few Indian Banks to raise its capital through American Depository shares in their international market which has received an overwhelming response for its issue of $175 mn. with a total order book of US D 2.2 bn. At the time of filling the prospectus, with the US Securities and Exchange Commission, the Bank had mentioned that the proceeds of the issue would be used to acquire a bank.

At the time of filling the prospectus with US Securities and Exchange Commission, the Bank had mentioned that proceeds of the issue would be used to acquire a bank.

As on March 31, 2000 bank had a network of 81 branches, 16 extension counters and 175 ATMs. The capital adequacy ratio was at 19.64 percent of risk-weighted assets, a significant excess of 9 percent over RBI's benchmark.

ICICI Bank has been scouting for a private banker for merger, with a view to expand its asset and client base and geographical coverage. Though it had 21 per cent of stake, the choice of Federal bank, was not lucrative due to the employee size (6600), per employee business is as low at Rs.161 lakh and a snail pace of technical up gradation. While, BOM had an attractive business per employee figure of Rs.2002 lakh, a better technological edge and had a vast base in southern Indian when compared to Federal bank, While all these factors sound good, a cultural integration would be a tough task ahead for ICICI Bank.

ICICI bank has announced a merger with 57 year old Bank of Madura, with 263 branches out of which 82 of them are in rural areas, with most of them in southern Indian. As on the day of announcement of merger (09-12-2000), Kotak Mahindra group was holding about 12percent stake in BOM, the Chairman BOM, Mr. K.M. Thiagarajan along with his associates was holding about 26 percent stake Spic groups has bout 4.7 percent, while LIXC and UTI were having marginal holdings. The merger will give ICICI Bank a hold on South Indian market, which has high rate of economic development.

The board of Directors at ICICI has contemplated the following synergies emerging from the merger:

FINANCIAL CAPABILITY: The amalgamation will enable them to have a stronger financial and operational structure, which is suppose to be capable of greater resource/deposit mobilization. And ICICI will emerge as one of the largest private sector banks in the country.

BRANCH NETWORK: The ICICI's branch network would not only increase by 264, but also increases geographic coverage as well as convenience to its customers.

Customer base: The emerged largest customer base will enable the ICICI bank to offer banking and financial services and products and also facilitate cross-selling of products and services of the ICICI group.

TECH EDGE: The merger will enable ICICI to provide ATMs, phone and the Internet banking and financial services and products to a large customer base, with expected savings in costs and operating expenses.

FOCUS ON PRIORITY SECTOR: The enhanced branch network will enable the Bank to focus on micro-finance activities through self-help groups, in its priority sector initiatives through its acquired 87 rural and 88 semi-urban branches.

The swap ratio has been approved in the ratio of 1:2 – two shares of ICICI Bank for every one share of BOM. The deal with BOM is likely to dilute the current equity capital byu around 12 per cent. And the merger is expected to bring 20 percent gains in EPS of ICICI Bank. And also the bank's comfortable Capital Adequacy Ratio (CAR) of 19.64 percetn has declined to 17.6 per cetn.

Will the merger of 57 year old BOM, south based old generation bank with a fast growing tech savvy new generation bank, help the latter? For sure, the stock merger is likely to bring cheer to shareholders and bank employees of BOM, and some amount off discomfort and anxiety to those of ICICI bank.

The scheme of amalgamation will increase the equity base of ICICI bank to Rs,.220.36 cr. ICICI bank will issue 235.4 lakh shares of Rs. 10 each to the share holder of BOM. The merged entity will have an increase of asset base over Rs.160 bn. The merged entity will have 360 branches and a similar number of

ATMs across the country and also enable the ICICI to serve a large customer base of 1.2 million customers of BOM through a wider network, adding to the customer base to 2.7 million.

They had gone with agreements in the following various aspects also in order to execute their business.

- ❑ Managing rural branches
- ❑ The M&A Terminology
- ❑ Leveraged Cash out
- ❑ White Knight
- ❑ Poison Pills
- ❑ Green Mail
- ❑ Golden Parachutes
- ❑ White Squire
- ❑ Leveraged Buyout (LBO)
- ❑ Managing Software
- ❑ Managing Human resources
- ❑ Managing Client base
- ❑ Entry norms

FUTURISTIC OUTLOOK

After viewing the merger syndrome, there could be a possibility that the following permutations and combinations of mergers in banking industry may take place in near future:

> *When size only matters, the PSB's which will shortly be loosing their public sector nature by there increased capital (as the government is planning to reduce its stake from 100 per cent to 33 per cent) are strong contenders to take over old generation private sector banks. Foreign Banks will not stay behind in overall one point financial services concept in the takeover bids.*

"In the new millennium, banks should strive to achieve significant increases in their productivity, efficiency, and reorganizing banks' setup towards thinner and leaner administrative offices;

Closing down and/or merging of unviable branches particularly in urban and metropolitan branches;

Forging of strategic alliances to take advantage of the geographic spread of branch network of banks; type of customer concentration with a view to developing niche markets suitable for each bank consistent with its ethos and culture;

Develop new products and services that would meet the emerging customer needs; Professional sing management structures that would be responsive to the changes in the business environment".

"Cyber banking and e-commerce would make large urban branch net work irrelevant. Many Banks will be forced to open more ATM's in the place of their branches in urban areas".

The market is seeing new products such as phone-banking, home banking, Finance against securities and time (FAST), credit cards etc. The more one goes closer to the customer the more one would get higher volumes and value addition in business. For all banks, repositioning for competitive advantage in the rapidly changing market place will call for large investments in information technology and communication networks."

The challenges in the new millennium for the banking industry are, therefore, enormous and can be met effectively only when the banking institutions also make knowledge as engine for growth. Embedding knowledge into products can enhance value. Connecting different knowledge sources can create innovative products. This is one of the reasons for the World Development Report, 1998-99 to devote to this aspect exclusively. Knowledge management is 90 per cent common sense and good management practice. One may find knowledge management is really about.

It is very relevant to again quote the works of the Governor of RBI, Mr. Bimal Jalan that set forth the direction in which Indian Banning should strive in the new millennium. "The primary sources of comparative advantage of nations today are skills and the ability to adapt and change. These factors determine that prospects fo prosperity and growth of an economy. It is important for the merging economies like India to base their growth on leadership in new technology, knowledge-based services, and manpower skills (as did the US and Germany in the second half of the nineteenth Century).

4

Core Banking and IT

*Dr. A.Selvaraj and K.R.Vijaysanthi

Banking system plays an important role in a country's economy. It promotes growth and development of the country. The commercial banks perform various important functions in the development of a country. They mobiise financial resources from non-productive channels to productive channels. Development of a country is not possible in the absence of networks of commercial banks. The development of present day developed nations has been possible through the sound commercial banking while developing countries have been analyzing the banking system in different sectors. The important and role of commercial banks in economic development are capital formation, loans and advances, enlarging market, allocation of funds, developing entrepreneurial skills, consumer loans, supply of money, innovation. Thus, the commercial banks have not to play an

* Reader in Commerce, Gobi Arts and Science College, Gobi.

** Project Associate, Department of Commerce, Gobi Arts and Science College, Gobi

important dynamic role in the economic development of the country. Banks are not only commercial but they are also providers of social banking, mass banking, innovative banking and development and investment banking in the country.

Indian banking has topped the charts in value creation in financial year 2007-2008 among all major economies, the global banking sector's average total shareholders return plumed by 93% in 2007, to 1.7% and was well below the 15.2% average TSR of all industries. Globally, the sector's market capitalization increased by a mere 2.4% to $ 8.3 trillion a stark change from 2006, when market cap grew by 31%. Since the end of 2007, shareholders returns in the banking industry, in general, have deteriorated rapidly: in less than three months, the sector's market cap has dropped by more than 15%, to $ 7 trillion from $ 8.3% trillion. Banks representing more than 75% of total banking market capitalization.

In the present trend the concept of core banking is very famous. This paper put forth some conceptual ideas regarding core banking.

BANKING AND IT

Economic value associated with goods and services has been subject to successive refinements, beginning with precious metal, followed by coinage, paper currency, bank deposits and the present day stored value smart cards. The complete dematerialization of value and its conversion into pure information was achieved by banking. Banks stored value as information - the information was valuable. It would be natural, then, that Banks would be the major users of Information Technology as it developed. So they are, globally.

In fact, IT spends by banks is considered to have stemmed the IT decline post Y2K and dotcom bust.

HISTORICAL OVERVIEW

It is almost impossible to view the core banking systems market without putting it into some sort of historical context.

By definition, it requires considerable effort and an awfully long time to develop a core banking system, even with today's technology. As such, new solutions do not come along very often and the shelf life of those systems that make it to market is far longer than would have been predicted at the outset. Systems, which have their roots in the 1970s, continue to gain new takers. The attributes of the older offerings are typically stability and breadth, constituting a low risk option. It is easy to knock the old systems, but they have attracted a huge amount of investment down the years.

The downside to the older systems is typically to do with technology and flexibility. On the technology front, they may well be tied to a proprietary operating system and/or database. They will probably be written in proprietary code, for which market resources are scarce. They will probably have a fairly heavy batch-processing component and they may not be able to support multiple-entities, so are unsuited for the current push towards centralized processing. In terms of flexibility, this could mean that they are difficult to amend, so that banks are hindered in how quickly they can get to market with a new product. Data extraction and integration are other commonly cited obstacles.

GLOBAL CORE BANKING MARKET TODAY

One of those exceptions is I-flex Solutions. The rewrite that produced Flex cube was remarkably successful, and it is hard to think of a new system that has a smoother entry into the market. There are now over 100 users and it has sold far and wide. A key competitor around the globe is Temenos, with Globus, as well as Misys, with its assorted offerings (Midas, Equation, and Opics). On the retail front, I-flex often clashes with Infosys, although the latter has still to break out of India and Africa with its application software.

There is no doubt that a lot of banks are now looking for centralized processing support. This applies to the largest banks (such as Citibank) as much as it does to the mid-tier (ING Bank is heading this way, for instance), and to a growing number of smaller banks. It also applies to banks across wholesale banking, trade finance and securities. For retail banking, a few banks have centralized cross-border (Citibank is an example) but in India the concept of centralization in this domain has still to do with moving from a decentralized retail branch to a single back office system at the centre, thereby potentially bringing a quantum leap forward in terms of customer service. Some banks will look for one system to handle most or all of their operations. They might tailor their processes to fit the platform. Banks that take this line are probably generalists - in other words, they try to offer a broad service rather than specialize in particular areas. A bank that wants to be a specialist in, for instance, trade finance, would probably buy or build a dedicated system, which was seen as **best of breed**. Despite the arrival of supposed rapid application development tools and techniques, there is still a strong push within most banks towards third party software.

CBS MARKET HEATING UP IN INDIA

Before the dawn of the new millennium, foreign (read MNC) banks and most of the new generation private banks in India had CBS systems in place. Increasing de-regulation of Indian Financial Market in the 1990's which allowed setting up of new private banks am facilitated expansion and entry of MNC banks unleashed a fierce competition for market share. Riding on the CBS backbone, came the technology enabled innovative products and alternate delivery channels from these MNC and new generation private banks which slowly started eating up into the market share of major government owned banks and old generation private banks. Interest de-regulation and maturing of capital and debt markets shifted the focus to retail banking. De-regulation and liberalization exposed Indian banks to various market risks whose management required timely information and sophisticated models. CBS is no longer a choice, but a compulsion driven by market reality. "It is a fact that banks are vying with one another in the implementation of core banking solutions. Today banks no longer reason it as to why they should have CBS in place.

They rather look at the risks associated with a situation of not having CBS and still are in a position to compete and survive in a market that is turning more and more aggressive. Movement to core banking is no longer an option but a necessity driven by market forces. It is the entry of government owned banks and the size of their implementations that has generated the heat in CBS market in India.

CBS IS JUST A BEGINNING NOT A PANACEA

Every bank that has moved onto the CBS bandwagon or is planning to do so, seems convinced that once the CBS is in place it will provide the competitive edge, help retain customers, enable cross selling, better risk management provide substantive business value. The expectations are certainly valid and realizable. "A centralized Core Banking System on its own will not deliver the benefits. The banks will need to leverage this powerful technology to generate benefits". "CBS is only an enabler for doing banking and not a magic wand does away with all weaknesses. Competitive edge is provided by Research and Innovation of new products and services, cost and convenience of transactions, customer relationship management, personal touch and counselling". Competition will be eventually between banks that are all on one CBS platform or the other. Then, it will be operational excellence and closeness with the customer that will be the differentiating factors. "Software doesn't run the bank. CBS or any software is a tool. Banks gain competitive edge only if they have gained the maturity to align technology with business".

ROI AND OBSOLESCENCE RISK

Measuring return on investment in IT has been so notoriously difficult that it prompted a banker to call IT an "Investment Trap"!

"Expenditure on technology should not be considered a capital expenditure but revenue expenditure." The solution, if acceptable, would definitely be equal in elegance to Einstein's mass energy equation, but not many bankers would buy it at this point of time. In fact, "In spite of rapid technological changes, it should be the endeavour of banks to ensure return of investments. The short implementation life cycle is critical to its success. The average pay back period is estimated at around 3.5 years, the average life for CBS in India can be estimated to be around 5 years".

Though estimates of average life span of a CBS product in Indian environment differ (CMC, TCS expect it to run beyond ten years, Polaris' estimate is 7-8 years and that of IBM, more than five years) almost everyone agrees that speed of implementation is a crucial factor to ensure ROI. "The sheer logistic of the exercise determines the timelines. Even elsewhere roll out of IT across geographies runs into several months and sometimes years. It would be interesting to compare this with the current major IT migration exercises like SWIFT upgrading to SWIFTNET in 200 countries and CLS rollout around the globe."

"Ready-made package needs lot of customization suiting Indian banking scenario and regulations. Therefore the life cycle envisaged has to be long term in order to extract ROI from CBS investments. Timeframes for CBS implementation are large as number of branches is very high". However, are optimistic that CBS implementation life cycle, even in the case of big Indian banks, can be brought down in the range of 12-24 months.

RFP: THE FIRST STEP IN DUE DILIGENCE PROCESS

Request for Proposal (RFP) is the first milestone in the due diligence process of CBS selection. It is also a stage where maximum variety of opinion is encountered. Two issues stand out:

BUSINESS PROCESS REVIEW BEFORE OR AFTER RFP?

Majority opinion favours BPR before drawing up of RFP and process adaptation post selection. "BPR needs to be completed before drawing up an RFP. Given that most banks implementing CBS are not just choosing a new CBS product but are making the radical change from stand alone single branch banking to CBS extensive BPR and a recasting of processes are required. In Indian Government owned banks processes for CBS environment do not exist at all currently." "It is always better to review the business process and then draw the RFP. However if in the selected product, favourable and improved features are present, then the process may also be adapted to the product".

"A business process review prior to RFP helps as most banks, when they move from" branch automation" to a "bank automation" phase, require organizational and process related changes to various areas of operation. Most core banking applications, having been implemented for customers globally, tend to evolve "best practices" over a period of time. An approach of blending "internal business process review did" with the best practices inbuilt in the core product would bring the best of both worlds in an implementation".

Ground reality is quite different. "Mapping current functionality without any BPR has been the rule rather than exception." This throws out a lot of customization requirements confides a senior executive of State Bank of India where retaining of maker/checker ideology as against post commit audit has caused a sizeable customization of FNS's Bancs solution with all its attendant risks and delays. Mapping current functionality also tends to favour domestic suppliers. Not that RFP focuses on current functionality alone. On the contrary, "Most of the RFPs issued in India are more of a wish list which banks issue at the first instance. Towards the walkthrough phase, banks get on with focusing on the functionality required on an immediate basis".

NEED FOR CONSULTANTS

For banks which are saddled with legacy applications, having a mix of manual, standalone and TBA packages co-existent, a plethora of satellite software for specific jobs and a weak IT management capability; putting in place a CBS solution is a highly complex task. There are a whole set of issues: drawing up an RFP, vendor/product selection, setting up the network and data center, deciding on customization/adaptation, change management, security policy, service level agreements (SLAs), hardware/infrastructure procurement, and sustaining the roll-out pace. Most bank managements do not have relevant experience and technology management capability to undertake all or some of these jobs on their own.

While there seems to be near consensus that banks definitely need the consultancy services of specialists in their respective areas of competence, having a general management consultant at the top to drive the entire CBS project evokes divergent opinions. "It is desirable to have one general consultant who capabilities, knowledge and expertise to integrate all the stages". Aruna Rao elaborates further: "One general management consultant is often the most practical way to go as specialists tend to disagree even among themselves. A critical project CBS selection cannot afford to have too many experts all pulling in different directions".

CONSULTANTS REVISITED: WHAT IS EXPECTED OF THEM?

First, the attributes:

- ❑ Knowledge of banking domain
- ❑ Experience of CBS selection and implementation
- ❑ Acquainted with current technologies and future trends
- ❑ Understands the values and benefits banks expect to achieve from CBS
- ❑ Can help translate his recommendations into successful implementation
- ❑ Integrity

Expected value addition in the areas of:

- ❑ Avoidance of pitfalls
- ❑ BPR
- ❑ Change management

- Help the bank "move up the learning curve" on the evaluation process
- Bringing in "feasible best practices"
- Evolve and impart quickest roll-out plan
- Security/business continuity issues

Banks report a gap in value addition expected and actually delivered. Sometimes the feeling of having been let down is mutual. This could be due to inappropriate expectation management by the consultant, vague scope definition or over dependence by the bank simply inferior performance.

EVALUATION AND SELECTION PROCESS

This is the most delicate part as commercials are involved. A whole lot of issues here:

1. VENDOR OR PRODUCT?

It is categorical that vendor selection must be done first and then the product, not simultaneously as has been the mode in India so far. Given the life span estimates of five to ten years for a CBS, it is of paramount importance that the CBS solution vendor has financial soundness and stability to be around for such a long period. Technical soundness and functional richness of a product can only be of use if the vendor continues to support it. His criteria for vendor selection:

- Financial strength and stability
- Commitment to product
- Commitment to geography
- Product evolution road map

It emphasizes the need for long term sustenance: "The entire gamut of core banking and associated success at the end of the day is driven by the strength of the relationship between the bank and the vendor and capability of the vendor to deliver and consistently deliver on a long-term basis". CBS Vendor evaluation with a view to long term partnership before product evaluation appears to be a commercially sound strategy.

2. REFINING IT FURTHER: SYSTEM INTEGRATOR LED CONSORTIUM

A CBS product implementation includes selection of hardware, sizing of hardware, benchmarking for performance on selected hardware, designing the network, sourcing network components, customization and configuration, data conversion and interfacing with other existing/third party software. Banks have experimented with separate evaluations for these related suppliers. Often, this approach has been found to result in delays. Selecting a Systems Integrator can cut down on these delays. Portability and inter-operability of software systems (both in system software and application software domains) are often statements of what is technically possible. There is always a native hardware and software platform on which the implementation consumes least time, effort and money and gives best performance. Though the CBS solution may not be tied to a particular hardware, in practice, large benefits accrue if the same set of all participating vendors collaborates in the CBS implementation. Learning and synergy levels realized in previous implementations help reduce pitfalls and largely eliminate the issues of inter-vendor logistics management. A System Integrator led consortium of various suppliers including the CBS vendor presents a Single Window approach to CBS implementation for the banks. The concept is catching up fast.

3. CO-OPERATION VS. COMPETITION

In CBS selection, every bank goes through a more-or-less similar exercise and often arrives at similar conclusions. The exercise costs quite a sum to each bank and also takes up a lot of time and effort. It is candid to admit: "That is generally true in every market around the globe. The ground reality is that there is intense competition for customers even within government owned banks. In such an environment it is not possible for banks to collaborate on product selection". It cites differences in the requirements of each bank and the learning opportunities for the bank as the reasons for rejecting this idea. "This is not true. The priorities and preferences vary from bank to bank depending on business mix, core competencies in line of business, customer Profiles, the skills and knowledge available within. The selection process is worth undergoing as bank management and the employees appreciate better what is involved in selection and implementation of CBSA and it also ensures the involvement of all concerned." It talks of an informal collaborative and knowledge sharing initiative among banks which needs to take off. He feels some collaboration among the banks on knowledge sharing in CBS evaluation and selection process is likely to happen in future when there is more learning across the industry.

It suggests that "A better way would be to have a third party hosted product selection portal in which latest information on all available products is disseminated in a systemic and uniform format in an authenticated, unbiased and independent way. Such portals could allow banks to get the basic information in a very structured manner at one place and complete the process in shorter time frames". Similar benefits could also be obtained in vendor selection and tracking from reliable market reports. It feels that reliable market reports on CBS vendors should be given a weight age to the extent of 20% -30% in Vendor evaluation matrix. Others would like to have customer references and customer feedback factored in as well.

4. ARE INDIAN BANKS LOOKING BEYOND DOMESTIC SUPPLIERS?

An expected answer from the biggest banking conglomerate in India, SBI and its associate banks. In the past it had taken Bank master from Kindle and is currently implementing Bancs from FNS. A similar yes from Bart Hellemans whose bank is the only site in India for Profile. It differs sharply: "In a global world, there is nothing like a domestic supplier. All major suppliers are operating on the global scale. For a bank, it is important to evaluate whether the vendor and its product are world class and whether they meet all its requirements". "Today, Indian solution providers in banking are replacing systems in developed countries". It feels that domestic vendors offer a comfort level which cannot be matched by overseas vendors. Bankers are, by nature, risk-averse, he says. Aruna Rao feels domestic vendors enjoy a cost advantage: "Overseas vendors are not cost effective in India and cannot compete against Indian vendors due to their high man day costs for implementation".

It has a word of advice for overseas vendors trying to enter Indian CBS market: "If Global CBS vendors set up base in India and assure support at domestic costs and their product offerings are superior, I am sure banks would be open to such solutions even at a little higher cost". "Banks need to look at both Indian and global vendors for there core banking implementation as they strive to achieve a right mix of global features with Indian banking requirements".

5. PRODUCT EVALUATION

It feels that, "Most CBS projects start with requirements which are incomplete and confusing. A confused request for proposal will lead to confused quotations by vendors". Successive rounds of vendor presentations and discussions, product walkthroughs and reference site visits are required to enable the Bank to refine the RFP. "Generally, at least version 3 of request for quotation is required before an acceptable request for quotation by the technical committee of the bank and vendors emerges," says Kaujalgi. At each iteration, some vendors are knocked off. It suggests that banks should classify their functional requirements (both existing and desired) as critical (must have), semi-critical (should have) and non-critical (nice to have). Customisation should be done only for critical requirements and BPR for others.

6. VENDOR RISK

To mitigate vendor risk, there is general consensus on Escrow arrangements, proper drawing up of the contract and Service Level Agreements (SLA). The ownership option (whether through internal build, getting one developed for exclusive use, acquiring IPR of an existing solution or through a joint venture with a vendor) is not found feasible. There have been and always will be banks that prefer to own their own software by getting it developed on a project basis. However, such software never makes the cut as a product it is highly customized to the owner. It is difficult to imagine a consortium of banks owning a single CBS platform. If such an entity existed it would fit into the description of just another CBS vendor with no special advantages at another bank outside the consortium". "World over, banks have realized the fact that banking solutions are best provided by software vendors. Development or ownership of a software solution is not in the ambit of bank's business and even Citibank, the most technology savvy bank, has realized that it is best entrusted to a software house that it has spun off from its own".

IMPLEMENTATION

"Initial effort driven from head office cannot be sustained over long periods. Quite often, the objectives of visibility/ accomplishment are perceived to be achieved with the first 20-25 branches. Consequently, the rule of diminishing returns takes away the enthusiasm and excitement out of the minds of key stakeholders and implementation managers". In addition, "Implementation at the first 20-25 branches raises the issue of BPR (Business Process Review) which most banks which have gone for CBS never planned for before implementing CBS (stand alone branch banking vs. CBS requires extensive BPR)".

EVOLUTIONARY ROAD MAP OF CBS

Technology forecasting is no better than weather forecasting. A few interesting instances –

1. BANKERS' WISH LIST

- ❑ Truly multi channel enabled with single sign on
- ❑ Scalability (better performance and large transaction volume handling)
- ❑ Seamless integration of satellite applications like trade finance, treasury
- ❑ Fraud alerts
- ❑ Straight Through Processing of inter-bank transactions
- ❑ Integration with e-payment systems such at RTGSs etc.
- ❑ Flexibility for product innovation

- ❑ Workflow automation
- ❑ Document Management

2. VENDORS' FORECAST

- ❑ "The technology architecture will evolve into Front office customer facing module, Middle office business rules/ decisions module, Multiple Back office data store glued together as a customer centric set of services with a one-to-many relationship."
- ❑ "CBS is likely to evolve into some kind of an ERP for banks with HR, Admin, Extensive MIS/Data warehousing, with cash and people optimization tools built in. CBS will probably be able to support extensive marketing campaign and cross selling campaigns for customers".
- ❑ "Anticipate and complete the solution for banks with respect to offering modules for:
  - Channels beyond branch and web
  - Handling analytics (CRM, profitability and risk)
  - Handling other areas like HR, payroll, administration.
  - Building the necessary customization and integration flexibility to make 30 day launches a reality
  - Making full integration with industry systems such as RTGS, PDO/NDS, and SFMS etc".

3. INTER-OPERABILITY, OPEN ARCHITECTURE & E-PAYMENTS SYSTEM

CBS solutions of future to be more open to allow easier interfacing with third party products and inter-operability between different CBS products. Interoperability between core banking and other complementary channels exists but there is not much in terms of interoperability among the CBS products. Current CBS products need to have the capability and the requisite architecture to support online real-time payments. Certain specific modules like payments, accounting, etc would need to be redesigned to handle this".

4. CBS DEPLOYMENT ON ASP

Almost everyone thinks it is a great concept whose time is yet to come in India.

"Long terms prospects for an ASP model in India is good (as the economics of this model are inescapable) while short and medium term prospects are not encouraging. The main problem seems to be of trust. The market is waiting for an impartial player to emerge with whom smaller banks will feel secure in housing their customer data and information. Globally the cost of competing with banks with deep pockets pushes smaller banks to ASPs. India is unlikely to be any different in this".

CONCLUSION

Developing concern for results and performance on the part of entire personnel in banks is a vital requirement. This too will be a challenge. Future of core banking will depend on there alertness, operational and capital efficiency, customer orientation and standard of services creation of larger and larger volumes of performing assets, attainment of optimum level of productivity profitability and overall performance. Many a CBS implementation in India proceeds at a quick pace till implementation reaches around 10-20 branches. The pace then drops down and picks up again after a couple of months. "A pause at the end of 20-25 branches is essential. It is important that the bank examines the implementation, draws appropriate lessons from it and then firms up a suitable action plan for roll out to other branches. At the end of 20 branches or so, the software would have been standardized on a set of processes. The bank then needs to communicate to all other branches the standardized processes and then roll out rapidly". These can be easily achieved, if generously the concept of core banking is implemented.

Reference

1) www.google.com
2) www.rbi.com

3) Ammannaya K.K. "Indian Banking: Post-reform transformation & future Challenges" Southern Economist, July, Vol. 47 No. 6, 2008
4) Choudhary C.M. recent trends in Indian Banking, sublime publications, Jaipur, Indian, 2004.
5) RBI annual report, 2006-2007
6) Sreekantaradhya, Banking and finance, Deep & Deep publications PVT. Ltd. New Delhi, 2004.

5

Customer Relationship Management in Banking & Finance

*R.Manigandadurai,

The biggest management challenge in the new millennium of liberalisation and globalization for a business is to serve and maintain good relations with the king-the customer. In the past, producers did not take their customers for granted because at that time customers were not demanding nor had many alternative sources of supply or suppliers. Since he was a passive customer, the producer dictated terms and had little customer commitment. But today there is a radical transformation. The changing business environment is characterised by economic liberalisation, increasing competition, high consumer choice, enlightened and demanding customer, more emphasis on quality and value of purchase. All these changes have made today's producer shift from traditional marketing to modern marketing. Modern marketing calls for more than developing a product, pricing it, promoting it and making it accessible to target customers.

*Lecturer in Commerce, Maharaja Arts & Science College, Nelambur

It demands building trust, a binding force and value added relationship with the customers to win their hearts. The new age marketing aims at winning customers for ever, where companies greet the customers, create products to suit their needs, work hard to develop life time customers through the principles of customer delight, approval and enthusiasm.

WHAT IS CUSTOMER RELATIONSHIP MANAGEMENT (CRM)

The process of developing a cooperative and collaborative relationship between the buyers and sellers is called customer relationship management shortly called CRM. CRM aims at focusing all the organizational activities towards creating and maintaining a customer. CRM is a new technique in marketing where the marketer tries to develop long term collaborative relationship with customers to develop them as life time customers. CRM aims to make the customer climb up the ladder of loyalty.

Simply put, Customer Relationship Management (CRM) is the term for a company-wide system used by businesses to seek, obtain, and maintain customers. CRM helps businesses manage customer relationships in a more organised way. A successful CRM system involves all people, processes, and information technology associated with marketing, sales, and customer service. According to CRM consultants, "The idea is to have the same information available to everyone in the company so that every product or service need of the customer is met. CRM implies that everyone in the enterprise is focused on the customer."

CUSTOMER FOCUS IN BANKING SERVICES

As the intense competition becomes a way of doing business, it is the customer who calls the shot in deciding the nature of products and services offered in the market. The customers are becoming demanding, dominant and selective. In fact the perceptions and the expectations of the customers have undergone a sea change, with the availability of banking services to the customers at their door steps through the help of technology. Marketing of customer services aims at two important goals: prosperity to the bank and satisfied customers. Banks offer tangible services like loan schemes, interest rates and kinds of account and the intangible services like behavior and efficiency of staff, speed of transactions and the ambience. The banks may need to include customer oriented approach or customer focus in their five areas of businesses such as Cash accessibility, asset security, money transfer, deferred payment and financial advices.

There are four strategies available to customer relations' managers:

- To win back or save customers
- To attract new and potential customers
- To create loyalty among existing customers and
- To up sell or offer cross services.

The future of banking business very much depends upon the ability of the banks to develop close relationship with the customers. In order to develop close relationship with the customers the banking industry has to focus on the technology oriented innovations that offer convenience to the customers. Today customers are offered ATM services, access to internet banking and phone banking facilities and credit cards. These have elevated banking beyond the barriers of time and space.

MARKETING OF BANKING SERVICES

Marketing of banking services means organizing right activities and programmes in rendering right services to the right people at the right place, at the right time at the right price and with right communication and promotion. Marketing of banking services embrace the following unique features

- Intangibility-they cannot be seen or possessed physically but can only be experienced.
- Inseparability-their production and consumption occur simultaneously.
- Variability-they are highly variable depending on the merit of customers.
- Perishability -they cannot be stored.

CRM OBJECTIVES IN BANKING SECTOR

The idea of CRM is that it helps businesses use technology and human resources gain insight into the behavior of customers and the value of those customers. If it works as hoped, a business can: provide better customer service, make call centers more efficient, cross sell products more effectively, help sales staff close deals faster, simplify marketing and sales processes, discover new customers, and increase customer revenues. It doesn't happen by simply buying software and installing it. For CRM to be truly effective an organization must first decide what kind of customer information it is looking for and it must decide what it intends to do with that information. For example, many financial institutions keep track of customers' life stages in order to market appropriate banking products like mortgages or IRAs to them at the right time to fit their needs. Next, the organization must look into all of the different ways information about customers comes into a business, where and how this data is stored and how it is currently used. One company, for instance, may interact with customers in a myriad of different ways including mail campaigns, Web sites, brick-and-mortar stores, call centers, mobile sales force staff and marketing and advertising efforts. Solid CRM systems link up each of these points. This collected data flows between operational systems (like sales and inventory systems) and analytical systems that can help sort through these records for patterns. Company analysts can then comb through the data to obtain a holistic view of each customer and pinpoint areas where better services are needed.

GLOLBALISED SCENARIO

"Change" is a continuous process and banking industry is no exception to this natural law. Change in the Indian banking industry is inevitable due to the implementation of the financial sector reforms and policies in the country. The main objective of financial sector reforms is to promote an efficient, competitive and diversified financial system in the country. Indian banking industry has undergone tremendous transformation after liberalization and globalisation process initiated from 1991. These changes have forced the Indian banking industry to adjust the product mix to effect the rapid changes in their process to remain competitive in the globalised environment.

COMPETITION FROM FOREIGN BANKS AND NEW PRIVATE SECTOR BANKS

The entry of more and more foreign banks and new private sector banks, with lean and nimble footed structure, better technology, market orientation and cost effective measures, have intensified the competition in the Indian banking industry. Financial Institutions have also started entering into the domain of banks. In recent years, the share of business of public sector banks has declined considerably. So there is a compelling need for the Indian banking industry to modify its marketing strategy to attract the customers and to withstand the stiff competition from foreign banks and new private sector banks.

TECHNOLOGICAL ADVANCEMENT

The advent of technology both in terms of computers and communications has drastically altered the methodology of banking business. In the banking sector, the technology has opened new vistas and in turn has brought new possibilities for doing the same work differently and in a most cost-effective manner. Technology helps to have 24 hours a day banking, all seven days in a week. Tele banking, Internet banking and E-banking have opened new business potentials and opportunities which hither to remained unexplored. All these technological advancement may pave the way for home banking rather than branch banking.

INNOVATION

Another important force of change in the Indian banking sector is innovation. Banks are innovative, pro-active now-a-days and offer top class service to customers. They play a dynamic role not only as a provider of finance but also as a departmental store of finance. As a result of this, new products like merchant banking, mutual funds, leasing, factoring, forfeiting, corporate advisory services and venture capital are emerging. These innovative services may augment revenue with cost effective measures.

DEVELOPMENT OF THE SKILLS OF BANK PERSONNEL

To meet the new challenges, banks have to devise novel ways of meeting the customer's demands. To help the banking staff to get sufficient exposure to technology, suitable packages relating to hardware and software applications in relation to their works are to be provided. Further, a separate marketing wing may be created in every bank to market their banking services. They must be trained suitably to keep pace with the changing environment. In order to meet the challenges, the Human Resource Department in banks has to prepare appropriate manpower plans and strategies.

INTEGRATING MULTIPLE CHANNELS

ATMs, phone banking and even Internet banking almost seems like a pass, customers are now demanding multiple channels and consistent 24x7 service across these channels irrespective of their location, thus making banking services more accessible. Responding to the customer needs, banks are developing more intensive knowledge about retail customers and corporate clients so that they can execute relationship management strategies. CRM (Corporate Client Relationship Management) is a CRM term that is now gaining weight in banking services. CRM is designed for a more complex product set used by fewer clients who are corporate entities. Execution of CRM and CRM relies on data and technology to create knowledge about the customer or the client.

Banks combine internal data with data obtained from external sources in order to create a repository, a data warehouse. This is further analyzed to create customer or client profiles to identify opportunities. This analysis results in customer intelligence that can be used to decide on actionable points to maximize business opportunity and minimize risk. Effective customer relationship management usage in financial services helps improve customer acquisition and increase cross-selling. But this has to be applied consistently across the entire enterprise. That is, for the project to succeed- there has to be one-view of the bank and a data warehouse in place.

CRM has evolved from being a technology-driven sophisticated tool for marketing to being a key component of business strategy in the financials services industry. Cross-selling possibilities are often cited as one of the CRM pay-offs. But CRM could work cross-purposes too. Imagine the credit card division of a large financial institution conducting a targeted marketing campaign to increase credit limits and getting a good response. After an exhaustive credit analysis of customer information, some other division runs a campaign persuading many of these customers to consolidate debt and reduce credit exposure and risk. The net result would be a loss for the institution and a confused customer.

This typically happens when customer data is not shared seamlessly across the organization in real-time. Many times customer information gathered at one channel is inaccessible at other channels. An ATM behavior of a customer is not co-related with his online behavior. Eventually, this calls for integration across all marketing, sales, and service channels and across all businesses. Look at these as various stops in a CRM continuum.

SHARED ATM NETWORKS

Some banks find it difficult to share their ATM network with competitors, as ATMs are being projected as the key differentiator while others are aggregating to achieve scale. Shared ATM networks are a global phenomenon. While ATMs are high on fixed costs, the variable costs are lesser, and as usage is high in shared networks, it increases profitability by maximising utilization. These networks evolve from being a proprietary one set up by individual banks. The ones that set up ATM infrastructure are called the acquiring banks- like UTI Bank in the Cashnet case. UTI has around 800 ATMs in its network. Standard Chartered and Citibank with its credit cards and debit cards base are called the issuing banks. These banks spur the growth in the network usage. The transaction fee paid by the users is shared among the issuing bank to the acquiring bank. Explains Dr P J Nayak, chairman, UTI Bank, "For shared ATM networks, we need to differentiate between issuing banks and the acquiring banks." SBI and its affiliate banks are slated to install about 1,500 NCR ATMs over the next 18 months. With this deployment, SBI will have the country's largest ATM network, with more than 3,000 machines. The contract includes hardware, site installation services and ATM network management services.

CUSTOMERS EXPERIENCE A BANK THROUGH MULTIPLE CHANNELS AND INTERACTION POINTS

Given that self-service channels typically cost between one and two orders of magnitude less than attended branch services, banks have been employing electronic service delivery technologies aggressively for the past 20 years. Thus, automated teller machines (ATMs), for example, have long become a ubiquitous feature not confined to bank locations. Besides the efficiency motives that drive banks to push these new technologies, they are responding to a younger generation of customers, which has embraced electronic channels wholeheartedly. As retail delivery technologies have become widely available, customers have grown used to accessing their bank services virtually everywhere, 24 hours a day, any day of the week (although most consumers are still transacting with bank employees at a branch at least once a month). While electronic networks power hundreds of thousands of ATMs, an even larger multitude of point-of-sale terminals and other electronic devices have cropped up at retail merchants' outlets. Traditional telephone access has given way to sophisticated call centers and interactive voice response. Thanks to the Internet and wireless technologies, online banking has been growing steadily since its inception. Contact less devices now link customer accounts for highway tolls, transit, and other proximity payment purposes. Push channels such as snail mail, e-mails, and faxes continue to be important conduits of banking delivery.

AIB'S CRM STRATEGY

AIB recognises that customers are the lifeblood of the business and that the way to protect and grow its customer base - and ultimately its profitability - is to build strong customer relationships through delivery of superior quality service and to meet customer needs better than the competition. The CRM approach adopted by AIB focuses on maximising value for the customer and the bank. Research has shown that the key drivers of customer loyalty are:

- ❑ positive staff attitude
- ❑ honesty, integrity, and reliability
- ❑ proactive advice and delivery of promise
- ❑ consistent delivery of superior quality service
- ❑ simplicity and ease of doing business
- ❑ good after-sales service
- ❑ a fair and efficient complaint resolution policy

CRM NEEDS & REQUIREMENTS

Personal Customer Needs	AIB Requires
Personal contact	Quality customer information
A knowledgeable reliable banker	Product knowledge
Relevant information	Consultative selling/relationship
Customised & timely solutions	Management skills
Value for Money	Proactive approach

Business Customer Needs	AIB Requires
A professional partnership approach	Strategic thinking
High levels of information	Understanding the business
Customised and highly responsive service	Industry knowledge
Quality customer information	Partnership skills

ROLES AND RESPONSIBILITIES

AIB has approximately 1500 Relationship Managers, each designated as the prime contact for an assigned group of customers. Relationship managers proactively contact customers and offer customised products and services in a timely manner. Understanding the customers growing needs for choice, convenience and an anytime/anywhere banking service, AIB provides access for customers to products and services through a number of other delivery channels such as the 24-hour call centre, internet and ATM network.

The relationship managers, branch service staff and call-centre staff have participated in CRM training and have developed their relationship and service skills, to enhance their customer interactions.

INFORMATION QUALITY MANAGEMENT

Accurate customer information is crucial to providing effective customer service. It is just as important to update customer information regularly as it is to get the information in the first place. Quality customer information provides a better understanding of what each customer wants so businesses can offer customers the right products and services, at the right time, through the right marketing channel. With poor quality customer information, a business may miss out on the potential to add value both for customers and its own business.

EXCELLENT INFORMATION QUALITY

There are 6 areas critical to building excellent information quality:

- ❑ Completeness - Is some information missing or incomplete?
- ❑ Conformity - Is all information uniform and does everyone understand it?
- ❑ Consistency - Does all the information make sense or do some parts conflict with others?
- ❑ Accuracy - Is all the information up-to-date and accurate?
- ❑ Integrity - Does the information make sense in terms of personal knowledge of the customer?
- ❑ Duplication - Is the same information being held in different places?

BUSINESS INTELLEGENCE

As part of the CRM Framework, AIB has set up a Business Intelligence Centre. A team of highly skilled analysts interpret customer information and distribute it to the appropriate relationship manager or business area for action. Their analysis of reported information focuses on key customer relationship management strategies including:

- ❑ Dynamic Customer Segmentation
- ❑ Customer needs analysis
- ❑ Customer Retention
- ❑ Customer Value Management
- ❑ Customer Contact Programmes
- ❑ Development of tailored propositions, encompassing the appropriate marketing mix

BUSINESS REPORTING AND RESULTS

Ongoing support and information for CRM is provided by way of weekly, monthly, and quarterly performance reports. Reports can help with day to- day customer contact planning, encourage sharing of best practices, and strengthen business performance. The success of AIB's CRM strategy is also measured through Annual Customer Service Research, Market Share Research and Annual Results. AIB had record levels of business in 2003, particularly in the areas of business lending and personal mortgages, as a result of having more time to engage customers in a more focused way. AIB customers can choose from an extensive range of financial products and services. Recent customer surveys show increased satisfaction towards the bank from customers around the country.

NEW HORIZONS FOR INSTITUTIONAL BANKING

In today's highly competitive worldwide foreign exchange markets, banks have been implored to focus internally on retaining their invaluable human capital, namely their key employees. Statements such as "Our assets depart nightly by the bank elevators" are now firmly enshrined in management guidelines. In fact, the truly most productive and desirable assets may not be present in the building at all! That is, the bonafide assets consist of a profitable customer base that is increasingly accessible even to non-traditional bank competitors via sophisticated technology.

BENEFITS OF CRM

Customers can now visit any branch and AIB customer service representatives can access customer information efficiently and securely. Customer service representatives can avoid double selling and offering unrelated products and services to customers. By listening and reacting to customers, businesses can develop customer centric products and services based on customer wants, tailored to their needs. Through its relationship management programme, AIB maintains and builds on existing customer relationships, adds value by retaining clients and cross sells products and services.

BENEFITS FOR CUSTOMERS

- Customers feel empowered if they have greater access to products and services e.g., 24-hour banking.
- There is a more coordinated and professional approach to customer contact.
- Targeted product and service offerings can be timed to coincide with customer events and life stages e.g., educational loans.
- With up-to-date customer information, businesses can prepare more personalised services.

BENEFITS FOR EMPLOYEES

- Employees have more time to serve customers and fulfill orders.
- Employees are empowered with the information to deliver high quality service and meet customer expectations.
- Employees have higher satisfaction ratings.

BENEFITS FOR AIB

- There is optimum use of resources.
- Customer satisfaction and loyalty is increased by providing consistent personalised experiences.
- There is improved customer acquisition, retention, and cross-selling.
- Managers are empowered with information that can help them manage customer relationships and make better decisions faster.
- Executives are empowered with information enabling them to capitalize on short windows of opportunity in the market.

CONCLUSION

The recent trend of globalisation and liberalization has posed serious problems to domestic banks. The entry of new foreign banks and private sector banks with their advanced knowledge base of automation in the banking operations and aggressive marketing strategies has pushed public sector banks to a tight corner. Potential customers have started moving towards foreign banks and private sector banks. To survive and succeed, banks must identify their marketing areas, develop adequate resources, convert these resources into healthy and efficient services and distribute them effectively satisfying the manifold tastes of customers. By developing and utilising an effective CRM system, AIB has positioned itself as a leading provider of superior quality financial products and services. AIB observed the changing financial services industry and its customers and adapted accordingly. It has been successful because AIB was flexible enough to change its overall business strategy. Staying abreast of current industry and market trends while focusing on your most valuable asset, your customers, is proving a smart way to stay ahead in business.

6

Customer Relationship Management in Banking Sector

*P. Pirakatheeswari,

Today, many businesses such as banks, insurance companies, and other service providers realize the importance of Customer Relationship Management (CRM) and its potential to help them acquire new customers retain existing ones and maximize their lifetime value. At this point, close relationship with customers will require a strong coordination between IT and marketing departments to provide a long-term retention of selected customers. Today, financial institutions can no longer rely on these committed relationships or established marketing techniques to attract and retain customers. As markets break down into heterogeneous segments, a more precisely targeted marketing technique is required, which creates a dialogue with smaller groups of customers and identifies individual needs. Also, before the Internet revolution, consumers largely selected their banks based on how convenient the location of bank's branches was to their

*Lecturer in Commerce, Sri Sarada College for Women (Autonomous), Salem.

homes or offices. With the advent of new technologies in the business of bank, such as Internet banking and ATMs, now customers can freely chose any bank for their transactions. Thus, the customer base of banks has increased, and so has the choices of customers for selecting the banks. This situation coupled with the pressures of competitive and dynamic markets has contributed to the growth of CRM in the Financial Services Sector.

Customer Relationship Management: The Concept

Customer Relationship Management is the establishment, development, maintenance and optimization of long-term mutually valuable relationships between consumers and the organizations. Successful customer relationship management focuses on understanding the needs and desires of the customers and is achieved by placing these needs at the heart of the business by integrating them with the organization's strategy, people, technology and business processes.

CRM is an integrated business strategy that places the customer at the centre of business consciousness. The new study based on only improving customer relationship and increasing customer loyalty. The needs and requirements of customers are relative to their life events. By being closely associated with the customer at all times during their lives, major events and at times of decision-making and most importantly being aware of it goes a ling way in increasing profitability of banks. At the heart of a perfect CRM strategy is the creation of mutual value for all the parties involved in the business process. It is about creating a sustainable competitive advantage by being the best at understanding, communicating and delivering and developing existing customer relationships in addition to creating and keeping new customers. So the concept of product life cycle is giving way to the concept of customer life cycle focusing on the development of products and services that anticipate the future need of the existing customers and creating additional services that extend existing customer relationships beyond transactions.

Management of Customer Relationship in Banking Sector in India

In banking and financial sector a customer is a care component which occupies prominent place in the new millennium. The banking business can not operate without customer and nor is the business done by acquiring a certain number of customers. No bank can possible meet all the needs of its customers given to the diversity of their wants. In such a situation, the secret key factor of the company's success is effective Customer Relationship Management (CRM).

CRM in Banking Sector as New Strategies

CRM is the latest catchword across the banking industry all over the globe. It provides complete solutions to the institution which includes technology, process, system arid most significantly, human resources. CRM provides solutions in terms of quality, cost abs delivery while bringing together the man and the machine. The game is "have a strong customer base or perish". The banks are willing to go to any extent to achieve this.

CRM is a customer driven business strategy designed to optimize profitability, revenue and customer satisfaction. CRM involves relationship marketing which is to establish, maintain, enhance relationships with customers and other partners so that the objectives of the parties involved are met. It is achieved by mutual exchange and fulfillment of promises. Thus, CBM provides a holistic view of the customer across all of an organisation's products and channels.

CRM Objectives in Banking Sector

The idea of CRM is that it helps businesses use technology and human resources gain insight into the behavior of customers and the value of those customers. If it works as hoped, a business can provide better customer service, make call centers more efficient, cross sell products more effectively, help sales staff close deals faster, simplify marketing and sales processes, discover new customers, and increase customer revenues. It doesn't happen by simply buying software and installing it.

CBM is based on the short-term orientation of the management of banking sector. Its focus was on short term a result which stresses on the following drives:

- To attract new customers
- To increase sales per customer
- To reduce cost through optimization of business process.
- To improve customer relationship
- To increase loyalty.

Need of CRM in the Banking Industry

A Relationship-based Marketing approach has the following benefits: -

- Over time, retail bank customers tend to increase their holding of the other products from across the range of financial products / services available.
- Long-term customers are more likely to become a referral source.
- The longer a relationship continues; the better a bank can understand the customer and his/her needs & preferences, and so greater the opportunity to tailor products and services and cross-sell the product / service range.
- Customers in long-term relationships are more comfortable with the service, the organization, methods and procedures. This helps reduce operating cost and costs arising out of customer error.

With increased number of banks, products and services and practically nil switching costs, customers are easily switching banks whenever they find better services and products. Banks are finding it tough to get new customers and more importantly, retain existing customers. According to a research by Reichheld and Sasser in the Harvard Business Review, 5% increase in customer retention can increase profitability by 35% in banking business, 50% in insurance and brokerage and 125% in the consumer credit card market. Therefore, banks are now stressing on retaining customers and increasing market share.

Private Banking and CRM

Private Banks have traditionally viewed themselves as exceedingly 'Customer Centric' offering what they believe to be highly personalized services to the High Net Worth Customers. However, changes in the customer behavior and accumulation of wealth are resulting in the needs of HNW customers becoming more diverse and complex in terms of the sorts of products they want, the channels through which they want to access them and the associated range of advice. The wealthier the customers, the more demanding they are - and the clients expect more and more from their banks. Competition for "Supremely elite" is increasing

Customer Experiences

The first step towards successfully winning, retaining and growing the profitability of private banking customers is to understand what their wants and needs are, so that the organization can be built around serving those needs. Only when an organization has done this and incorporated this into its strategy can it start to design its value proposition and a customer experience that will enable it to achieve a differentiated competitive position in the private banking market, and more importantly, do so in an economically viable way.

The Basic Customer Experience

There is a basic 'generic' customer experience that many private banking customers are seeking. To be a credible player in the market, a private bank must be able to deliver this 'base' experience. This represents a common set of needs that are shared by most HNW customers. Therefore, the private bank must have the capabilities required to meet these needs for the majority of its customer base. All customers, regardless of wealth levels, have similar emotional needs, which drive their need for advice and their purchase of products. Different wealth levels impose different priorities on meeting these needs and open up new avenues for doing so.

Take a simple example, HNW customers can afford on it to fund their retirement, so their priorities may be associated with growing wealth, rather than preserving it, allowing them to choose a product option with a higher risk/reward ratio. If this is true, it means all HNW customers start with a basic, common set of what they want and need from a bank, which might include: -

- Personal, long-term relationship
- Advice combining industry expertise and knowledge of personal circumstances
- High quality, consistent quality
- Security, privacy, confidentiality

At this basic level, grouping together these core wants and needs produces a set of generic characteristics that an HNW individual seeks from an organization before he or she will even consider placing any of his or her wealth with it. Underlying these generic characteristics is a set of capabilities covering organization, process and technology, which the private bank must process to operate in the high net worth market.

Customer Satisfaction - A Critical Component of Profitability

The basic role of CBM is to provide maximum satisfaction to customers in the banking services. It is found that on an average, the customers of banks that give personalized service are far more satisfied than the ones which adhere to traditional services.

Managing the Customer Satisfaction Process presents an organized, systematic method of identifying, measuring, managing, and monitoring customer requirements and satisfaction to improve profits and beat the competition. This course defines each step of the customers satisfaction management process and equips you with powerful research, quality, and planning tools to carry out the improvement process in your department and company. We will learn how to identify

- Customer requirements;
- Expectations for quality and satisfaction and to assess and measure critical customer needs;
- Market segmentation;
- Competitive structure and
- Employee perceptions.

The importance of customer service for capturing business in banks have become a focus point in all stages of marketing of banking service, since all most all banks offering more or less the same product with little changes in nomenclature. Here the concept of enhancing the customer satisfaction is a pivotal point to attract more and more people to banking by a particular bank. Exceptional customer service of greater customer retention which in turn results in high profitability. Customer loyalty is major contribution to sustainable profit growth. A seamless integration of the entire component in the service profit chaises- employee satisfaction, value creation, customer satisfaction, customer loyalty and profit and growth-links all the critical dynamics of top customer services.

Sadly, nature companies often forget or forsake the thing that made them successful in the first place, a customer centric business model. They lose focus on the customer and start focusing on the bottom line and quarterly results. They look for ways to cut cost or increasing revenues, often at expenses of the customer. They forget that satisfying customer needs and continuous value innovation is the only path to sustainable growth. This creates opportunities for new smaller companies to emulate and improve upon what made their bigger competition. It has become challenging and tough job for banks in retaining the existing customer box and winning the new customer. Otherwise sustaining in the banking business is a tough phenomenon. Bankers are in the people business and it is the goal of the bankers to make customer happy to achieve their target. So achieve this challenging task of customer satisfaction, bankers are turning to technology for help.

Changing Perception of Customer

The customer perception is changing day by day. Peter Drucker said twenty five years ago-"The purpose of business is to attract and retain a customer". It sounds simple but too many business and paradigms shifts towards customer focus for the past five decade.

1950's to 1960's	SERVICING THE CUSTOMER
1960's to 1980's	SATISFYING THE CUSTOMER
1980's to 1990's	PLEASING THE CUSTOMER
1990's to 2000 A.D	DELIGHTING THE CUSTOMER
2000 A.D and beyond	RETAINING THE CUSTOMER

Bankers and Customer Relationship

Today the relationship between the bankers and customer has come under the sharp focus both at the bankers and as well as at the customers ends. Many customers are not only wanting but are expecting better service. The factors viz, lack of competition, administered regime, insulted economy which lendered market forces to the customer.

The dominant questions, which are bothering the mends of bank management today is now to improve customer service and competitive advantages.

PARADIGM SHIFT SCENARIO IN INDIA

Before 1991	**After 1991**
Sellers market	Buyers market
Protected market	Open market
Not many global brands	Increase in global brands
Patient customer	Demanding customer

Friendly competition	Cut throat competition
Limited choice of customer	Increasing choice of customer
Limited T.V promotion	Extensive T.V promotion
Limited role of service	Increase role of service
Gaining new customer	Retaining existing customer
Transaction	Relationship
Standard of living	Quality of life

The Need for a Standardized Infrastructure in Banking

For the customer, the lack of integration can mean frustrating delays, inconsistency data across channels and a less than-satisfactory experience and dis-satisfied customers vote with their feel. Bank loose more than 10% of their customer each year. For employers, the each of integrated customer data prevents them from delivering great service, which contributes to low employees moral and increases turnover. Many banks experience 40% annual turnover at the branch level and as even higher percentage at call centers. Perhaps, the biggest challenge lies in the growing expectations of bank customers. They now expect to now more freely among their branch bank and other challenges such as ATM's and internet banking and their expectation this experience to be seamless and consistent.

Mapping the Customer Needs

In the present day banking, through the banking services are technology driven and major role is played by technology in all decision on customer service, the tested methods like customer decision on customer service, the tested methods like customer survey continue to help the management in identifying the customer needs is important before providing the service, so that the actual requirement of the particular segments of the customer is met with. This will help the management to have an insight into the customer needs and attitudes. In order to identify the customer needs, the banks have to develop a proactive approach. Such approach, will not only enhance the image of the bank in the customer view point, but also presides a satisfaction to the bank for having served the customer needs.

Knowledge about the Needs of Customers

CRM cannot be implemented properly unless full knowledge about the needs and requirements of the customers are provided. It has been noticed that constant interaction between the bank and the customers is the key factor.

Change of Organisation Structure for Better Servicing

The financial sector reforms have bought about a need for restructuring of banks in providing good customer service. The number of innovative financial products offered by banks is increasing steadily. The public sector banks are still continuing with old patterns in their structure. This structure is hampering customer services. In these days of super specialization public sector banks have to regret their structure by classifying the banking as rural banking and commercial banking. In such case they can compete effectively with new breed of private sector banks. On account of new structure and cost effective business techniques, the new private sector banks have become strong competitors to public sectors banks. The business process re-engineering, business process out sourcing and support services implemented in new breed of banks have helped them in concentrating more on "customer centric banking". The new banking structure has helped for extending more efficient and effective services to customer resulting in making a brand for the bank itself.

Therefore, it is imperative for the public sector banks to restructure their organization for catering better service to customers and say good-bye to the age old practices. New structure will help to migrate the low value customer to low cost channels, where there is a cost increase due to high volume. Channel migration is an important aspect in re-structuring. This enable banks to services the high value customer more effectively.

Technology is the Key

Technology has thrown new challenges in the banking sector and new issues have started cropping up which is going to pose certain problems in the near future. The new entrants in the banking are with computer background. However, over a period of time they would acquire banking experience. Whereas the middle and senior level people have rich banking experience but their computer literacy is at a low level. Therefore, they feel the handicap in this regard since technology has become an indispensable tool in banking.

Foreign banks and the new private sector banks have embraced technology right from the inception of their operations and therefore, they have adapted themselves to the changes in the technology easily. Whereas the Public Sector Banks (PSBs) and the old private sector banks (barring a very few of them) have not been able to keep pace with these developments. In this regard, one can cite historical, political and other factors like work culture and working relations (which are mainly governed by bipartite settlements between the managements and the staff members) as the main constraints. Added to these woes, the PSBs were also saddled with some non-viable and loss-making branches, thanks to the social banking concept thrust upon them by the regulatory authorities in 1960s.

Customer Retention

Customer retention is also an important on CRM in banks. The observations and experience reveal that retention of old customers is more profitable that acquiring new ones. This is because a happy and satisfied old customer brings in many other new customers, it has been realised that it pays more to keep your existing customer content which results in cross selling and repurchase of products. Retention is definitely the "buzz" word for businesses today. Customer retention has business leader's attention and leaving most wondering how other businesses are approaching this seemingly complex business function. A web search of "customer retention" results in thousands of available web sites all with the real solutions for customer retention. Researchers, analysts, and consultants have developed a multiple selection of theories, programs, and practices for customer retention. Businesses today readily share their experience in improving customer retention. Most solutions point to business culture, staff training, and sales methodology along with tracking and responding to customer demographics. In simple terms, customer retention is all about the customer and the customer's experience.

Knowledge of Bankers

Knowledge of bankers is also an important issue of CRM in present banking. To motive and train the staff to do so is the first step in implementation of CRM in Indian banking. The motivation must come from the side of management in the form of regular training in behavioral and functional aspect of banking.

The issues surrounding the collaboration of knowledge and delivery have to do with the management of the data and processes involved as well as some very emotional aspects of the customer's relationship with the bank and the extent to which individual customers perceive the bank as a threat to their privacy. To build on the full strength of this collaboration, banks need to completely understand the issues surrounding the use of knowledge, and then tread lightly.

Data acquisition through customer interaction is determined by the delivery channels, themselves, or through some integrated channel management architecture. Institutions are already collecting most of the available information today such as customer identity, accounts, channels, transactions performed, time of day, and all the pieces of information that have some value to the institution. Such basic information is included in the transactions that are sent to the core banking system or to some external system such as a credit processor.

For now, there seems to be no need to collect additional information that is not currently acquired. What is required is the use of the data in managing the relationship with the customer in a more fulfilling way.

The shift to the existing use of data comes in the form of the centralized acquisition (or processing) of this information ***outside of the transactional sense.*** Along with the use of transactional information by the systems that perform the basic units of work, specialized applications collect and analyze information about the customer interaction, itself, to give insight into customer behavior. Banks can also collect and store information about nontrivial transactions to provide continuity among customer contacts. So if a customer has an unresolved problem, that information is available at all appropriate channels. While many institutions are currently performing such analysis within a given channel (online banking navigation behavior, for example), the next step includes analysis of the customer's behavior across all delivery channels in the network. This enables gauging behavior in a broader context, analysis of all external providers of service, and analysis of how the customer uses these products.

Powerful Customer Knowledge Systems for the Future

The pace of implementation of integrated delivery channel architectures will quicken and eventually prevail at top banks. The deployment of powerful customer knowledge systems will also increase as more and more useful information can be distilled from the myriad of resources in the bank IT network. As these two infrastructures evolve, the integration between them will also increase. Already, many institutions use information gleaned from customer knowledge systems to suggest new products to customers at the branch teller. Nonetheless, Tower Group believes that much of the use of information between the knowledge systems and the delivery channels has yet to be fully realized. With most of the technology in place, banks must begin to form strategies around the use of information in the day-to-day contact with its customers.

As the capability to build on this flow of information grows, it has the potential to outpace the customer's acceptance of the bank's knowledge. Privacy is an emotional issue and, so, not entirely rational. Technology and policy can only go so far in ensuring that the use of information at the point of contact is not intrusive to the customer's comfortable level of privacy. Relationship training is more important than before as banks begin to learn more about their customers and use that information to bring financial value to them.

Ultimately, the management of customer information at the point of interaction is about service, about keeping the customer happy and simply put, about keeping the customer. It's about strengthening the relationship and showing the customer that the bank's knowledge can lead to real benefit. It's about increasing the bank's benefit as well, and doing it in a way that does not sacrifice the customer's long-term well-being. Finally, it's about trust as a result of knowing the customer and not as an excuse for misusing information.

Steps initiated:

Some of the banks have started to introduce new strategies for proper CRM which can be stated below:

1. With the advent of IT, ATM and net banking have become a reality. Many Indian banks have introduced "anywhere banking". An account holder can transact business anywhere in the country in select branches.
2. The loan seeker needs not to make trips to the bank. Today, the banker is going to the door step of a prospective loan seeker and offering him different repayment options.
3. Some foreign banks have started displaying works of famous artists just to create the difference.
4. An executive of foreign bank feels bankers have to follow the basics of the hotel and airline industry to put customers at ease and in an environment he relates to.
5. Hospitality such as offering coffee to customers is followed in some banks.

6. Some of the oldest private sector banks of our nation have made revolutionary changes and launched products just too offered quality service to the customers.
7. Interiors are part of marketing efforts of banks these days to bring in retail customers and hold on them. There is a bit of life style in banking these days.

Suggestion for Improvement

- Banks should realize that the customer is the focus point to improve the business.
- Banks have to evolve plans and strategies to cater better service and enhance satisfaction levels and try to create a brand image.
- Skill of personnel working, training program to be developed among the staff.
- Customer service should be the main motto for the improvement of the business.
- Technology implementation should be speed-up, such as computerization, electronic banking through email, tele-banking, mobile phone banking and wide net of ATM's through channel negotiation process.

Banking Industry is in midst of a major transformation. Mega Tectonics in the Banking Industry can be summarized as follows:

1. Banks are going global. To be successful it is important that banks understand local culture and preferences.
2. Banks in order to be profitable are offering a variety of innovative products. It is important for the Banks to know how the various products are performing and how successful is their promotional campaigns on target segment.
3. Banks are reaching to their customers through multiple channels like ATM, web banking, mobile banking, telebanking in addition to the traditional Bank Branch. Customer data in silos is a challenge to the bank.

4. Banks are operating in wafer thin margin under changing regulatory and competitive landscape.

Banks need systems to manage its customer base and meet the challenges of growth.

- It is important that Banks get a 'Single version of Truth' for the customers they serve.
- It is important that Banks get a '360 degree View' of their customers. This will allow banks to have a deeper understanding of the customer's interaction with the various sections of the bank. It is important to understand the credit worthiness of its customers. A customer may have a banking account, home account, personal loan account, mutual funds demat accounts all with the same bank. Unless the Bank has a 360 degree view of the customer, it will not be able to have a holistic view of the customer profile and cross sell or up sell other products and services. Similarly the Bank will not be able to advice its customer on whether they have a high risk or a low risk investment portfolio. They need to have a complete understanding of their customers need in order to get a greater share of their wallets.
- Banks need to know how effective their campaign promotions are. They need to know which product is performing well at what segment of the market.
- Banks need to maintain their Knowledge and share their insights with various sections of their employee as relevant. There has to be only one version of the truth. How often do we see that various sections of the bank are totally naive of what they have already sold to a customer?
- Banks need to know how though effectively schedule and dispatch bank representatives for products such as Loans, Personal Banking etc.
- In Wealth Management, Banks need to know what portfolios to invest in. How the underlying assets are performing and how to rehash their portfolios.

- Bank need analytics that can help them predict customer interest in them as well as scorecards that indicate how well they are performing against their goals

Conclusion

All the above factors will help to increase customer service. Ultimately should prove that they are presiding essential service as already branded for development to the economy. Banking can be mysterious for consumers and how they interact with their finances can be a complex matter. The challenges faced by banks and their customers are many but the trick lies in de-mystifying complex financial relationships. Technical solutions deployed by banks today are flexible, user-friendly and meant to facilitate specific workflow and requirements in implementation processes. In order to simplify lives, banks have begun to implement end-to-end technologies through all departments with the intention of removing human error from processes. Previously existing manual environments could not have been adequate for future visions, growth plans and strategies. In this day and age, customers enjoy complete luxury in terms of customized technical solutions and banks use the same to cement long-term, mutually-beneficial relationships.

7

E-Banking: Risks and Responses

*P. Janaki

Banking has come a long way from the time of ledger cards and other manual filing systems. Most banks today have Electronic systems to handle their daily voluminous tasks of information retrieval, storage and processing. Irrespective of whether they are automated or not, banks by their nature are continually involved in all forms of information management on a continuous basis. The Computer is of course an established tool for achieving a competitive edge and optimal resource allocation. The most obvious banking application of Computers is customer service. Computerized banks respond immediately to requests from customers for Statement of Accounts, Balance and Account activity enquiries. With Signature and Image verification systems, the time taken to offer typical cashier services like receiving and paying out of cash, is minimized. With advent of Automatic Teller Machines (ATM), banks are able to serve customers outside the banking hall. Furthermore, computers help banks to reduce the cost of doing

*Lecturer in Commerce, Vellalar College for Women, Thindal, Erode

business. Although, the effectiveness of the Information Technology deployment in banks is another matter, the fact remains that IT usage is now a reality. This is to be expected in view of the huge amount of information being handled by banks on a daily basis. On the customer's side, cash is withdrawn or deposited, cheques are deposited or cleared, statement of accounts are produced, etc. At the same time, banks need up-to-date information on accounts, credit facilities, interest, deposits, charges, income, profitability indices and other financial control information.

E-banking

Internet banking (or E-banking) means any user with a personal computer and a browser can get connected to his bank's website to perform any of the virtual banking functions. In internet banking system the bank has a centralized database that is web-enabled. All the services that the bank has permitted on the internet are displayed in menu. Any service can be selected and further interaction is dictated by the nature of service. The traditional branch model of bank is now giving place to an alternative delivery channels with ATM network. Once the branch offices of bank are interconnected through terrestrial or satellite links, there would be no physical identity for any branch. It would a borderless entity permitting anytime, anywhere and anyhow banking. The network which connects the various locations and gives connectivity to the central office within the organization is called intranet. These networks are limited to organizations for which they are set up. SWIFT is a live example of intranet application.

Internet banking in India

The Reserve Bank of India constituted a working group on Internet Banking. The group divided the internet banking products in India into 3 types based on the levels of access granted. They are:

i) Information Only System: General purpose information like interest rates, branch location, bank products and their features, loan and deposit calculations are provided in the banks website. There exist facilities for downloading various types of application forms. The communication is normally done through e-mail. There is no interaction between the customer and bank's application system. No identification of the customer is done. In this system, there is no possibility of any unauthorized person getting into production systems of the bank through internet.

ii) Electronic Information Transfer System: The system provides customer- specific information in the form of account balances, transaction details, and statement of accounts. The information is still largely of the 'read only' format. Identification and authentication of the customer is through password. The information is fetched from the bank's application system either in batch mode or off-line. The application systems cannot directly access through the internet.

iii) Fully Electronic Transactional System: This system allows bi-directional capabilities. Transactions can be submitted by the customer for online update. This system requires high degree of security and control. In this environment, web server and application systems are linked over secure infrastructure. It comprises technology covering computerization, networking and security, inter-bank payment gateway and legal infrastructure.

Automated Teller Machine (ATM): ATM is designed to perform the most important function of bank. It is operated by plastic card with its special features. The plastic card is replacing cheque, personal attendance of the customer, banking hour's restrictions and paper based verification. There are debit cards. ATMs used as spring board for Electronic Fund Transfer. ATM itself can provide information about customers account and also receive instructions from customers - ATM cardholders. An ATM is an Electronic Fund Transfer terminal capable of handling cash deposits, transfer between accounts, balance enquiries, cash withdrawals and pay bills. It may be on-line or Off-line. The on-line ATM enables the customer to avail banking facilities from anywhere. In off-line the facilities are confined to that particular ATM assigned. Any customer possessing ATM card issued by the Shared Payment Network System can go to any ATM linked to Shared Payment Networks and perform his transactions.

Credit Cards/Debit Cards: The Credit Card holder is empowered to spend wherever and whenever he wants with his Credit Card within the limits fixed by his bank. Credit Card is a post paid card. Debit Card, on the other hand, is a prepaid card with some stored value. Every time a person uses this card, the Internet Banking house gets money transferred to its account from the bank of the buyer. The buyers account is debited with the exact amount of purchases. An individual has to open an account with the issuing bank which gives debit card with a Personal Identification Number (PIN). When he makes a purchase, he enters his PIN on shops PIN pad. When the card is slurped through the electronic terminal, it dials the acquiring bank system - either Master Card or VISA that validates the PIN and finds out from the issuing bank whether to accept or decline the transactions. The customer can never overspend because the system rejects any transaction which exceeds the balance in his account. The bank never faces a default because the amount spent is debited immediately from the customers account.

Smart Card: Banks are adding chips to their current magnetic stripe cards to enhance security and offer new service, called Smart Cards. Smart Cards allow thousands of times of information storable on magnetic stripe cards. In addition, these cards are highly secure, more reliable and perform multiple functions. They hold a large amount of personal information, from medical and health history to personal banking and personal preferences.

Security Precautions

Customers should never share personal information like PIN numbers, passwords etc with anyone, including employees of the bank. It is important that documents that contain confidential information are safeguarded. PIN or password mailers should not be stored, the PIN and/or passwords should be changed immediately and memorised before destroying the mailers. Customers are advised not to provide sensitive account-related information over unsecured e-mails or over the phone. Take simple precautions like changing the ATM PIN and online login and transaction passwords on a regular basis. Also ensure that the logged in session is properly signed out.

Risks and Responses

One of the issues currently being addressed is the impact of e-banking on traditional banking players. After all, if there are risks inherent in going into e-banking there are other risks in not doing so. It is too early to have a firm view on this yet. Even to practitioners the future of e-banking and its implications are unclear. It might be convenient nevertheless to outline briefly two views that are prevalent in the market. The view that the Internet is a revolution that will sweep away the old order holds much sway. Arguments in favour are as follows:

E-banking transactions are much cheaper than branch or even phone transactions. This could turn yesterday's competitive advantage - a large branch network - into a comparative disadvantage, allowing e-banks to undercut bricks and mortar banks. This is commonly known as the "beached dinosaur" theory. E-banks are easy to set up so lots of new entrants will arrive. 'Old-world' systems, cultures and structures will not encumber these new entrants. Instead, they will be adaptable and responsive. E-banking gives consumers much more choice. Consumers will be less inclined to remain loyal. E-banking will lead to an erosion of the 'endowment effect' currently enjoyed by the major UK banks. Deposits will go elsewhere with the consequence that these banks will have to fight to regain and retain their customer base. This will increase their cost of funds, possibly making their business less viable. Lost revenue may even result in these banks taking more risks to breach the gap.

Portal providers are likely to attract the most significant share of banking profits. Indeed banks could become glorified marriage brokers. They would simply bring two parties together – eg buyer and seller, payer and payee. The products will be provided by monolines, experts in their field. Traditional banks may simply be left with payment and settlement business – even this could be cast into doubt. Traditional banks will find it difficult to evolve. Not only will they be unable to make acquisitions for cash as opposed to being able to offer shares, they will be unable to obtain additional capital from the stock market. This is in contrast to the situation for Internet firms for whom it seems relatively easy to attract investment.

There is of course another view which sees e-banking more as an evolution than a revolution. E-banking is just banking offered via a new delivery channel. It simply gives consumers another service (just as ATMs did). Like ATMs, e-banking will impact on the nature of branches but will not remove their value. Experience in Scandinavia (arguably the most advanced e-banking area in the world) appears to confirm that the future is 'clicks and mortar' banking. Customers want full service banking via a number of delivery channels. The future is therefore 'Martini Banking' (any time, any place, anywhere, anyhow). Traditional banks are starting to fight back.

The start-up costs of an e-bank are high. Establishing a trusted brand is very costly as it requires significant advertising expenditure in addition to the purchase of expensive technology (as security and privacy are key to gaining customer approval). E-banks have already found that retail banking only becomes profitable once a large critical mass is achieved. Consequently many e-banks are limiting themselves to providing a tailored service to the better off. Nobody really knows which of these versions will triumph. This is something that the market will determine. However, supervisors will need to pay close attention to the impact of e-banks on the traditional banks, for example by surveillance of:

- strategy
- customer levels
- earnings and costs
- advertising spending
- margins
- funding costs
- merger opportunities and threats, both in the UK and abroad.
- About the risks banks, and building societies, whether new or old, are running. The risk factors are discussed in the following heads:
  - strategy
  - business
  - security
  - reputation
  - operations

Even though the risk based approach to banking supervision is known to all, it is necessary to give different weightage and emphasis to the above factors for E-banking.

Strategic Risk

On strategic risk E-banking is relatively new and as a result, there can be a lack of understanding among senior management about its potential and implications. People with technological, but not banking, skills can end up driving the initiatives. E-initiatives can spring up in an incoherent and piecemeal manner in firms. They can be expensive and can fail to recoup their cost. Furthermore, they are often positioned as loss leaders (to capture market share), but may not attract the types of customers that banks want or expect and may have unexpected implications on existing business lines.

Banks should respond to these risks by having a clear strategy driven from the top and should ensure that this strategy takes account of the effects of e-banking, wherever relevant. Such a strategy should be clearly disseminated across the business, and supported by a clear business plan with an effective means of monitoring performance against it.

Business Risks

Business risks are also significant. Given the newness of e-banking, nobody knows much about whether e-banking customers will have different characteristics from the traditional banking customers. They may well have different characteristics – eg I want it all and I want it now. This could render existing score card models inappropriate, thus resulting in either higher rejection rates or inappropriate pricing to cover the risk. Banks may not be able to assess credit quality at a distance as effectively as they do in face to face circumstances. It could be more difficult to assess the nature and quality of collateral offered at a distance, especially if it is located in an area the bank is unfamiliar with (particularly if this is overseas). Furthermore as it is difficult to predict customer volumes and the stickiness of e-deposits (things which could lead either to rapid flows in or out of the bank) it could be very difficult to manage liquidity.

Of course, these are old risks with which banks and supervisors have considerable experience but they need to be watchful of old risks in new guises. In particular risk models and even processes designed for traditional banking may not be appropriate.

Operations Risk

Banks face three main types of operations risk:

- volume forecasts
- management information systems and
- outsourcing

Accurate volume forecasts have proved difficult - One of the key challenges encountered by banks in the Internet environment is how to predict and manage the volume of customers that they will obtain. Many banks going on-line have significantly misjudged volumes. When a bank has inadequate systems to cope with demand it may suffer reputation and financial damage, and even compromises in security if extra systems that are inadequately configured or tested are brought on-line to deal with the capacity problems.

As a way of addressing this risk, banks should:

- undertake market research,
- adopt systems with adequate capacity and scalability,
- undertake proportionate advertising campaigns, and
- ensure that they have adequate staff coverage and develop a suitable business continuity plan.

In brief, this is a new area, nobody knows all the answers, and banks need to exercise particular caution.

The second type of operations risk concerns management information systems. Again this is not unique to E-banking. I have seen many banks venture into new areas without having addressed management information issues. Banks may have difficulties in obtaining adequate management information to monitor their e-service, as it can be difficult to establish/ configure new systems to ensure that sufficient, meaningful and clear information is generated. Such information is particularly important in a new field like e-banking. Banks are being encouraged by the FSA to ensure that management have all the information that they require in a format that they understand and that does not cloud the key information with superfluous details.

Finally, a significant number of banks offering e-banking services outsource related business functions, e.g. security, either for reasons of cost reduction or, as are often the case in this field, because they do not have the relevant expertise in-house. Outsourcing a significant function can create material risks by potentially reducing a bank's control over that function. Outsourcing is of course neither new nor unmanageable but banks should be mindful of the FSA's guidance on outsourcing, which addresses these risks.

Security

Security issues are a major source of concern for everyone both inside and outside the banking industry. E-banking increases security risks, potentially exposing hitherto isolated systems to open and risky environments. Both the FSA and banks need to be proactive in monitoring and managing the security threat. Security breaches essentially fall into three categories; breaches with serious criminal intent (e.g. fraud, theft of commercially sensitive or financial information), breaches by 'casual hackers' (e.g. defacement of web sites or 'denial of service' - causing web sites to crash), and flaws in systems design and/or set up leading to security breaches (e.g. genuine users seeing / being able to transact on other users' accounts). All of these threats have potentially serious financial, legal and reputation implications.

Many banks are finding that their systems are being probed for weaknesses hundreds of times a day but damage/ losses arising from security breaches have so far tended to be minor. However some banks could develop more sensitive "burglar alarms", so that they are better aware of the nature and frequency of unsuccessful attempts to break into their system. The most sensitive computer systems, such as those used for high value payments or those storing highly confidential information, tend to be the most comprehensively secured. One could therefore imply that the greater the potential loss to a bank the less likely it is to occur, and in general this is the case. However, while banks tend to have reasonable perimeter security, there is sometimes insufficient segregation between internal systems and poor internal security. It may be that someone could breach the lighter security around a low value system, e.g. a bank's retail web site, and gain entry to a high value system via the bank's internal network. We are encouraging banks to look at the firewalls between their different systems to ensure adequate damage limitation should an external breach occur. As ever though, the greatest threat so far has been from the enemy within – ie your own employees, contractors and so on.

It is easy to overemphasize the security risks in e-banking. It must be remembered that the Internet could remove some errors introduced by manual processing (by increasing the degree of straight through processing from the customer through banks' systems). This reduces risks to the integrity of transaction data (although the risk of customer's incorrectly inputting data remains). As e-banking advances, focusing general attention on security risks, there could be large security gains. The banks have to deal with emerging threats effectively. Financial institutions need as a minimum to have a strategic approach to information security, building best practice security controls into systems and networks as they are developed a proactive approach to information security, involving active testing of system security controls (e.g. penetration testing), rapid response to new threats and vulnerabilities and regular review of market place developments, sufficient staff with information security, expertise active use of system based security management and monitoring tools and strong business information security controls. These are the issues line supervisors will be raising with their banks as part of their on-going supervision; or, for new applicants, will need to be given adequate assurances about.

Reputational Risks

This is considerably heightened for banks using the Internet. For example the Internet allows for the rapid dissemination of information which means that any incident, either good or bad, is common knowledge within a short space of time. Internet rumours can easily become self-fulfilling prophecies. The speed of the Internet considerably cuts the optimal response times for both banks and regulators to any incident. Banks must ensure their crisis management, particularly PR, processes are able to cope with Internet related incidents (whether they be real or hoaxes).

Any problems encountered by one firm in this new environment may affect the business of another, as it may affect confidence in the Internet as a whole. There is therefore a risk that one rogue e-bank could cause significant problems for all banks providing services via the Internet. This is a new type of systemic risk and is causing concern to e-banking providers. Overall, the Internet puts an emphasis on reputational risks. Never before has the bank's shop window (ie its site) been so important. One last reputational risk will be familiar to us all. That is whether the products being sold over the net are being marketed in such a way that the bank will be protected against future charges of miss-selling. As in the physical, so in the virtual world. Banks need to be sure those customers' rights and information needs are adequately safeguarded and provided for.

Conclusion

Have a clear and widely disseminated strategy that is driven from the top and takes into account the effects of e-banking, together with an effective process for measuring performance against it. Take into account the effect that e-provision will have upon their business risk exposures and manage these accordingly. Undertake market research, adopt systems with adequate capacity and scalability, undertake proportional advertising campaigns and ensure that they have adequate staff coverage and a suitable business continuity plan. Ensure they have adequate management information in a clear and comprehensible format. Take a strategic and proactive approach to information security, maintaining adequate staff expertise, building in best practice controls and testing and updating these as the market develops. Make active use of system based security management and monitoring tools. Ensure that crisis management processes are able to cope with Internet related incidents. Certainly there are risks. But there are also opportunities, and significant potential benefits for consumers, banks and regulators.

8

E-Banking Challenges and Opportunities

*Dr. A. Jayakumar and N.Kanimozhi

Electronic banking is the wave of the future. It provides enormous benefits to consumers in terms of the ease and cost of transactions. But it also poses new challenges for country authorities in regulating and supervising the financial system and in designing and implementing macroeconomic policy. E-banking is a generic term for delivery of banking services and products through electronic channels, such as the telephone, the internet, the cell phone, etc. The concept and scope of E-banking is still evolving. It facilitates an effective payment and accounting system thereby enhancing the speed of delivery of banking services considerably. While E-banking has improved efficiency and convenience, it has also posed several challenges to the regulators and supervisors. Several initiatives taken by the government of India, as well as the Reserve Bank of India (RBI), have facilitated the development of E-banking

*Department of Commerce, Periyar University, Salem
*Project Fellowship, Periyar University, Salem

in India. The government of India enacted the IT Act, 2000, which provides legal recognition to electronic transactions and other means of electronic commerce. The RBI has been preparing to upgrade itself as a regulator and supervisor of the technologically dominated financial system. It issued guidelines on risks and control in computer and telecommunication system to all banks, advising them to evaluate the risks inherent in the systems and put in place adequate control mechanisms to address the risks. The existing regulatory framework over banks has also been extended to E-banking. It covers various issues that fall within the framework of technology, security standards, legal and regulatory issues.

WHAT IS ELECTRONIC BANKING?

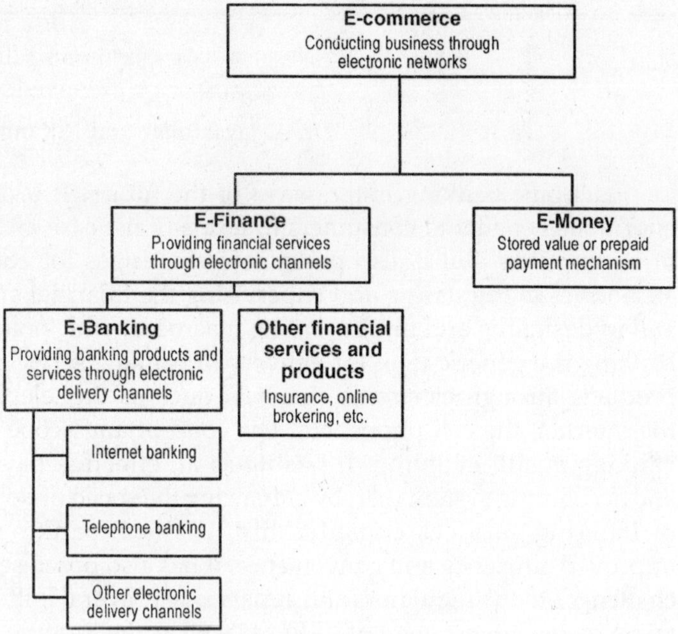

Figure 8.1. *Electronic Banking*

Electronic banking has been around for some time in the form of automatic teller machines and telephone transactions.

More recently, it has been transformed by the Internet, a new delivery channel for banking services that benefits both customers and banks. Access is fast, convenient, and available around the clock, whatever the customer's location (see illustration above). Plus, banks can provide services more efficiently and at substantially lower costs. Electronic banking also makes it easier for customers to compare banks' services and products, can increase competition among banks, and allows banks to penetrate new markets and thus expand their geographical reach. Some even see electronic banking as an opportunity for countries with underdeveloped financial systems to leapfrog developmental stages. Customers in such countries can access services more easily from banks abroad and through wireless communication systems, which are developing more rapidly than traditional "wired" communication networks.

The flip side of this technological boom is that electronic banking is not only susceptible to, but may exacerbate, some of the risks—particularly governance, legal, operational, and reputational—inherent in traditional banking. In addition, it poses new challenges. In response, many national regulators have already modified their regulations to achieve their main objectives: ensuring the safety and soundness of the domestic banking system, promoting market discipline, and protecting customer rights and the public trust in the banking system. Policymakers are also becoming increasingly aware of the greater potential impact of macroeconomic policy on capital movements.

TYPES OF E-BANKING

1. Various information on different products and services offered to customer and members of public in general it mighty receive and reply to customers queries through e-mail.

2. Simple transactional websites which allow customer to submit their instructions applications for different services, queries on their account balances etc, but they do not permit any fund-based transactions on their accounts.

3. Fully transactional websites which allow the customers to operate on their accounts for transfer of funds, payment of different bills, subscribing to other products of the bank and to transact purchase and sale of securities

FEATURES OF E-BANKING

- Removes the traditional geographical barriers
- Improves customer access
- Facilitates the offering of more services
- Attracts new customer
- Provides services offered by competitors
- To integrate with other banks or total banking system
- Maintaining Demat account.

The expansion of banking business would call for a massive increase in manpower requirements even if one were to assume that there would be some improvement in productivity. Productivity many will have to come through changes in work technology, more specifically through mechanization and computerization. These are no longer luxuries. Nor can they be regarded as anti labour. They are essential ingredients for maintaining accurate accounts and expeditious clearance of transactions. If the banking system is not to collapse under the weight of its own business, there is not escape from having more efficient data processing and information retrieval methods. Better customer service, the more expeditious handling of cheques, the early reconciliation of inter branch entries are all crucially dependent on the early adoption of mechanized accounting and data processing. The branch expansion programme opportunities for employment and manpower development.

Banking industry in developed countries has kept pace with the economic developments. The development economics have also tried to acquire the advanced banking networks taking full advantages of various inventions in the electronics, computers and telecommunications fields. The development of online access of information and networking of computers helps cope up with rapidly increasing volumes of transaction by linking branch office terminals with mainframe computers located in a head office. These core systems forming large integrated networks in many countries are the nerve centers of branch banking and now extend well beyond transaction processing, accounting and provision of management information. They are under constant development and modification primarily to reduce unit costs and to eliminate unnecessary paper output. For example, achieve ledgers are now stored electronically in mass storage units in some banks and management information is produced on microfiche and visual display units rather that on paper reports.

E-BANKING COMPONENTS

E-banking systems can vary significantly in their configuration depending on a number of factors. Financial institutions should choose their e-banking system configuration, including outsourcing relationships, based on four factors:

- Strategic objectives for e-banking
- Scope, scale, and complexity of equipment, systems, and activities
- Technology expertise; and
- Security and internal control requirements.

Financial institutions may choose to support their e-banking services internally. Alternatively, financial institutions can outsource any aspect of their e-banking systems to third parties. The following entities could provide or host (i.e., allow applications to reside on their servers) e-banking-related services for financial institutions:

- Another financial institution,
- Internet service provider,
- Core banking vendor or processor,
- Managed security service provider,
- Bill payment provider,
- Credit bureau and
- Credit scoring company.

E-banking systems rely on a number of common components or processes. The following list includes many of the potential components and processes seen in a typical institution:

- Website design and hosting,
- Firewall configuration and management,
- Intrusion detection system or IDS (network and host-based),
- Network administration,
- Security management,
- Internet banking server,
- E-commerce applications (e.g., bill payment, lending, brokerage),
- Internal network servers,
- Core processing system,
- Programming support, and
- Automated decision support systems.

These components work together to deliver e-banking services. Each component represents a control point to consider. Through a combination of internal and outsourced solutions, management has many alternatives when determining the overall system configuration for the various components of an e-banking system. However, for the sake of simplicity, this booklet presents only two basic variations. First, one or more technology service providers can host the e-banking application and numerous network components as illustrated in the following diagram. In this configuration, the institution's service provider hosts the institution's website, Internet banking server, firewall, and intrusion detection system. While the institution does not have to manage the daily administration of these component systems, its management and board remain responsible for the content, performance, and security of the e-banking system.

TRENDS IN ELECTRONIC BANKING

Internet banking is gaining ground. Banks increasingly operate websites through which customers are able not only to inquire about account balances and interest and exchange rates but also to conduct a range of transactions. Unfortunately, data on Internet banking are scarce, and differences in definitions make cross-country comparisons difficult. Even so, one finds that Internet banking is particularly widespread in Austria, Korea, the Scandinavian countries, Singapore, Spain, and Switzerland, where more than 75 percent of all banks offer such services (see chart). The Scandinavian countries have the largest number of Internet users, with up to one-third of bank customers in Finland and Sweden taking advantage of e-banking.

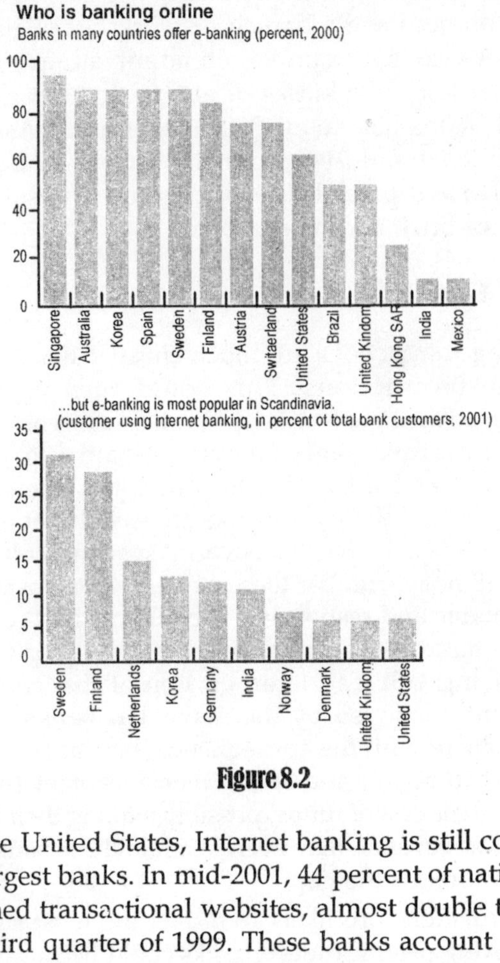

Figure 8.2

In the United States, Internet banking is still concentrated in the largest banks. In mid-2001, 44 percent of national banks maintained transactional websites, almost double the number in the third quarter of 1999. These banks account for over 90 percent of national banking system assets. The larger banks tend to offer a wider array of electronic banking services, including loan applications and brokerage services. While most U.S. consumers have accounts with banks that offer Internet services, only about 6 percent of them use these services. To date, most banks have combined the new electronic delivery channels with traditional brick and mortar branches ("brick and click" banks), but a small number have emerged that offer their products and services predominantly, or only, through electronic distribution channels. These "virtual" or Internet-only banks do not have a branch network but might have a physical presence, for example, an administrative office or nonbranch facilities like kiosks or automatic teller machines. The United States has about 30 virtual banks; Asia has 2, launched in 2000 and 2001; and the European Union has several—either as separately licensed entities or as subsidiaries or branches of brick and mortar banks.

FAVOUR OF E-BANKING

E-banking transactions are much cheaper than branch or even phone transactions. This could turn yesterday's competitive advantage - a large branch network - into a comparative disadvantage, allowing e-banks to undercut bricks-and-mortar banks. This is commonly known as the "beached dinosaur" theory. E-banks are easy to set up so lots of new entrants will arrive. 'Old-world' systems, cultures and structures will not encumber these new entrants. Instead, they will be adaptable and responsive. E-banking gives consumers much more choice. Consumers will be less inclined to remain loyal. E-banking will lead to an erosion of the 'endowment effect' currently enjoyed by the major UK banks. Deposits will go elsewhere with the consequence that these banks will have to fight to regain and retain their customer base. This will increase their cost of funds, possibly making their business less viable. Lost revenue may even result in these banks taking more risks to breach the gap.

Portal providers, are likely to attract the most significant share of banking profits. Indeed banks could become glorified marriage brokers. They would simply bring two parties together - eg buyer and seller, payer and payee. The products will be provided by monolines, experts in their field. Traditional banks may simply be left with payment and settlement business - even this could be cast into doubt. Traditional banks will find it difficult to evolve. Not only will they be unable to make acquisitions for cash as opposed to being able to offer shares, they will be unable to obtain additional capital from the stock market. This is in contrast to the situation for Internet firms for whom it seems relatively easy to attract investment.

CHALLENGES IN E-BANKING

- Customer data going online the system must be secured.
- Retaining customer is more important than cost-reduction
- Integrate easily and quickly disparate systems (software and hardware) currently in use.
- To support business transactions every minute of every day.

OPPORTUNITIES IN E-BANKING: READY OR NOT, HERE WE COME

It has always been a chicken-and-egg dilemma in business. Either firms wait for the market to mature until customers are ready for the products and services. Or, firms can go ahead and offer the products and services, hoping that their customers will catch on soon. The same is true for new products and services that have emerged — and continue to emerge — in the world of electronic banking (e-banking). Whether first-movers or latecomers, there is one partner in the e-banking game that is not waiting for the chicken to lay the egg, or wait for the egg to hatch into a chick. Technology providers are always up on their toes, like chicken ready to catch the early worm. Technology providers include companies who provide the hardware, software and services solutions that enable banks to offer e-banking products and services to their clients. These providers are either computer companies or infrastructure providers like telephone companies.

Some banks, they said, are just waiting in the sidelines, ready to offer the e-banking services whenever the market is ready. The banking sector is one of the major industry sectors for some technology providers. Think number crunching and expect Big Blue's mainframe computers to be behind every centavo transaction happening in the background.

Felix Cua, HP Phils. Manager for financial services, told Business World Online that his company is currently beefing up its financial services team in anticipation of growth. In terms of e-banking in particular, both IBM and HP claim they have readily available solutions to enable local banks to offer e-banking. Technology providers in general noted that prospects for e-banking in the country depend on two factors: the aggressiveness of the banks and the acceptance of the local market.

RECENT TECHNOLOGICAL DEVELOPMENT

Absorption and effective utilization of new technologies will involve changes in structure organization, systems as well as attitudes of people working in banking industry. The following are the recent direction of the RBI with respect to technology up gradation.

1. IMPLEMENTATION OF CENTRALIZED FUNDS MANAGEMENT SYSTEM: The CFMS provides for a centralized viewing of balance positions of the account holders across different accounts maintained at various locations of RBI. While the first phase of the system covering the Centralized Funds Enquiry system (CFES) has been made available to the users. The second phase covering the Centralized Funds Transfer System (CFTS) would be made available by the middle of 2003. So far, 54 banks have implemented the system and the treasuries/funds management branches.

2. CERTIFICATION AND DIGITAL SIGNATURE: The midterm review of October 2002 indicated the need for information security on the network and the use of Public Key Infrastructure (PKI) by banks. The Controller of Certifying

Authorities, Government of India, have approved the Institute for Development and Research in Banking Technology (IDRBT) as a Certification Authority (CA) for Digital Signatures, consequently, the process of setting up of Registration Authorities (RA) under the CA has commenced at various banks. In addition to the Negotiated Dealing System (NDS), the Electronic Clearing Service (ECS) and Electronic Fund Transfer (EFT) are being enhanced in terms security by means of implementation of PKI and digital signatures using the facilities offered by the CA (Certification authority).

3. COMMITTEE ON PAYMENT SYSTEM: In order to examine the entire gamut of the process of reforms in payment and settlement system, the RBI set up a committed of real time gross settlement in 2002. The committee, after examining the various aspects relating to the payment and settlement system, submitted its report in September 2002 along with draft payment system bill. The draft bill provides, interalia, legal basis for netting, apart from empowering RBI to have regulatory and over sign powers over payment and settlement systems of the country.

4. MULTI- APPLICATION SMART CARDS: Recognizing the need for technology based payment products and growing importance of smart card based payment flows, a pilot project for multi application smart cards in conjunction with the few banks and vendors under the Ministry of Communication and Information Technology, Government of India, has been initiated by the RBI. The project is aimed at the formulation of standards multi application smart cards on the basic inter-operable system and technological components of the entire system.

CONCLUSION

While electronic banking can provide a number of benefits for customers and new business opportunities for banks, it exacerbates traditional banking risks. Even though considerable work has been done in some countries in adapting banking and supervision regulations, continuous vigilance and revisions will be essential as the scope of e-banking increases. In particular, there is still a need to establish greater harmonization and coordination at the international level. Moreover, the ease with which capital can potentially be moved between banks and across borders in an electronic environment creates a greater sensitivity to economic policy management.

REFERENCE

1. www.imf.org/external/pubs/ft/fandd/2002/09/nsouli.htm
2. www.easternbookcorporation.com/moreinfo. php?txt_searchstring
3. Parameswaran.r., "computer applications in business" s.chand & co.
4. Reynoids.k., "e-commerce " shroff publishers & distributors pvt. ltd., Calcuttacedric.c., "internet and e-commerce" bpb publications, New Delhi.
5. www.Zawya.Com/E-Banking
6. www.bworldonline.com/onlineexclusives/ebank/inside.
7. Ffiec.gov/ffiecimfobase/booklets/e-banking/ebanking_00_intro _def.html

9

Emerging Identity Theft: A Challenge to E-Banking

*Dr. Ayub Khan Dawood and Prof. Devamaidhan

In terms of financial losses, identity theft was surpassed all other types of cyber crime. According to a study by Fraud Advisory Panel of UK, identity fraud in all forms would have costed US $ 221 bn across the world. According to the National Criminal Intelligence Squad of UK, the British economy suffered a loss 1.3 bn during 2002, as a result of identity theft. A study conducted by Aberdeen Group during 2003 reported that identity theft in all its forms is on track for $2 bn in financial losses by the end of 2005. Privacy experts in the US estimate that identities of one million people have been stolen this year. And these numbers are growing with each passing day.

*Reader in Commerce, Department of Commerce, Quaide Milleth College, Chennai .

*Dept of Management Studies, University of Madras, Chennai

Identity Fraud

Identity fraud occurs when someone steals your personal information and uses it as their own. In this, fraudster steals another person's identity information like credit card numbers, social security numbers, driving license numbers, and ATM cards. Using the stolen personal information of others, identity thieves carry out the fraud by opening bank accounts or obtaining credit cards in the names of victims, or they might obtain payments. Next by impersonating the victim, they spend as much money of the victim as possible, normally in a very short time period. They may order for goods or services in the name of the victim. After running up a huge bill, normally up to the credit limit of the victim or after using up the balance in the victim's bank account, the thief moves on to another victim. One of the common practices among identity thieves is to affect a false change of address of the victim in the records of their banks and credit card issuing agencies. This facilitates the identity thieves to get around the cheque made by suppliers and creditors. The change of address also prevents the victims from knowing about the deals that are taking place in their name. Identity theft is not only applicable to individuals, but also it is directed against companies and government organizations. In fact, one of the most prevalent frauds is obtaining social security benefits by assuming false identity. The department for work and pensions of UK estimated that they must have lost 50 mm due to the identity fraud during 2001-02.

Types of Identity Frauds

Research into identity theft has discovered a number of ways in which a fraudster carries out identity theft. Fraud advisory panel of UK distinguishes them as application fraud; account take-over, wholesale assumption of victim's identity, business identity. Stolen identity information is some cases is being used for dangerous criminal activities like terrorism as in the case of the 9/11 incident.

Application Fraud

Normally, the fraudster obtains bits and pieces of personal information about the victim from old utility bills or financial dealings or social security number. Then, the perpetrator applies for financial products or credit cards in the name of the victim. Normally, a false change of address of victim is affected. Then the fraudster makes use of this information to obtain credit cards or to open bank accounts in the name of the victim. According to the Association for Payment Clearing services, application fraud cost UK in 2002.

Account Take-over

In this kind of fraud, the fraudster collects sufficient information about the victim like bank account number, PIN or / and dupes the bank by impersonating as the victim. In this, after collecting victim's information, the thief impersonating as the victim, informs the victims bank that the address of the victim has changed. He then orders a credit card to be sent to his new address. Once the credit card is received, the fraudster will have a field day. Account take-over fraud cost in 2002.

Assumption of Wholesale Identity

By assuming the identity of a person, the fraudsters can obtain false identification papers or passport. In many cases, it was found that the fraudster assumed the identity of a dead person for obtaining fraudulent claims or social security benefits. The simple procedure the thieves follow here is obtaining a certified copy of the victims birth certificate, which is legal and then basing on that, apply for identification documents including passports, driving license and insurance. Once in possession of the documents including passports, driving license and insurance. Once in possession of the documents, a fraudster can use any or all of them to secure a wide variety of benefits for himself at the cost of the victim.

In one case, a former police sergeant was declared bankrupt in 1995. His dead nephew had the same name. He stole his dead nephew's identity and borrowed $10 mn to finance his businesses. Eventually he was caught and sentenced to seven years imprisonment but his lenders, between them lost around $3.5mn. According to the Department for Work and Pensions, UK, the overall cost of this fraud is 22 mn pounds of which 50mn is due to wholly fictitious identities.

Assuming Business Identity

By assuming the identity of businesses, a fraudster can dupe customers, suppliers or any other person dealing with that business. He can use company invoices to get goods and services. On Internet, he can set up a duplicate website and then collect payments from the unsuspecting customers or their credit card information. In a recent case, fraudsters obtained identification documentation relating to a company, including VAT certificates, invoices, and company stationary and placed some orders with the suppliers. Suppliers carried out normal checks. But the sophisticated fraudster even had telephone numbers similar to one connecting to a reputed call center "High street bank call center". Fraudsters asked the suppliers to speak to the call center and confirm whether the funds have been released or not. Fraudsters even arranged for that confirmation. On the basis of the confirmation, the suppliers delivered goods worth $1,00,000 to an address in London. The goods were stolen immediately.

Uses of Identity Theft

In most cases of identity theft, the aim of the fraudster is to steal and enjoy the proceeds of the crime. But in a small number of cases, identity theft is being used for other purposes. All 19 of the terrorists responsible for 9/11 had stolen SS numbers. This enabled them to open bank accounts, transfer money and obtain driving licenses.

Methods of Stealing

The predominant method of stealing personal information is by making use of Internet and computer technology. In addition to technology, identity thieves also make use of social engineering methods like dumpster driving and sweet talking. In some cases the fraudsters were purchasing personal identification information from unscrupulous employees of database organizations or credit card organizations or from hackers.

Technology: Advantage Fraudsters

It is the technology that gave boost to new kinds of businesses and new ways of conducting business. Internet and Web technologies have changed the way the businesses are conducted. E-Commerce is growing at a very fast rate. Unfortunately, the security measures have not kept pace with the development of technology or the growth of new business models. Despite security being available, there are a number of loopholes in all these technologies. Further, technological sophistication of fraudsters is as good as any technology specialist, and in some cases, even better. In the present scenario, money can be transferred by e-mail, telephone call or fax in a fraction of a second, from anywhere to anywhere in the world. This speed offered by technology is one of the main reasons for the growth of identity theft. Technology also makes it very difficult to gather evidence sustainable in the court of law. The sophisticated are well aware of this and they get emboldened to carry out the crime with impunity.

Social Engineering

Social engineering is prevalent in all parts of the world. This is typically used by many organizations for market intelligence, especially for information about the competitors. Social engineering has become a potent tool in cyber crime and many fraudsters are using it to steal personal information. Social engineering techniques can range from dumpster driving to making the victim give the details himself. Studies have shown that students are particularly vulnerable for this type of crime.

The Insider

Organizations today have a lot of financial information about the organization itself, the employees, customers and suppliers. In the context of identity theft, the threat is equal from insiders i.e., the employees, as from outsiders. This implies that all organizations handling personal information like database organizations, financial organizations like banks, and credit card companies must take all possible precautions to safeguard the information from possible abuse by the employees. Bribery of insiders or employees by fraudsters and organized gangs is one phenomenon that is on the rise.

Victims Realize Later

The victims are normally unaware of the fact that their identities are stolen. They realize this only when they apply for a credit card or bank loan and their applications are turned down for low credit rating. Sometimes, they come to know when they are going through their monthly bank or credit card statements. But by then the damage is total and in most cases, irrevocable. From past experiences, it has been seen that the fraudsters in possession of the victim's identity incur huge debts in the name of victims within a very short time span. The unfortunate thing is, it is the victim's responsibility to prove to the credit rating agencies and all other agencies involved that it is the fraudster who had done it. And that is a Herculean task. Identity theft can make a law abiding innocent citizen, a criminal overnight, at lease officially on paper. Identity theft is a violation of people's privacy. It devastates their credit and it takes a long time to repair that damage.

Legal Position

Unfortunately, in many countries assuming the identity of another person is not an offence. For example, even in UK use of false identity is not a criminal offence. It becomes a criminal offence only when one can prove that there is some kind of conspiracy to commit a crime or fraud or if a criminal act has taken place.

Prevention and Detection at Personal Level

Internet buying is safe only on secured websites. People should check their credit history periodically. Checking every month is highly recommended but at least once in three months is a must. It is always advisable to cancel unused credit cards with the company and destroy them. One should never leave the valet with credit cards or driving licenses in the car or any place where they are likely to be stolen. One must carry only cards that are necessary. In case of loss of any cards, the matter should be immediately reported to the issuing company and police, to prove to the creditors that the first step was taken. Further, one must not give one's credit card number or other information on telephone to any one. One should also be careful about items like pre approved credit card applications, bank statements, new checks being sent by post on home address, as they contain a lot of financial information, through which any clever thief can gain access to victims finances. Further one should "opt out" of programs that allow financial institutions to share data. One should be very careful when purchasing anything on the Internet. Unless one is very sure about the security, important financial information like credit card numbers or personal information like Social Security Numbers must never be disclosed. If somebody asks you for this information through e-mail or on the phone, one must not divulge the same. It could be a social engineering technique being employed by hackers. You may disclose the information if you are absolutely sure about the person who is asking for the information. Simple things like shredding old bills or reports will certainly reduce the risk of becoming an identity theft victim.

Prevention and Detection at Organisational Level

One should clearly remember that most identity theft incidents take place because of insiders or with active assistance from insiders. Organizations must verify and vet all employees with access to personal information. Job rotation has been found to be effective in uncovering identity frauds. Education of employees about all aspects of identity theft will also help a lot in identifying such incidents. It is always advisable to lock hard copies of personal information. The unwanted material containing personal information must be shredded. All organizations must have a written information protection policy in place. The procedures for transmission of personal information must be clearly laid down, taking into account all aspects of security that must be strictly enforced. As far as the customers are concerned, credit reference checks must be carried out and they must also be asked to produce original documents for identification.

Technical Measures

Smart cards with micro chip technology can be effectively used for prevention of identity theft. Smart cards are being used in France and the credit card fraud using identity theft is negligible there, compared to other countries. Use of encryption systems reduces the chances of identity theft. Encryption can prevent and frustrate hackers on the prowl. In many places data mining was found to be another technology that can assist the early detection. However, these systems must be continuously assessed, evaluated and upgraded, as the intelligent scammers are also finding ways of circumventing such technologies.

Measures by Government

After recognizing the severity and magnitude of identity theft, most of the governments are enacting stringent laws.

Further, most state governments in the US are no longer using SS numbers on the driving licenses. They are also urging people who have SS numbers on the driving licenses to change them. Some universities are allotting different enrollment numbers to students and are changing the practice of students using the SSN as the enrolment number. Governments and private organizations are also taking steps to protect the employees who blow the whistle on identity frauds. Governments and private organizations are cooperating in this regard in most of the countries and are taking many positive legal, technological, and operational steps to control identity theft.

Conclusion

Identity theft can happen to anyone, even to people who are conscious of the crime. It can affect organizations and government agencies also. The main aim of fraudsters in 99% of the cases is financial gain. In some cases the motives could be different. This is one crime which is growing in spite of strict legislations by most of the countries. Undoubtedly, this is the costliest of all crimes in terms of the money involved. Effective preventive measures by individuals, companies and other organizations can certainly bring down the crime. The cooperation between organizations and the government is also yielding positive results. At the individual level, one can take all the precautions to reduce the chance of becoming a victim of identity theft.

Reference

1. Norman A Willox, 2002, Journal of Economic Crime Management, www.jecm.org.
2. Fraud Advisory Panel, 2003, Identity theft: Do you know the signs? www.fraudadvisorypanel.org.
3. Linda Wenger, 2002, Specialist says identity theft is becoming and extreme problem, Washington Evening Journal.

4. Sam Boush, 2002, Identity theft: Growing problem on campus, www.tecrime.com.
5. Erin Quinn, 2002, Theft Cases become more common, San Angleo Standard Times.
6. Abby Heisey, 2002, Identity theft concern causes student reaction, The Digital Collegian.

10

Financial and Banking Sector Reforms

*Dr. N. Piramela

Without a sound and effective banking system in India it cannot have a healthy economy. The banking system of India should not only be hassle free but it should be able to meet new challenges posed by the technology and any other external and internal factors. For the past three decades India's banking system has several outstanding achievements to its credit. The most striking is its extensive reach. It is no longer confined to only metropolitans or cosmopolitans in India. In fact, Indian banking system has reached even to the remote corners of the country. This is one of the main reasons of India's growth process. The government's regular policy for Indian bank since 1969 has paid rich dividends with the nationalization of 14 major private banks of India.

Not long ago, an account holder had to wait for hours at the bank counters for getting a draft or for withdrawing his

*HOD of Commerce, Dhanalakshmi Srinivasan College of Arts and Science for Women, Perambalur

own money. Today, he has a choice. Gone are days when the most efficient bank transferred money from one branch to other in two days. Now it is simple as instant messaging or dial a pizza. Money has become the order of the day. The first bank in India, though conservative, was established in 1786. From 1786 till today, the journey of Indian Banking System can be segregated into three distinct phases. They are as mentioned below:

- Early phase from 1786 to 1969 of Indian Banks
- Nationalization of Indian Banks and up to 1991 prior to Indian banking sector Reforms.
- New phase of Indian Banking System with the advent of Indian Financial & Banking Sector Reforms after 1991.

The last decade witnessed the maturity of India's financial markets. Since 1991, every governments of India took major steps in reforming the financial sector of the country. The important achievements in the following fields is discussed under separate heads:

- Financial markets
- Regulators
- Banking system
- Non-banking finance companies
- Capital market
- Mutual funds
- Overall approach to reforms
- Deregulation of banking system
- Capital market developments
- Consolidation imperative

FINANCIAL MARKETS

In the last decade, Private Sector Institutions played an important role. They grew rapidly in commercial banking and asset management business. With the openings in the insurance sector for these institutions, they started making debt in the market.

Competition among financial intermediaries gradually helped the interest rates to decline. Deregulation added to it. The real interest rate was maintained. The borrowers did not pay high price while depositors had incentives to save. It was something between the nominal rate of interest and the expected rate of inflation.

REGULATORS

The Finance Ministry continuously formulated major policies in the field of financial sector of the country. The Government accepted the important role of regulators. The Reserve Bank of India (RBI) has become more independent. Securities and Exchange Board of India (SEBI) and the Insurance Regulatory and Development Authority (IRDA) became important institutions. Opinions are also there that there should be a super-regulator for the financial services sector instead of multiplicity of regulators.

BANKING SYSTEM

Almost 80% of the business are still controlled by Public Sector Banks (PSBs). PSBs are still dominating the commercial banking system. The RBI has given licences to new private sector banks as part of the liberalisation process. The RBI has also been granting licences to industrial houses. Many banks are successfully running in the retail and consumer segments but are yet to deliver services to industrial finance, retail trade, small business and agricultural finance. The PSBs will play an important role in the industry due to its number of branches and foreign banks facing the constraint of limited number of branches. Hence, in order to achieve an efficient banking system, the onus is on the Government to encourage the PSBs to be run on profession lines.

DEVELOPMENT FINANCE INSTITUTIONS

FIs's access to SLR funds reduced. Now they have to approach the capital market for debt and equity funds.

Convertibility clause no longer obligatory for assistance to corporate sanctioned by term-lending institutions. Capital adequacy norms extended to financial institutions. DFIs such as IDBI and ICICI have entered other segments of financial services such as commercial banking, asset management and insurance through separate ventures. The move to universal banking has started.

NON BANKING FINANCE COMPANIES

In the case of new NBFCs seeking registration with the RBI, the requirement of minimum net owned funds, has been raised to Rs. 2 crores.

Until recently, the money market in India was narrow and circumscribed by tight regulations over interest rates and participants. The secondary market was underdeveloped and lacked liquidity. Several measures have been initiated and include new money market instruments, strengthening of existing instruments and setting up of the Discount and Finance House of India (DFHI).

The RBI conducts its sales of dated securities and treasury bills through its open market operations (OMO) window. Primary dealers bid for these securities and also trade in them. The DFHI is the principal agency for developing a secondary market for money market instruments and Government of India treasury bills. The RBI has introduced a liquidity adjustment facility (LAF) in which liquidity is injected through reverse repo auctions and liquidity is sucked out through repo auctions.

On account of the substantial issue of government debt, the gilt- edged market occupies an important position in the financial set- up. The Securities Trading Corporation of India (STCI), which started operations in June 1994 has a mandate to develop the secondary market in government securities.

Long-term debt market: The development of a long-term debt market is crucial to the financing of infrastructure. After bringing some order to the equity market, the SEBI has now decided to concentrate on the development of the debt market.

Stamp duty is being withdrawn at the time of dematerialization of debt instruments in order to encourage paperless trading.

CAPITAL MARKET

The number of shareholders in India is estimated at 25 million. However, only an estimated two lakh persons actively trade in stocks. There has been a dramatic improvement in the country's stock market trading infrastructure during the last few years. Expectations are that India will be an attractive emerging market with tremendous potential. Unfortunately, during recent times the stock markets have been constrained by some unsavoury developments, which has led to retail investors deserting the stock markets.

MUTUAL FUNDS

The mutual funds industry is now regulated under the SEBI (Mutual Funds) Regulations, 1996 and amendments thereto. With the issuance of SEBI guidelines, the industry had a framework for the establishment of many more players, both Indian and foreign players. The Unit Trust of India remains easily the biggest mutual fund controlling a corpus of nearly Rs.70,000 crores, but its share is going down. The biggest shock to the mutual fund industry during recent times was the insecurity generated in the minds of investors regarding the US 64 scheme. With the growth in the securities markets and tax advantages granted for investment in mutual fund units, mutual funds started becoming popular. The foreign owned AMCs are the ones, which are now setting the pace for the industry. They are introducing new products, setting new standards of customer service, improving disclosure standards and experimenting with new types of distribution. The insurance industry is the latest to be thrown open to competition from the private sector including foreign players. Foreign companies can only enter joint ventures with Indian companies, with participation restricted to 26 per cent of equity. It is too early to conclude whether the erstwhile public sector monopolies will successfully be able to face up to the competition posed by the new players, but it can be expected that the customer will gain from improved service.

The new players will need to bring in innovative products as well as fresh ideas on marketing and distribution, in order to improve the low per capita insurance coverage. Good regulation will of course be essential.

OVERALL APPROACH TO REFORMS

The last ten years have seen major improvements in the working of various financial market participants. The government and the regulatory authorities have followed a step-by-step approach, not a big bang one. The entry of foreign players has assisted in the introduction of international practices and systems. Technology developments have improved customer service. Some gaps however remain (for example: lack of an inter-bank interest rate benchmark, an active corporate debt market and a developed derivatives market). On the whole, the cumulative effect of the developments since 1991 has been quite encouraging. An indication of the strength of the reformed Indian financial system can be seen from the way India was not affected by the Southeast Asian crisis.

However, financial liberalization alone will not ensure stable economic growth. Some tough decisions still need to be taken. Without fiscal control, financial stability cannot be ensured. The fate of the Fiscal Responsibility Bill remains unknown and high fiscal deficits continue. In the case of financial institutions, the political and legal structures have to ensure that borrowers repay on time the loans they have taken. The phenomenon of rich industrialists and bankrupt companies continues. Further, frauds cannot be totally prevented, even with the best of regulation. However, punishment has to follow crime, which is often not the case in India.

DEREGULATTION OF BANKING SYSTEM

Prudential norms were introduced for income recognition, asset classification, provisioning for delinquent loans and for capital adequacy. In order to reach the stipulated capital adequacy norms, substantial capital was provided by the Government to PSBs. Government pre-emption of banks' resources through statutory liquidity ratio (SLR) and cash reserve ratio (CRR) brought down in steps. Interest rates on the deposits and lending sides almost entirely were deregulated. New private sector banks allowed promoting and encouraging competition. PSBs were encouraged to approach the public for raising resources. Recovery of debts due to banks and the Financial Institutions Act, 1993 was passed, and special recovery tribunals set up to facilitate quicker recovery of loan arrears. Bank lending norms liberalized and a loan system to ensure better control over credit introduced. Banks asked to set up asset liability management (ALM) systems. RBI guidelines issued for risk management systems in banks encompassing credit, market and operational risks. A credit information bureau being established to identify bad risks. Derivative products such as forward rate agreements (FRAs) and interest rate swaps (IRSs) introduced.

CAPITAL MARKET DEVELOPMENTS

The Capital Issues (Control) Act, 1947, repealed, office of the Controller of Capital Issues were abolished and the initial share pricing were decontrolled. SEBI, the capital market regulator was established in 1992. Foreign institutional investors (FIIs) were allowed to invest in Indian capital markets after registration with the SEBI. Indian companies were permitted to access international capital markets through euro issues.

The National Stock Exchange (NSE), with nationwide stock trading and electronic display, clearing and settlement facilities was established. Several local stock exchanges changed over from floor based trading to screen based trading.

PRIVATE MUTUAL FUNDS PERMITTED

The Depositories Act had given a legal framework for the establishment of depositories to record ownership deals in book entry form. Dematerialization of stocks encouraged paperless trading. Companies were required to disclose all material facts and specific risk factors associated with their projects while making public issues.

To reduce the cost of issue, underwriting by the issuer were made optional, subject to conditions. The practice of making preferential allotment of shares at prices unrelated to the prevailing market prices stopped and fresh guidelines were issued by SEBI.

SEBI reconstituted governing boards of the stock exchanges, introduced capital adequacy norms for brokers, and made rules for making client or broker relationship more transparent, which included separation of client and broker, accounts.

BUY BACK OF SHARES ALLOWED

The SEBI started insisting on greater corporate disclosures. Steps were taken to improve corporate governance based on the report of a committee.

SEBI issued detailed employee stock option scheme and employee stock purchase scheme for listed companies. Standard denomination for equity shares of Rs. 10 and Rs. 100 were abolished. Companies given the freedom to issue dematerialized shares in any denomination. Derivatives trading starts with index options and futures. A system of rolling settlements introduced. SEBI empowered to register and regulate venture capital funds. The SEBI (Credit Rating Agencies) Regulations, 1999 issued for regulating new credit rating agencies as well as introducing a code of conduct for all credit rating agencies operating in India.

CONSOLIDATION IMPERATIVE

Another aspect of the financial sector reforms in India is the consolidation of existing institutions, which is especially applicable to the commercial banks. In India the banks are in huge quantity. First, there is no need for 27 PSBs with branches all over India. A number of them can be merged. The merger of Punjab National Bank and New Bank of India was a difficult one, but the situation is different now. No one expected so many employees to take voluntary retirement from PSBs, which at one time were much sought after jobs. Private sector banks will be self-consolidated while co-operative and rural banks will be encouraged for consolidation, and anyway play only a niche role.

In the case of insurance, the Life Insurance Corporation of India is a behemoth, while the four public sector general insurance companies will probably move towards consolidation with a bit of nudging. The UTI is yet again a big institution, even though facing difficult times, and most other public sector players are already exiting the mutual fund business. There are a number of small mutual fund players in the private sector, but the business being comparatively new for the private players, it will take some time.

CONCLUSION

Convergence in the financial sector, the new buzzword internationally. Hi-tech and the need to meet increasing consumer needs is encouraging convergence, even though it has not always been a success till date. In India organizations such as IDBI, ICICI, HDFC and SBI are already trying to offer various services to the customer under one umbrella. This phenomenon is expected to grow rapidly in the coming years. Where mergers may not be possible, alliances between organizations may be effective. Various forms of bancassurance are being introduced, with the RBI having already come out with detailed guidelines for entry of banks into insurance. The LIC has bought into Corporation Bank in order to spread its insurance distribution network. Both banks and insurance companies have started entering the asset management business, as there is a great deal of synergy among these businesses. The pensions market is expected to open up fresh opportunities for insurance companies and mutual funds.

11

Financing of Higher Education – Issues and Prospectus

*Dr. V. Murugan

India being agriculture country, it has wide opportunity for higher education. Education plays vital role in every life. India's higher education is in a commendable position. India is the second largest higher education system in the world. India occupies third largest skilled man power. Both higher education and skill develops in our Indian economy.

Education Meaning

Education is the process by which people not only acquire knowledge and information, but also values. It also inculcates the ability to live and interact with social groups, as well as participated in cultural life and leisure activities. Higher education is considered essential for any nation's cultural, social and economic development.

*Dept. of Corporate Secretaryship, Maharaja College for Women, Perundurai

Higher Education Scenario

In the olden days, several universities were established such Nalanda, Taxila and Vikramsila were crowned as higher learning universities. It attracted students from all over the countries as well as Korea, China, Indonesia, Ceylon, Burma and Nepal. In India, three universities were set up in the metropolitan city of Bombay, Calcutta and Madras in 1857. In 1887, the fourth university was established after 30 years. The fifth and sixth universities set up in Mysore and Benaras in 1916. All the universities were started with the help of London University. In 1920 many universities were established for research purposes. The system includes approximately 304 universities, including 62 "Deemed Universities". 11 open universities, 14,600 colleges, 10 million students and 0.5 million teachers. During the year 2006, the quality of higher education was conducted in the universities. For this, world universities were ranked. The rankings of the world universities are shown below.

Table 11.1: *World Universities Rankings*

Countries	Top 20	Top 50	Top 100	Top 200
China	1	2	2	6
Hongkong	0	2	3	4
India	0	0	2	3
Japan	1	2	3	11
Other Asia	1	1	3	9
Sub total	3	7	13	33
Australia	1	6	7	13
Canada	0	3	3	7
Newzeland	0	1	2	2
U.K	4	8	16	30
U.S	11	22	33	55
Total	19	47	74	140

Each new column subsumes the previous column, a university in the top 20 is also in the top 50, 100 and 200.

Source: Ramesh Takur, The Hindu, December 9th 2006, P.14.

Modern higher education in India standard with the establishment of Hindu College in Calcutta in 1817. In the whole of the then British empire, Calcutta University was the first to confer the bachelor's degree to women in 1883. Ms.Kadambini ganguly and Ms.Chandramuki Basu were the first recipients of this honour. The strong growth in the number of universities and institutions were much higher in the 1950s and 1960s primarily because of the relatively small number of such institutions existing planned expansion of higher education started only after independence. During the year 1970s and 1980s, the growth of higher educational institutions was slow. During 1990s onwards, the higher educational institutions were started fastely, because more demand for higher education. This growth occurred mainly in the private sector educational institutions.

The India becomes second rank in providing higher education in the world. The literacy rates in the Indian states are low. All the Indian states are not having statisfiable literacy rates. Some of the southern and northern states literacy rates are shown below.

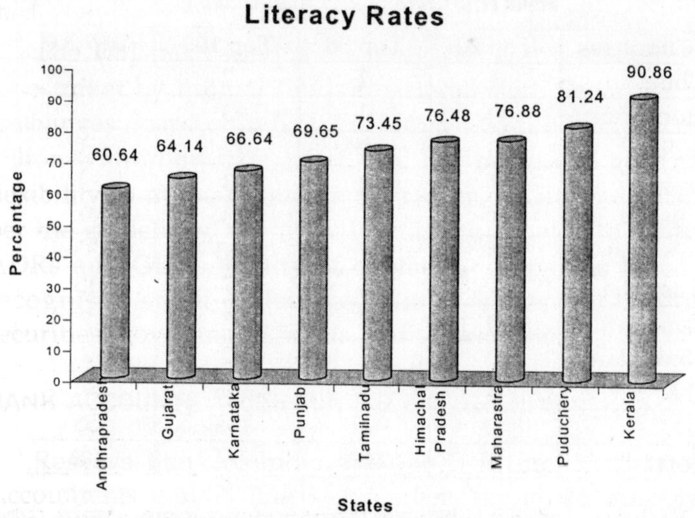

Source: The Hindu, Independent India at 60, dated on August 15th 2007, P.20.

FINANCING OF HIGHER EDUCATION

The expenditure on higher education is medium level in our India. Which comes as the percentage of gross national product (GNP), had fallen from 0.98 percent in 1980-81 to 0.35 percent in 1994-95. The share of higher education in the union budget's total provision for education has fallen form 28.19 percentage in 1990-91 to 17.7 percent in 2003-04.

Table 11.2: *Details of public expenditure on higher education (Including Technical Education) as percentage of budget.*

Year	Higher	Technical	Higher and Tech
1990-1991	1.58	0.51	2.09
1991-1992	1.43	0.48	1.91
1992-1993	1.42	0.47	1.90
1993-1994	1.42	0.47	1.89
1994-1995	1.40	0.47	1.87
1995-1996	1.35	0.45	1.80
1996-1997	1.30	0.44	1.74
1997-1998	1.31	0.44	1.75
1998-1999	1.39	0.47	1.86
1999-2000	1.61	0.48	2.09
2000-2001	1.79	0.49	2.29
2001-2002	1.31	0.41	1.72
2002-2003	1.31	0.42	1.72
2003-2004	1.18	0.42	1.60

Source: Southern Economist, April 1st and 15th, 2008, P.32.

The public expenditure on higher education was increased from a level of 17.15 crores in 1950-51 to 9562 crores in 2004-05, by a increasing 550 times. It was a good commence during the1950s with a original growth rate of 7.5 percent per year. It was considered as golden period during the 1690s with a real growth rate of 11 percent per annum. But it was suffered by some of the problems during the 1970s with the annual growth rate declining to 3.4 percent and recovered during the 1980s with annual growth rate of 7.3 percent. Expenditure on higher education was increased to 9562 crores. The total allocation for the education sector during 2008-2009 is Rs.34.400 crores. The amount Rs.34.400 crores is more than the amount allotted during the year 2007-2008. (i.e.Rs. 28,674). This shows 20 percent increase during the year 2008-2009. This is shown in the following table.

Allocations for education in the first five year plan were 7.2 percent of the total outlay. In the tenth five year plan, it has further come down to 0.29 percent. Privatization in the sphere of higher education was stressed in the country paper submitted by the union HRD minister at the world conference in higher education, held in Paris on October 5-9, 1998. Then the Mukesh Ambani and Kumaramangalam Birla committee submitted its report in 2000, recommending a greater level of privatization in higher eduction.

Private institutions, particularly in areas of management, engineering have been increasing in large numbers raising issues if accesses, equity, quality and regulation. The entry of Foreign institutions creating it all the more complex. Interestingly, higher education is facing some challenges at a juncture when it is anticipated to play a greater role in improving the nation's competitiveness in the global knowledge economy.

Institutes for Higher Education

There were several institutes for higher education in our India. At the advent of India's independence, there were 19 universities and 591 colleges for higher education. Knowledge is power. It is knowledge that will drive success in the 21st century. India has the opportunity to become a knowledge of society. Following the prime minister's announcement, an IIM at Shillong three ISSERS at Mohali, Pune and Kolkatta and an IIIT at Kanchipuram have started functioning. Government will establish one central university in each of the hitherto uncovered state. We propose to make a beginning in 2008-09 by establishing 16 central universities. In addition to the central government has proposed to set up three IITS in Andhra Pradesh, Bihar and Rajashtan. Two IISERS at Bhopal and Tiruvanandhapuram; and two schools of planning and

Architecture at Bhopal and Vijayawada. More institutes of higher education, as promised by prime minister will be established during the eleventh plan period.

Finance minister has promised to make a grant of Rs. 5 crores to the Decan college Post Graduate and Research Institute Pune, which is one of the oldest intuitions of modern learning in India. An amount of Rs. 10 crores, have been given to information technology ministry to set up national knowledge centers is very appreciable step. The budgets have given importance to promote higher education in our country. The higher education provides a highly creative and knowledge based society.

Science and Technology

We must encourage our children to take care in science and research and development, ministry of science and technology will introduce a scheme called Innovation in Science Pursuit for Inspired Research (INSPIRE) that will include scholarships for young learners (10-17 years), scholarships for continuing science education (17-22 years) and opportunities for research careers (22-32 years). For this, Rs.85 crores, were allocated during the year 2008-09, to built a knowledge society.

The recommendations of the national knowledge commission, submitted form time to time, are under active consideration. Some of them have been incorporated in the eleventh plan. Government has accepted an important recommendation to inter connect all knowledge institutions through an electronic digital broadband network. This will encourage sharing of resources and collaborative research. The central government gave Rs.100 crores to the Ministry of Information Technology for establishing the National Knowledge Network.

Issues of Higher Education

1. As per the eleventh five year plan only 20 percent of youth taking of higher education. Balance 80 percent not studying higher education.

2. Higher Education is still not attractive as it is considered unaffordable and graduates are not ensured of a job.
3. The Higher Education and Technical Education in India are privatized in many ways.
4. The private institutions are charging unbelievable cost for Higher Education.
5. The private institutions are willing in large numbers changing the very face of higher and technical education.
6. The private are not interested to provide seats to socially and economically weaker sections in the society.
7. The National Institute of Education Planning and Administration (NIEPA) observed in 2000 that the danger of opening up of the education sector under the auspices of the WTO-GATS regime is that it might result in the draining of resources of privatizing country.
8. The Higher Education and research sector is over regulated and lower funded. It has been falling steadily behind the world average.
9. Due to globalization of Higher Education, the commodification of Indian Higher Education bound to have an adverse effect on our culture, the ethos of social welfare and even quality of India Education System.
10. The entire Higher Education System in India has thus been thrown into a dangerous situation, which was never witnessed before. The World Bank has published a report on higher Education in developing countries, titled peril and promise.
11. During the past two decades, the expansion of the higher education system, specially the professional education, has occurred to the extent of 90 percent is in the private sector.

PROSPECTUS OF HIGHER EDUCATION

1. The "New Education Policy" was introduced by the Rajeev Gandhi, with this policy privatization of higher education was moved strongly.

2. The Finance Minster Mr.P.Chindambaram has given a boom to education sector, because he has promised 20 percent increase in fund allotment for higher education. He allotted funds for education from Rs.28,674 crores in 2007 to Rs.34,400 crores in financial year 2008-09.
3. Globalization provides wide market place for talented, higher educated candidates. Talented candidates are in great demand in the global market place.
4. The comparative advantage of the higher education sector lies in its identity as the custodian and manager of knowledge-based networks that give it a global mandate and reach.
5. The internalization of higher education, increase in the quality of higher education arising from ever increasing competitive pressure can naturally be anticipated.
6. For developing nations like India which are finding it difficult to raise adequate t resources for providing higher and technical education. Internationalization will provide easier access to facilitate for higher education available elsewhere, particularly in the developing nations.
7. High growth in the enrolment of women higher education with the changing the attitudes in favour of gender equity and setting up of special situations for women.
8. Another important prospectus of the higher education system in the last two decades is the growth of distance and open learning. In addition to the open universities, virtually every major university, some large colleges and several private institutions offer a large verity of degree, diploma and certificate level programmes in the distance mode.
9. The migration from one country to other in search of technical education and higher education can be expected in the future.
10. The availability of bank finance for higher and technical education is on the rise, as a banks are in the progress of easing relevant norms.

11. Recently, Finance Minister gave strict instruction to all banks to provide educational loan to all eligible candidates. The Finance said around four lakhs students were received bank loan during year 2008-2009. The Tamilnadu State becomes, first state to provide maximum bank loan for higher education.

12

Impact of Bank Credit on Self-Help Groups

*B. SeethaDevi

Economic progress of any country would be achieved through social development. Women constitute equal share with men in total population of our country and in few regions, women's share outnumbered men in total population. Therefore women's empowerment cannot be ignored while devising various policies for rural and socio-economic development. Right from the independence, in fact even in the pre-independence era, rural development vis-à-vis poverty alleviation had been considered as a major challenge to our country. Initially, it was assumed that various poverty alleviation programmes could be able to enhance income level of the rural masses but these programmes failed to achieve the target because 'trickle down' effect of economic growth. Lack of participatory approach in planning and execution of these programmes result in complete failure to improve socio-

*HOD of commerce, Bharathiyar Arts & Science Collage for Women, Deviyakurchi, Attur, Salem(D.T)

economic condition of the poor masses for which these were evolved. At this point of view, micro financing is being looked upon as the instrument that can be considered as the golden stick for poverty alleviation and rural development. Micro finance is recognized as a key strategy for addressing issues of poverty alleviation and Women empowerment. The Women become economically self - reliant, contribute directly to the well being of their families, play a more active role in decision making and are able to control systematic gender inequalities.

Emergence of Self-Help Groups

Although women constitute half of world's population yet they are the largest group, which is excluded from the benefits of social and economic development. Women constitute a strong labour force, which needs to be mobilized and encouraged to make an effective contribution to the development process. In India, the work participation rate of women is less than half that of men. Despite efforts made towards economic empowerment of women, majority of the active female population continues to be confined to micro, small-scale enterprises and the informal sector. The Ninth Five Year Plan adopted the strategy of Women's Component Plan under which not less than 30 per cent of funds/benefits were earmarked for all the women-related sectors and women-specific programmes. The Tenth Five Year Plan also undertook steps to further strengthen the policy of Women's Component Plan. The Working Group on Empowerment of Women for the Eleventh Five Year Plan, constituted by the Planning Commission in 2006, has emphasized the strengthening of Self-Help Groups and community-based organizations for the empowerment of women. Special attention needs to be given to increasing employment opportunities and productive resources of women through special financial intermediaries, building women's competitiveness and increasing economic exchanges among women entrepreneurs. Poverty and unemployment are the major problems of any under developed countries, to which India is no exception. In India, at the end of Ninth Five Year Pan 26.1% of the population was living below poverty line. In the rural area 27.1% of the population was living under poverty. The overall unemployment rate is estimated to 7.32%. The female unemployment rate is 8.5%. The rate of growth of women unemployment in the rural area is 9.8%. This is because of the low growth rate of new and productive employment. In the end of IX Plan the rate of growth of implemented various schemes to reduce poverty and to promote the gainful employment. But the more attractive scheme with less effort is "Self-Help Group". It is a tool to remove poverty and improve the rural development.

Importance of the Study

Women's participation is significant in rural development. They put their entrepreneurial skills in all the rural employment activities such as agriculture, poultry, sheep rearing, diary, firewood cutting and selling etc. Though they put their heart and soul in rural employment activities, their economic status is not yet improved. Though they have enough entrepreneurial potential, due to poor financial strength; they are unable to convert their entrepreneurial dream into reality.

In the context of designing programmes for the poor, micro finance is recognized and accepted as one of the new development paradigms for alleviating poverty through socio-economic empowerment of the poor. The operational framework of micro finance, therefore, essentially rests on the premises that; formation of a self employment enterprise is a viable alternate means of alleviating poverty, lack of access to assets or credit acts as a constraint on the existing and potential micro-enterprises, the poor are capable of saving despite their poor income level. Therefore, micro-finance could be referred to as an institutional mechanism of providing credit support in small amount and usually linked with small groups along with other complementary support such as training and other related services to the people for enabling them to take up economic activities. Self-Help Group is one such aspect of bottom-up strategy calling for mass action at the local level.

The Self-Help Groups Bank linkage programmed is the major. Which is implemented by commercial banks now for increasing the Volume and out reach of micro credit. The Self-Help Groups linkage programme has so far helped in extending from banking services to more than 45 lakh poor households in India by March 2001, making it the large micro finance innovative in the world today in terms of outreach. The mission of NABARD is to link one million Self-Help Groups with the overall banking systems by the year 2008, facilitating access of hundred million rural poor to formal credit system. In this context the researcher has made an attempt to study the socio-economic impact of self-help groups in Namakkal district. The study is expected to reveal the opinion of the members on the Self-Help Groups in Namakkal district.

Objectives

The main objectives of the present study to study the working of Self-Help Groups. To study the attitude level of the members towards socio-economic impact of Self-Help Groups in Namakkal District. To find out the problems and give suitable suggestions to the members of Self-Help Groups in Namakkal District.

Research Design

This study is descriptive in nature based on survey method, confined to Self-Help Groups in Namakkal district. The researcher had a discussion with the officials of the banks and members of the Self-Help Groups in Namakkal district. Based on the discussion, an interview schedule was prepared. The adequate information contained in the interview schedule has been tested and the necessary changes were incorporated in the revised interview schedule in the light of the experience gained from the pilot study. A pilot study was conducted with 10 members. The scope of the study was confined to members of the women Self-Help Groups in Namakkal district only. By adopting convenience sampling, 150 respondents were selected from the Vennanthur block of Namakkal district. The required data were collected from both primary and secondary sources. The interview schedule was employed for the collection of primary data. The necessary secondary data was collected from the books, government reports and periodicals.

Framework of Analysis

The understanding of the perception level of the members of Self-Help Groups may help the authorities to formulate policies and programmes for further improvement. The attitude level of the members of Self-Help Groups can be examined with help of their demographic variables. The profile of the members of Self-Help Groups such as age and education were considered in conjunction with this study. In order to study the attitude level of the members of Self-Help Groups, various statistical tools such as chi-square test and analysis of one-way variance have been employed. The analysis of one-way variance and chi-square test has been employed to study the association between the demographic variables of the respondents and their attitude with the socio-economic impact of Self-Help Groups.

Profile of Respondents

Age Composition of the Respondents

The age composition of the respondents is given below (Refer Table 12.1).

Table 12.1: *Distribution of Respondents by Age*

Age	Number of Respondents	Percentage
Up to 25	47	31.33
26-35	63	42.00
36-45	24	16.00
46 and above	16	10.67
Total	150	100.00
Source: Primary Data.		

It is observed that the predominant age group of the respondents was 26-35 years. A good majority of the remaining respondents were distributed in the age group up to 25 years. 16 percent and 10.67 percent of the sample members were in the age group of 36-45 years and above 46 years respectively.

Educational Status of the Respondents

Table 12.2 shows the educational status of the members of Self-Help Groups in Namakkal district.

Table 12.2: *Distribution of Respondents by Educational Status*

Educational Status	Number of Respondents	Percentage
Up to S.S.L.C	61	40.67
H.Sc	36	24.00
Degree	40	26.67
Post graduation	13	08.67
Total	150	100.00
Source: Primary Data		

A predominant literacy group (40.67 percent) of the members of Self-Help Groups was up to S.S.L.C qualifications. 24 percent and 26.67 percent of the respondents were distributed in the H.Sc and degree qualifications respectively. 8.67 percent of the respondents were in post graduation qualifications.

Members' Attitude with the Impact of Self-Help Groups

Age and Acceptance with the Socio-Economic Impact of Self-Help Groups

The association between age and acceptance could be complex. Generally one would expect that as the person would grow older he would get greater satisfaction with his occupation. Therefore, the sample members from different age groups were requested to state their acceptance with the socio-economic impact of Self-Help Groups in Namakkal district and an attempt has been made to find out the relationship between age and acceptance.

The calculated X^2 test value (25.97) is greater than the table value (12.59) at 5 percent level of significance. The test

Table 12.3: *Respondents' Acceptance with the Socio-Economic Impact of Self-Help Groups*

Age	Level of Acceptance			Total
	Agreed	Partially Agreed	Disagreed	
Up to 25	22	15	10	47
26-35	29	20	14	63
36-45	11	8	5	24
46 and above	5	6	5	16
Total	67	49	34	150

proves that there is a significant association between the acceptance levels of sample members belonging to different age groups with the socio-economic impact of Self-Help Groups in Namakkal district. Therefore, the null hypothesis is rejected.

Education and Acceptance with the Socio-Economic Impact

The predominant literacy group of the sample members (40.67 percent) was up to S.S.L.C qualifications. It becomes important to examine how the educational status of the members influences their acceptance on the socio-economic impact of Self-Help groups in Namakkal district. An attempt has been made to find out the association between educational status and acceptance.

Table 12.4: *Relationship between Respondents' Education and Acceptance: ANOVA*

Source of Variation	D.F	Sum of Squares	Mean Squares	Calculated Value	Table Value at 5 %	Significance
Between Groups	2	136.50	68.25	1.31	4.26	Not Significant
Within Groups	9	466.50	51.89			
Total	11	603.00	54.81			
Source: Primary Data						

The calculated F value (1.31) is less than the table value (4.26) at 5 percent level of significance. The test proves that there is no significant association between the acceptance levels of sample members belonging to different educational status with the socio-economic impact of Self-Help Groups in Namakkal district. Therefore, the null hypothesis is accepted.

Findings

1. The predominant age group of the respondents was 26-35 years. A good majority of the remaining respondents were distributed in the age group up to 25 years. About 40.67 percent of the members of Self-Help Groups having S.S.L.C qualifications.

2. There is a significant association between the acceptance levels of sample members belonging to different age groups with the socio-economic impact of Self-Help Groups. However, there is no significant association between the acceptance levels of sample members belonging to different educational status with the socio-economic impact of Self-Help Groups.

3. Recognition, survival of family, loan facility, economic independence, and entrepreneurial status were the motivating factors of the sample members to join Self-Help Groups in Namakkal District. About 44.67 percent of the respondents were agreed with the socio-economic impact of Self-Help Groups.

4. Ranging from 35 percent to 40 percent of the sample members were agreed about the role Self-Help Groups in increasing level of saving, removal of social disparities, increasing the level of income of the members and provision of entrepreneurial status to members.

5. Ranging from 41 percent to 45 percent of the sample members were agreed about the role Self-Help Groups in improving the standard of living and social status, developing competency level, sharing of information, developing self confidence, nation building, thrift management, eradication of poverty and uses of latent resources.

6. Ranging from 46 percent to 50 percent of the sample members were agreed about the role Self-Help Groups in improving economic independence, upliftment of the society, power emancipation, improving mutual help, participation in social development activities, developing problem solving capacity, employment generation, women empowerment and increasing responsibility.

7. Above 50 percent of the respondents were agreed about the role Self-Help Groups in team building, developing decision making skills and increasing social contact. About 41.34 percent of the sample members were partially agreed about the role of Self-Help Groups in building team spirit.

8. Family problems, financial problems, lack of social recognition, problems in marketing and problems with large scale organizations were the problems encountered by the members of Self-Help Groups.

9. Access to financial options, arrangements for marketing, demarcation of business, recognition of business, recognition in the family and social recognition were the suggestions of the sample members to improve the performance of Self-Help Groups in Namakkal District.

Suggestions

1. About 41.33 percent of the respondents views that their family members and public do not recognize their joining in Self-Help Groups. It affects the members psychologically and discourages their involvement in Self-Help Groups. Therefore it is advised that the family members and others should come-out with openness and understand their role in the economic upliftment of the family and the society too. This kind of understanding and encouragement leads to total involvement of the members with the Self-Help Groups.

2. About 36.67 percent of the members of the Self-Help Groups in Namakkal District are facing stiff competition from branded products and also from large-scale units producing the typical products. It is suggested that as that of small scale unit's reservation of certain products should be exclusively

made for Self-Help Groups in order to protect them from the competition of small and large scale units.

3. It is suggested that the Sate government should come forward to constitute a federation for marketing the products of Self-Help Groups through public distribution system.

4. In order to improve the socio-economic status and stability of the Self-Help Groups, they should change their production pattern from conventional goods to fancy goods. Apart from producing goods and services like broomsticks and craft goods they should produce goods and services like garments and hotels etc.

5. In countries like India, still there is an absence of encouragement and recognition especially for women entrepreneurs because women are considered as weaker section of the society and also there is a feel prevails those women are meant for housewives rather than being a successful entrepreneurs. In order to change this kind of attitude and promote more number of Self-Help Groups, the government should extent their unlimited assistance in the form of loans, subsidies, training and orientation programme etc to attract the members as well as the society.

Conclusion

Self-Help Groups occupy a crucial role in the process of women-empowerment and have crossed several milestones with enduring results. Empowerment of women and their families especially from the poorest sector through awareness programs, capacity building and strengthening their livelihoods by widening the choices and income generation programs is the objective of the Self-Help Groups. In this aspect we can say that the Self-Help Groups is the key factor for the community development. They have achieved a remarkable task in the employment, national income, export, removal of social disparities, and improvement of the society. When the authorities consider the above suggestions it is no doubt that the self-help groups in Namakkal district will be gained with better performance. The researcher has suggested suitable measures to improve the performance of Self-Help Groups. If this study provokes the people concerned to take some positive measures in order to improve it, the researcher will feel amply rewarded.

References

1. M. Karunakar and S. Saravanan, 'Impact of Micro finance on SHQS in Tamilnadu' Vol. 47, No.1, Southern Economist, May.1, 2008, P. 37.
2. P. Rajendran and K. Karthikeyen, 'Impact of NPAS on Micro Banking Variables' Vol. 47, No.2, Southern Economist, May.15, 2008, P. 10.
3. K. K. Thipathy, 'Micro credit intervention Poverty alleviation, Kurukshetra, Vol. 54, No. 11, Sept. 2004.

13

Micro Finance and NABARD in India – A Pragmatic View

* K. Nagarajan & ** Rst. Kiruthika

The proposed Micro Finance Services Regulation Bill defines, Micro Finance services as "providing financial assistance to an individual or an eligible client, either directly or through a group mechanism for:

i) an amount not exceeding rupees fifty thousand in aggregate per individual for, small and tiny enterprise, agriculture and allied activities (including for consumption purposes of such individual), or

ii) an amount not exceeding rupees one lakh fifty thousand in aggregate per individual for housing purposes, or

iii) such other amounts, for any one of the purposes national at items (i) and (ii) above or other purposes, as may be prescribed."

* Lecturer in Commerce, Department of Commerce, K.S.R. College of Arts and Science, Tiruchengode

** Lecturer in Commerce, Department of Commerce, A.V.S College of Arts and Science, Ramalingapuram, Salem

Micro finance is the extension of very small loans to the unemployed, to poor entrepreneurs and to others, living in poverty who are not considered bankable. Apart from credit, micro finance included micro savings, micro insurance and other financial institutions. This concept is best known for its application in the rural areas of Bangladesh which was introduced by Dr. Muhammad Yunus. As far as Indian rural economy is concerned, agriculture contributes more than 20 per cent of gross domestic product and it ensures livelihood support to nearly two-thirds of country's population. The micro finance system is focused on economically weaker section particularly, agricultural and allied activities. It has successfully enabled extremely impoverished people to engage in self-employment projects that allow them to generate on income and, in many cases, begin to build wealth and exit poverty.

ROLE OF NABARD IN MICRO FINANCE

The Indian financial institutions consist of both formal and informal institutions. As far as formal sector is concerned, NABARD has been playing a vital role in operations of micro finance in India. The bank has set-up a new department known as "Micro Credit Innovations Department (MCID)" to provide focused attention on micro financial activities. In order to give a new approach to rural finance, NABARD had introduced the 'Self-Help Groups' (SHGs) in 1992. Self-Help Group can be defined as a self-governed, peer controlled informal group of people with similar socio-economic background and having a desire to collectively perform a common purpose. In this context, the bank had launched the SHG-Bank Linkage Programme in February 1992 which could be considered as landmark development in banking with the poor. This Programme is a major plank of the strategy for delivering financial services, to the poor in a sustainable manner. The search for such alternatives started with internal introspection regarding the innovations which the poor had been traditionally making, to meet their financial services needs. It was observed that the poor tended to come together in a variety of informal ways for pooling their savings and dispensing small and unsecured loans at varying costs to group members on the basis of need.

Table 13.1: *Progress of SHG-Bank Linkage Programme*

Year	No. of SHGs financed during the year (in lakh)	Cumulative No. of SHGs financed (in lakh)
2001 - 02	1.98	4.61
2002 – 03	2.56	7.17
2003 – 04	3.62	10.79
2004 – 05	5.39	16.18
2005 – 06	6.20	22.38
2006 - 07	6.87	29.25
Source: www.nabard.org		

Initially there was a slow progress in the programme, up to 1999 as only 32,995 groups were credit linked during the period 1992 to 1999.

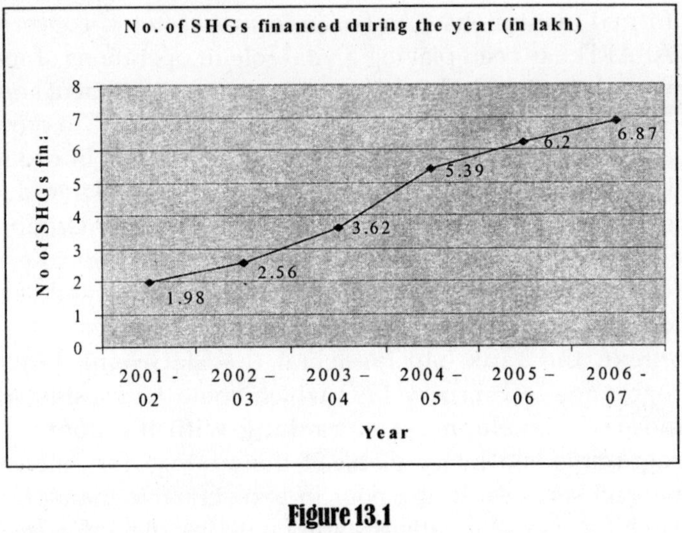

Figure 13.1

Since then the programme has been growing rapidly and the number of SHGs financed increased from 81,780 in 1999-2000 to more than 6.20 lakh in 2005-06 and 6.87 lakh in

2006- 07. At present, the bank has managed a Micro Finance Development Fund of Rs. 200 crore and it is fully utilized for micro financial activities in India.

Table 13.2: *Region wise Performance of Micro Credit upto 31st March 2007*

Region	No. of SHGs Linked	Cumulative Bank Loan (Rs. in million)
1. Northern Region	1,82,018	6,175.47
2. North-Eastern Region	91,754	2638.90
3. Eastern Region	5,25,881	16,045.91
4. Central Region	3,32,729	10,928.91
5. Western Region	2,70,447	9,148.99
6. Southern Region	15,22,144	1,35,469.24
Source: www.nabard.org		

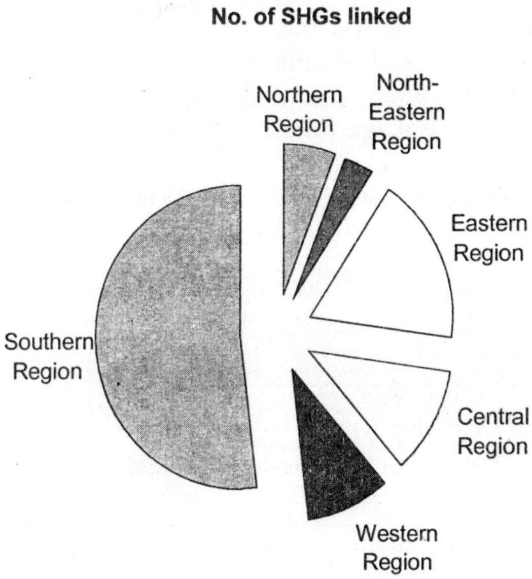

Figure 13.2

In terms of scope, the micro financial sector in India is concentrated in the Southern states, viz., Tamil Nadu, Andhra

Pradesh, Karnataka and Kerala. They encompass more than 70 per cent of micro credit activities.

SHG-BANK LINKAGE PROGRAMME

The performance of Indian micro financial sector may evidenced by the number of SHGs financed by banks and financial institutions. The significant success of this programme was due to the active involvement of over 700 NGOs, 266 banks, along with policy support from Government of India, Reserve Bank of India and NABARD. This programme covered 587 districts in 24 states and union territories of the country.

During the period April 2005 to March 2006, 6,20,109 new SHGs were financed by banks to the tune of Rs 44.99 billion by way of loans. Cumulatively, banks have lent Rs. 113.97 billion to 22,38,565 SHGs. NABARD has extended a refinance of Rs 10.68 billion to banks during 2005-06 bring the cumulative refinance amount to Rs 41.60 billion. About 32.98 million poor households have gained access to formal banking system through SHG bank linkage programme.

Table 13.3: *SHG-Bank Linkage Programme in India*
(As on 31st March 2007)

Particulars	Position
1. Number of SHGs linked	29,24,973
2. Percentage of Women groups	90 %
3. Number of Participating Banks	498
4. Number of Districts covered	587
5. Number of Poor Household assisted (in lakh)	409.5
6. Bank Loan (Rs. in billion)	180.41
7. Refinance (Rs. in billion)	54.59
Source: www.nabard.org	

During the financial year 2006 - 07, 6,86,408 new SHGs were financed by banks, to the tune of Rs. 66.43 billion by way of loans. Cumulatively, banks have lent Rs. 180.41 billion to 29,24,973 SHGs. NABARD has extended a refinance and it brings the cumulative refinance amount to Rs. 54.59 billion. About 40.95 million poor household have gained access to formal banking system through SHG-Bank linkage programme. Besides SHG-Bank linkage programme, NABARD has been encouraging various other credit delivery innovations, such as Grameen bank replication, NGO Networking, Credit Unions, SHG Federations and others. With a view to deepening the activities relating to banking with the poor, NABARD is keeping an internal mission, to reach 20 million families of rural poor during the next 10 years.

ROLE OF MFIs IN MICRO FINANCE

The new types of Micro Financial Institutions (MFIs) are being launched in India. Micro financial institutions are those which provide thrift, credit and other financial services and products of very small amount, mainly to the poor in rural and semi-urban areas for enabling them, to raise their income levels and improve living standards. They concentrate exclusively in the field of micro finance and adopt products, policies and procedures which can enable them to deliver their securities in a profitable manner. They also educate, local communities about the opportunity to improve their lives with micro finance. These institutions differ in size and reach; some serve a few thousand clients in their immediate area, while others serve hundreds of very poor people through hundreds of braches covering large regions.

Table 13.4: *Highlights of leading MFIs in India*

Name of MFI	Mode of Lending	Real Interest Rate	Overdues	% of borrowers below poverty line
1. SHARE	Group	Unrestricted	Nil	100%
2. SEWA	Group	Unrestricted	5%	Most
3. SHREYAS	Group	Unrestricted	N.A	95%
4. MYRADA	Group	Unrestricted	N.A	Most
5. BASIX	Group	Unrestricted	10%	Most
Note: N.A = Not Available				

The majority of micro financial institutions in India are trust and societies. They play a vital role in improving the financial access, particularly in rural India. These institutions have easy access to low cost funds, mobilized through savings, bank deposits from rural households. Performance of many of them in this field is remarkable.

INDIAN SCENE OF MICRO FINANCE

With 75 million poor households potentially requiring financial services, the micro finance market in India is, amongst the largest in the world. Estimate of household credit demand varies from a minimum of Rs.2,000 to Rs.6,000 in rural areas. Given that 80 per cent of poor households are located in rural areas, total credit demand rages between Rs.255 billion and RS.500 billion. Supply of micro financial services, however, falls significantly short of demand.

FURTHER MEASURES FOR IMPROVEMENT

The following suggestions are offered to improve the micro financial activities in India.

- The SHG-Bank linkage programme has made a, significant progress over the years. The present coverage is, however, insignificant when compared to the large population of the rural poor in the country. Efforts by banks, in providing financial services to the poor are being supplemented by NGOs.
- The various types of micro financial institutions, have to be established, to provide liberal financial services to the weaker section people.
- In order to propagate the concept and services of micro finance, the bankers have to organize workshop, conference or awareness programmes successfully.
- The bank need to devise new lending products, innovative systems and simple procedures to reduce the cost and time of lending for providing credit to the poor.

- The systematic efforts are required to be made for documentation of several innovative micro finance practices being adopted in different parts of India.
- Finally, there is a need for establishing, an apex organization exclusively for Micro Finance at the national level which should function for advocacy of micro finance.

CONCLUSION

Today, micro finance plays a major role in the development of many Asian nations, particularly in India. It attempts to unleash forces transforming lives from debt-driven to self-driven, so as to trigger growth in rural economies. But, the fact, however, is that most of the financial products used by the banking system were primarily developed for the business enterprise and urban population. The banks did not involve themselves wholeheartedly, in the spectrum of micro finance. In the changed economic scenario, banking systems would need to changing its attitude, innovate and evolve new products, which are appropriate and accessible for the rural poor. If so, there is no doubt, that the micro finance for the rural mass can lead to, sustainable development in the country.

REFERENCES

1. Basu, Kishanjit and Jindal, Krishnan (eds.), Micro Finance – Emerging Challenges, New Delhi: Tata McGraw-Hill Publishing Company Limited, 2000.
2. Chavan, Pallavi and Ramkumar, R., Micro Credit and Rural Poverty – An Analysis of Empirical Evidences, Economic and Political Weekly, March 9, 2002.
3. Desai, B.M., A study of SHGs and Linkage Programme, Indian Journal of Agricultural Economics, Vol.55, No.1, January-March, 2000.
4. Jerinabi, U., Micro Credit Management by Women's Self-Help Groups, New Delhi: Discovery Publishing House, 2006.

5. Kaladhar, K., Micro Finance in India: Design, Structure and Governance, Economic and Political Weekly, Vol.42, October 18-24, 1997.
6. Lalitha, N., Mainstreaming Micro Finance, New Delhi: Mohit Publications, 2003.
7. www.nabard.org

14

Micro Financing of Indian Commercial Banks

* Dr. N. Shaik Mohamed, Kavitha Shanmugam
and Dr. Jamaludeen

Background

Since the 1950s, various governments in India have experimented with a large number of grant and subsidy based poverty alleviation programmes. But these mandatory and dedicated subsidized financial programmes, implemented through banking institutions, have not been fully successful in meeting their social and economic objectives. This is due to the fact that, these programmes were not sustainable, perpetuated the dependent status of the beneficiaries, depended ultimately on government employees for delivery,

*Reader in Commerce, Jamal Mohamed College, Trichy

*Senior Lecturer, MBA Department, SRM University, Chennai

*Reader in Commerce, Urmu Dhanalakshmi College, Trichy

led to misuse of both credit and subsidy and were treated as poverty alleviation interventions. Banks also did not look upon them as a profitable commercial activity. According to a 1995 World Bank estimate, in most developing countries the formal financial system reaches only the top 25% of the economically active population, the bottom 75% have no access to financial services apart from moneylenders.[2]

Introduction to Microfinance

Microfinance is defined as, a process of providing financial services to both poor and low-income households, which include loans, deposits, insurance and pensions. It is a powerful developmental tool in creating high gains and raising the people's standard of living.[3]

Microfinance Institution is defined "as an institution that provides financial services to the poor". These institutions play a crucial role, in the economic empowerment of the poor people especially in the rural areas. Today there are more than 10,000 institutions engaged in these activities and serving the poor.

Microfinance: Services: Micro Finance is much broader than just micro credit. It includes other financial services such as

- Savings
- Remittances
- Risk mitigation products
- Financial counseling
- Lifecycle planning products

Features of Micro-Finance

The main features of the micro-finance services are:

1. It is a tool for empowerment of the poorest; the higher the income and better the asset position of the borrower, the lower the incremental benefit from further equal doses of micro-credit is likely to be.
2. Delivery is normally through Self Help Groups (SHGs).

3. It is essentially for promoting self-employment; the opportunities of wage employment are limited in developing countries - micro finance increases the productivity of self-employment in the informal sector of the economy - generally used for (a) direct income generation (b) rearrangement of assets and liabilities for the household to participate in future opportunities and (c) consumption smoothing.
4. It is not just a financing system, but a tool for social change, specially for women - it does not spring from market forces alone - it is potentially welfare enhancing - there is a public interest in promoting the growth of micro finance - this is what makes it acceptable as a valid goal for public policy.
5. Because micro credit is aimed at the poorest, micro-finance lending technology needs to mimic the informal lenders rather than the formal sector lending. It has to: a) provide for seasonality (b) allow repayment flexibility (c) eschew bureaucratic and legal formalities (d) fix a ceiling on loan sizes.

Service Providers in the Micro Credit Sector

- Self Help Groups (SHGs)
- Formal Banks
- Non-Governmental Organisations
- Microfinance Institutions
- Government Programs
- Money Lenders[5]

The Microfinance sector in India

The microfinance sector in India, has been perceived by policymakers, particularly the Reserve Bank of India, as a useful channel for expanding access to various financial services for low-income persons and those in the informal sector. The poor in India define the micro-finance market. The Planning Commission estimate of 1993-94 says, 36% of the population or 320 million people live below the poverty line - there would be 140-150 million women alone living below the poverty line. Assuming that only 30% of the country's poor women are ready to adopt micro-finance as a method of poverty alleviation, it is estimated that 40-45 million poor women would need credit. India's microfinance sector has an outreach of 36.8 million borrowers, about 50% of the estimated potential, MFIs had close to 10 million customers and a cumulative outstanding portfolio of $769 million. The efficiency and profitability indicators of Indian MFIs are highly favourable compared to Asian benchmarks. Several leading MFIs have begun to operate on a national scale.[6]

India's Microfinance based Poverty Alleviation Programmes

As part of the poverty alleviation measures, the Government of India (GOI) launched the Swarnjayanti Gram Swarozgar Yojana (SGSY) in 1999, where the major emphasis is on self-help group (SHG) formation, social mobilisation and economic activation through micro-credit finance. Up to March 2003, 13.38 lakh groups were constituted in 33 states and union territories, of which 33,436 SHGs only could take up economic activities for their economic sustenance.[7] Simultaneously, the government supports the National Bank for Agriculture and Rural Development (NABARD) to take up activities such as group formation, micro-finance and economic activation. Besides this, the Rashtriya Mahila Kosh (RMK that is, National Credit Fund for Women) and the Department of Women and Child Development have their own programmes, under which micro credit is being provided for economic empowerment of the rural poor.

The year 2001 to 02 marked a decade of self-help group-bank linkage programme in India. With the growing importance of the micro-credit through SHG-bank linkage in India, the Reserve Bank of India in 1996 included financing to SHGs as a mainstream activity of banks under their priority sector lending. The government bestowed national priority to the programme, through its recognition in the 1999 budget.

It has been estimated that India has the world's largest micro-finance programme in terms of out-reach, with 7.8 million households accessing credit through 17,085 branches of the formal banking system under the micro-credit finance programme.

The micro-credit programmes focus on organisation of the rural poor at the grassroots level through a process of social mobilisation, which enables the poor build their own organisations (SHGs) consisting of 10 to 20 persons, in which they participate fully and directly and take decisions on all issues concerning poverty eradication.

Impact of micro-finance in India

While the Government of India tries to widen the micro-credit reach for the million poor in India through the self-employment scheme, namely, SGSY, the NABARD envisages reaching banking services to one-third of the very poor in India, that is, a population of about 100 million rural poor through one million SHGs by 2007-08.

With NABARD support, bank loans were provided to 197,653 new SHGs during 2001-02 and repeat finance was provided to 41,413 existing SHGs during the year. Overall, the NABARD'S SHG-bank linkage programme benefited four million families covering an estimated 20 million poor in 2001-02.

The Potential of India's Micro Financing

Micro-finance is an innovative credit delivery mechanism that ensures viable financial services for the needy. It has the potential to address issues like actualising equitable gains from the development on a sustained basis and can play a vital role in developing nations in fighting poverty.

The micro-finance scene in India is dominated by SHG-bank linkage programme. Though the groups existed even before the linkage programme (under the SGSY and NABARD's SHG-bank linkage programme), the banks could not recognise their potential as business clients and both operated independently in most of the cases, without knowing the strength of the other. Intervening to forge a linkage, besides SGSY, the NABARD has helped in the emergence of a very strong micro-finance movement in the country.

The SHG-bank linkage programme was conceived with the objectives of supplementary credit delivery services for the un-reached poor, building mutual trust and confidence between the bankers and the poor and encouraging banking activity both on thrift, as well as credit and sustaining a simple and formal mechanism of banking with the poor. The linkage programme combines the flexibility, sensitivity and responsiveness of the informal credit system with the technical and administrative capabilities and financial resources of the formal financial sector which rely heavily on collective strength of the poor, closeness of effective social mobilisation functions contributing to an overall empowerment process.

India has a strong potential, to promote the women as key decision-makers through encouraged local leadership, which can be facilitated by complete involvement and participation of poor women in micro-credit programmes. This will succeed only with the coordination among the government, banks, participating members and micro credit finance institutions. Micro-finance can be a powerful tool in initiating a cyclical process of growth and development. Micro-finance activity can improve the access of rural poor to financial services. The micro-finance interventions help in inculcating necessary habits for economic independence and self-reliance. Appropriate and participatory credit plans, by the members of a group can help in social and economic empowerment. Increased access signifies the overcoming of isolation of rural women in terms of their access to financial services and denial of credit due to absence of collateral security. The pool of savings generated out of very small but regular voluntary contributions improves access of the poor women to bank loans. It could also help in strengthening poor families' resistance to external shocks and reducing dependence on moneylenders. The group utilizes its corpus to disburse loans of small amount amongst the needy members. In the beginning, the members meet out their consumption needs out of their own fund and afterwards they obtain loans from the Banks for taking up some economic activities for their sustained living.

Microfinance Investments of Commercial Banks in India

Banks in India have begun to enter the microfinance lending market, and many are partnering with regional microfinance institutions. Increasingly, loans as small as $100 are being made by mainstream Indian banks such as ICICI, HDFC, and UTI, and often contain unconventional covenants typical of microfinance transactions.[8] Founded in 1977, HDFC had net income for 2005 of about $200 million and 24 rural partners. Recent partnerships include: Ujjivan, Bellwether microfinance fund, Avishkar-Goodwell Fund, Lok Capital, and Activists for Social Alternatives. Another example of a commercial bank that has partnered with local MFIs is ICICI, which has 72 such partnerships. ICICI Bank had net income in 2005 of about $500 million, and operates 614 branches and 2200 ATMs. Through about 100 rural partnerships, its portfolio of microfinance investments stood at $227 million and 1.2 million clients at year end 2005. A prominent partner of the bank is Spandana. The Andhra-Pradesh-based microfinance institution disbursed loans of $3.4 million in 2004 at an effective rate of 30%, of which 9.25% went to ICICI. In addition, in November 2005, ICICI tied up with the Grameen Foundation USA to create microfinance lender Grameen Capital India. ICICI has been micro lending since 2001.

Mumbai-based UTI began in 1994, and is 72% publicly-owned. It had net income in 2005 of $104 million, and operates 450 branches and more than a thousand ATMs throughout India. In its Annual Report 2005-2006, reference is made to increasing microfinance activities by offering new services to rural clients. UTI works closely with the Grameen Koota program, which has outstanding loans of $3.2 million, as well as, SKS Microfinance of India.

Functioning of Microfinance Institutions in India

As far as the formal financial institutions are concerned, there are Commercial Banks, Housing Finance Institutions (HFIs), NABARD, Rural Development Banks (RDBs), Land Development Banks and Co-operative Banks (CBs). As regards the Co-operative Structures, the Urban Cooperative Banks (UCB) or Urban Credit Cooperative Societies (UCCS) are the two primary co-operative financial institutions operating in the urban areas. There are about 1400 UCBs with over 3400 branches in India having 14 million members. Their total lending outstanding in 1990-91 has been reported at over Rs 80 billion with deposits worth Rs 101 billion. Similarly there exist about 32000 credit cooperative societies with over 15 million members with their total outstanding lending in 1990-91 being Rs 20 billion with deposits of Rs 12 billion.

Few of the UCCS also have external borrowings from the District Central Cooperative Banks (DCCBs) at 18-19 percent. The loans given by the UCBs or the UCCS are for short term and unsecured except for few which are secured by personal guarantees, the most effective security being the group or the peer pressure.

The Constraints

Some of the main reasons for the constraints associated with micro credit are:

Non-productive loans and procedural delays for productive loans: Since most of the poor and needy are illiterate and prefer loans for consumption rather than productive purposes, majority of the poor find it hard to get loans sanctioned for taking up economic activities, even if they want to. Sometimes, the loanees are asked to furnish some documents and collateral security against the loan sanctioned, contrary to the directives of the Government and the RBI.

Inflexibility and delay: The rigid systems and procedures for sanctioning loans and disbursing them to the beneficiaries result in a lot of delay in time for the borrowers, which de-motivate them.

High transaction costs: Although the interest rate offered to the borrowers is regulated, the transaction costs in terms of the number of trips to be made, the documents to be furnished etc. plus the illegal charges demanded by the lending institutions clandestinely, result in increasing the cost of borrowing, thus, making it less attractive to the borrowers. **Social obligation, not a business opportunity:** Micro-finance has been seen as a social obligation rather than a potential business opportunity.

High interest rates: Sometimes, a few financial institutions charge the beneficiaries of a group high interest rate which makes the repayment difficult for the very poor. The poorest of the poor are, therefore, unable to access the micro-finance benefits.

Lack of training: In most of the cases, it has been found that members of a group take up certain economic activities for their sustenance which are not preceded by relevant training.

Conclusion

Typically in a world without health insurance a common place experience such as malaria or a funeral can quickly deplete a low income household's few reserves, forcing the victim to take on new loans or deplete productive assets, both of which reduce future income.[9] As more sophisticated financial institutions enter microfinance, India needs to develop an integrated regulatory structure from a fragmented one now. India should develop a diverse and robust, but well-regulated microfinance sector.

References

1. http://www.microfinanceindia.org/
2. www.rmk.nic.in/chap1.htm
3. http://www.cgap.org/about/faq01.html
4. http://www.blueorchard.ch/en what_is_microfinance.asp
5. Sumit Kumar Chaudhari and Rupesh Kumar Madhogaria, "Vikram Ahula's SKS Microfinance Pvt. Ltd. The Making of a

Successful Microfinance Institution", The Icfai Journal of Entrepreneurship Development, Vol. IV, No.1, 2007, pp. 76.

6. http://www.symbiotics.ch/en/rss_microfinance.asp?id=b1114
7. http://www.businessdayonline.com/economic-watch/5552.html
8. http://microcapitalmonitor.com/cblog/index.php?/archives/340-Commercial-Banks-in-India-Delve-into-Microfinance-Investments.html
9. http://www.socialedge.org/admin/discussions/responsibility/microfinance-who-uses-it-and-why-march-2005/?searchterm=microfinance

15

Performance of Urban Co-operative Banks in Thanjavur District: An Empirical Investigation

R.P.Ramesh*, T. Anuja** and K.Devanadhen***

Co-operative bank mobilize the deposits and provide finance to the entrepreneurs, urban cooperative banks have emerged as the main functionaries to meet the banking and credit needs in urban, semi urban and rural areas. They do it with simplicity, close contacts, local feel and involvement. The Co-operative banks including Urban Co-operative Banks (UCBs) have been forced to work hard to retain their members/ customers and to enlarge their clientele base. The existence of bank branches nearby and the availability of bank services combined with the competitive propagation of savings

* Senior Lecturer in Commerce, Dept. of Commerce, PRIST University, Thanjavur.

** Lecturer in Commerce, Dept. of commerce, PRIST University, Thanjavur.

*** Lecturer in Commerce, Directorate of Distance Education, Annamalai University, Annamalai Nagar.

and credit products by individual bankers have developed the banking habits among the people of rural / semi-urban / urban centers at large. The spurt in number of bank users has become an opportunity for the Co-operative banks including UCBs to overcome the threat posed by the competition duly erupted by the presence of commercial banks in their erstwhile domain of rural and semi-urban centers.

Financially strong and organizationally vibrant, viable credit institutions are imperative for dispensation of adequate and timely credit. The cooperative banks therefore to be sensitive to concepts of cost effectiveness, commercial orientation, professionalization, accountability etc. In the present study an attempt is made to examine the viability of the urban cooperative banks in Thanjavur by an analysis of the various parameters. Out of five urban cooperative banks in Thanjavur district, three cooperative banks are selected for the purpose.

They are:

1. The Nicholson Cooperative Town Bank Ltd., (NCTB) (Est. 1905)
2. The Karunthattangudi Dravidian Co-Operative Urban Bank Ltd.,(KDCUB) (Est. 1919)
3. The Pattukkottai Co-Operative Urban Bank Ltd., (PCUB) (Est. 1977)

In the following, Section II comprises review of literature, section III deals with the sources of data and methodology. Section IV discusses results and analysis through CAMEL Model and in the final section describes suggestions and conclusion.

1. Review of Literature

To build the conceptual framework for the application of CAMEL Model, we may draw on the following literature:

Barr and Siems (1996) tried to predict bank failures in the US, using eh data from December 1984 to June 1987 Using Camel Model. They used technical efficiency measure, Using DEA in their predication model. Along with their DEA results, which represent Management Quality "M" in the CAMEL rating, they used financial ratios representing soundness of Capital, Asset Quality, Earnings and Liquidity. They found that the use of The DEA Efficiency Score in the regression increased the accuracy of the classification results from 89% to 92.4% and the new model was superior to the earlier early-warning models.

Godse (1996) examined the application of new model CAMEL, i.e., "Capital Adequacy, Assets Quality, Management, Earning Quality, Liquidity, Systems and Control", for evaluating the performance of banks.

Rao and Datta (1998) made an attempt to derive rating based on CAMEL. In their study, based on theses five groups (C-A-M-E-L), 21 parameters in all were developed. After deriving separate rating for each parameter, a combined rating was derived for all nationalized banks (19) for the year 1998. The study found that Corporation Bank has the best rating followed by Oriental Bank of Commerce, Bank of Baroda, Dena Bank, Punjab National Bank, etc. and the worst rating was found to be of Indian Bank preceded by UCO bank, United Bank of India, Syndicate Bank and Vijaya Bank.

Prasuna (2004) analysed the performance of Indian banks by adopting the CAMEL Model. The performance of 65 banks was studied for the period 2003-04. The author concluded that the competition was tough and consumers benefitted from it. Better services quality, innovative products, better bargains are al greeting the Indian customers. The coming fiscal will prove to be a transition phase for Indian banks, as they will have to align their strategic focus to increasing interest rates.

Veni (2004) studied the capital adequacy requirement of banks and the measures adopted by them to strengthen their capital ratios. The author highlighted that the rating agencies give prominence to Capital Adequacy ratios of bank while rating the bank's certificate of deposits, fixed deposits and bonds. They normally adopt CAMEL Model for rating banks. Thus, Capital Adequacy is considered as the key element of bank rating.

Satish, Jutur Sharath and surrender (2005) adopted CAMEL model to asses the performance of Indian Banks. The authors analysed the performance of 55 banks for the year 2004-05, Using CAMEL Model. They concluded that the Indian banking system looks sound and information technology will help the banking system grow I strength while going into future. Banks' Initial Public Offer will be hitting the market to increase their capital and gearing up for the Basel II norms.

Bodla and Richa Verma (2006) study the performance of SBI and ICICI through CAMEL Model for the period 2000-01 to 2004-05. The author concluded that SBI has an edge over its counterpart ICICI in terms of Capital Adequacy. However, the ICICI has edge over SBI regarding assets Quality, earning quality and management quality. The liquidity position of both the banks is sound and does not differ significantly.

The primary objective of this paper to describe the CAMEL Model of rating Cooperative banks so as to catch up the comparative performance of banks.

2. Data and methodology

The basic data required for the study is collected from the annual reports of the respective bank for the year 1998-99 to 2006-07.

CAMEL is basically a ratio-based model for evaluating the performance of banks. Various ratios forming this model are available in Exhibit 1 below. These ratios are explained as follows.

Exhibit 1: CAMEL Model	
C: Capital Adequacy	• Capital Adequacy Ratio • Debt-Equity Ratio • Advances to Assets • G-Secs to Total Investment
A:Assets Quality	• Gross NPAs to Net Advances • Net NPAs to Net Advances • Total Investment to Total Assets • Net NPAs to Total Assets

M: Management Efficiency	• Total Advances to Total Deposits • Business per Employee • Profit per Employee
E: Earning Quality	• Operating Profits to Average Working funds • Spread to Total Assets • Net Profit to Average Assets. • Interest Income to Total Income • Non-Interest Income to Total Income
L:Liquidity	• Liquid Assets to Total Assets • G-Secs to Total Assets • Liquid Assets to Demand Deposits • Liquid Assets to Total Deposits

Capital Adequacy

Capital is seen as a cushion to protect depositors and promote the stability and efficiency of financial system around the world. Capital Adequacy reflects the overall financial condition of the banks and also the ability of the management to meet the need for additional capital. It also indicates whether the bank has enough capital to absorb unexpected losses. Capital Adequacy Ratios act as indicators of bank leverage. The following measure Capital Adequacy.

a. Capital Adequacy Ratio (CAR)

The banks are required to maintain the Capital Adequacy Ratio (CAR) as specified by RBI from time to time. As per the latest RBI norms, the bank in India should have a CAR at 9%. It is arrived at by dividing the sum of Tier-I, Tier-II and Tier-III capital by aggregate of Risk Weighted Assets (RWA) symbolically:

Tier–I : Capital includes equity capital and free reserves.

Tier–II: Capital comprises of subordinate debts of 5-7 years tenure, revaluation reserves, general provisions and loss reserves, hybrid debt capital instruments ad undisclosed reserves and cumulative perpetual preference shares.

Tier–III: Capital comprises of short-term subordinate debt.

The higher the CAR, the stronger is considered a bank, as it ensures high safety against bankruptcy.

b. Debt-Equity Ratio

This ratio indicates the degree of leverage of a bank. It indicates how much of the bank business is financed through debt and how much through equity. This is calculated as the proportion of total outside liability to net worth. "Outside Liabilities" includes total borrowings, deposits and other liabilities. "Net Worth" includes equity capital and reserves and surplus. Higher ratio indicates less protection for the creditors and depositors in the banking system.

c. Advances to Assets

This is the ratio of the Total Advances to Total Assets. This ratio indicates a bank's aggressiveness in lending which ultimately results in better profitability. Higher ratio of Advances/Asset is preferred. Total advances also include receivables. The Value of total Assets is excluding the revaluation of all the assets.

d. Government Securities (G-Secs.) to Total Investments

The percentage of investment in government securities to total investments is a very important indicator, which shows the risk-taking ability of the bank. It indicates a bank's strategy as being high profit-high risk or low profits-low risk. It also gives a view as to the availability of alternative investment opportunities. Government Securities are generally considered as the most safe debt instrument, which, as a result, carries the lowest return. Since Government Securities are risk-free, the higher the G-Secs. to investment ratio, the lower the risk involved in a bank's investments.

Assets Quality

The quality of assets is an important parameter to gauge the strength of the bank. The prime motto behind measuring the assets quality is to ascertain the component of Non-Performing Assets (NPAs) as percentage of the total assets. This indicates what types of advances the bank has made to generate interest income. Thus, assets quality indicates the type of the debtors the bank is having. The following ratios are necessary to assess assets quality:

a. Gross NPAs to Net Advances

It is a measure of the quality of assets in a situation, where the management has not provided for loss on NPAs. Here the Gross NPAs are measured as a percentage of Net Advances. The lower the ratio shows better the quality of advances.

b. Net NPAs to Net Advances

It is most standard measure of assets quality. In this ratio, Net NPAs are measured as a percentage of Net Advances. Net NPAs and Gross NPAs net of provisions on NPAs and interest in suspense account.

c. Total Investments to Total Assets Ratio

Total investment to total assets indicated the extent of deployment of assets in investment as against advances. This ratio is used as tool to measure the percentage of total assets locked up in investments, which, by conventional definition, does not form part of the Core Income of a bank. A higher level of investment means lack of credit off-take in the economy. This ratio is calculated by dividing total investments by total assets of a bank. A higher ratios means that the bank has conservatively kept a high cushion of investments to guard against NPAs. However, this affects its profitability adversely.

d. Net NPAs to Total Assets

This ratio indicates the efficiency of the bank in assessing credit risk and, to an extent, recovering the debts. This ratio is arrived at by dividing the Net NPAs by total Assets. Total assets considered are net of revaluation reserves. Lower the ratio better is the performance of the bank.

Management Efficiency

Management efficiency is another important element of the CAMEL Model. The ratios in this segment involve subjective analysis to measure the efficiency and effectiveness of management. The management of the bank takes crucial decisions depending on its risk perception. It sets vision and goals for the organization and sees that is achieves them. This parameter is used to evaluate management efficiency as to assign premium to better quality banks and discount poorly managed ones. The ratios used to evaluate management efficiency are described as under:

a. Total Advances to Total Deposits

This ratio measures the efficiency and ability of the bank's management in converting the deposits available with the bank (excluding other funds like equity capital, etc.,) into high earning advances. Total deposits include demand deposits, savings deposits, term deposits and deposits of other banks. Total Advances also include the receivables.

b. Business per Employee

This ratio shows the productivity of human forces of the bank. It is used as a tool to measure the efficiency of all the employees of a bank in generating business for the bank. It is arrived at by dividing the total business by total number of employees. Higher the ratio, the better it is for the bank. By business, we mean the sum of total Deposits and Total Advances in a particular year.

c. Profit per Employee

This ratio shows the surplus earned per employee. It is arrived at by dividing the profit after tax (PAT) earned by the bank by the total number of employees. The higher the ratio, the higher the efficiency of the management.

Earning Quality

The quality of earning is a very important criterion that determines the ability of a bank to earn consistently, going into the future. It basically determines the profitability of the banks. It also explains the sustainability and growth in earnings in the future. This parameter gains importance in the light of the argument that much of a bank's income is earned through non-core activities like investments, treasury operations, corporate advisory services and so on. The following ratios try to assess the quality of income in terms of income generated by core activity – income from lending operations.

a. Operating Profits to Average Working Funds Ratio

This ratio indicates how much a bank can earn from its operations net of the operating expenses for every rupee spent on working funds. This arrived at by dividing the operating profits by average working funds. Average Working Funds (AWF) are the total resources (total assets or liabilities) employed by a bank. It is daily average of total assets/liabilities during a year. The higher the ratio, the better it is. This ratio determines the operating profits generated out of working funds employed. The better utilization of funds will result in higher operating profits. Thus, this ratio will indicate how a bank has employed its working funds in generating profits. Banks which use their assets efficiency will tend to have a better average than the industry average.

b. Spread or Net Interest Margin (NIM) to Total Assets

NIM, being the difference between the interest income and the interest expended as percentage of total assts, shows the ability of the bank to keep the interest on deposits low and interest on advances high. It is an important measure of a bank's core income (income from lending operations). A higher spread indicates the better earnings given the total assets. The interest income includes dividend income and interest expended includes interest paid on deposits, loan from the RBI, and other short-term and long-term loans.

c. Net Profit to Average Assets

Profit to average assets indicates the efficiency of the banks in utilizing their asses in generating profits. A higher ratio indicates the better income generating capacity of the assets and better income generating capacity of the assets and better efficiency of management. It is arrived at by dividing the net profit by average assets, which is the average of total assets in the current and previous year. Thus, this ratio measures the return on assts employed. Higher ratio indicates better earning potential in the future.

d. Interest Income to Total Income

Interest Income is a basic source of revenue for banks. The Interest income to total income indicates the ability of the bank in generating income from its lending. In other words, this ratio measures the income from lending operations as a percentage of the total income generated by the bank in a year. Interest income includes income on advances, interest on deposits with the RBI, and dividend income.

e. Non-Interest Income to Total Income

A fee-based income account for a major portion of a bank's other incomes. The bank generates higher fee income through innovative products and adapting the technology for sustained service levels. This stream of revenue is not dependent on the bank's capital adequacy and consequent potential to generate income is immense. Thus, this ratio measures the income from operations, other than lending, as percentage of the total income, Non-interest income is the income earned by the banks excluding income o advances and deposits with the RBI. The higher ratio of non-interest income/total income indicates the increasing proportion of fee-based income.

Liquidity

Liquidity is very important for any organisation dealing with money. Banks have to take proper care I hedging liquidity risk while at the same time ensuring that a good percentage of funds are invested in higher return generating investments, so that banks can generate profit while at the same time provide liquidity to the depositors. Among a bank's assets, cash investments are the most liquid. The ratios suggested to measure liquidity under CAMEL Model are as follows:

a. Liquid Assets to Total Assets

Liquid Assets include cash in hand, balance with the RBI, balance with other banks (both in India and abroad), and money at call and short notice. Total assets include the revaluations of all the assets. The proportion of Liquid assets to Total Assets indicates the overall liquidity position of the bank.

b. G-Secs to Total Assets

Government securities are the most liquid and safe investments. This ratio measures the G-Secs as a proportion of total assets. Banks invest in government securities primarily to meet their SLR requirements, which are around 25% of net demand and time liabilities. This ratio measures the risk involved in the assets held by a bank.

c. Liquid Assets to Demand Deposits

This ratio measures the ability of a bank to meet the demand from deposits in a particular year. It is arrived at by dividing the liquid assets by total demand deposits. Demand deposits offer high liquidity to the depositor and hence banks have to invest these assets in a highly liquid form. The liquid assets include cash in hand, balance wit the RBI, Balance with other banks (both in India and abroad) and money at call and short notice.

d. Liquid Assets to Total Deposits

This ratio measures the liquidity available to the deposits of a bank. Total deposits include demand deposits, savings deposits, term deposits and deposits of other financial institutions. The liquid assets include cash in hand, balance wit the RBI, Balance with other banks (both in India and abroad) and money at call and short notice.

In order to have a comprehensive view, the growth of each ratio covered by CAMEL is calculated by Annual Compound Growth Rate (ACGR) Method for the last nine years. The Annual Compound Growth Rate (ACGR) is calculated by using SPSS software and statistically defined as:

Where Y = dependent variables (deposits, advances, etc.), a = constant, b = Slope of trend lines (growth rate), t = time.

Estimate of b (slope of trend lie or rate of change) has been arrived as follows:

In this equation, g (growth rate) has been obtained by taking antilogarithm of log (1 + g) and subtracting 1 from the same. The resultant value would be multiplied by 100 to express growth rate in percentage terms.

The significance of the difference between the performances of two banks is verified with the help of F-test. The F-ratio is calculated as:

Where, q = number of banks, N= total number of observations (number of banks X number of time series observations for each ratio), CESS = Combined sum of squared errors when both the bands and their observations are used to estimate the regression equation above (for each ratio); MESS = Sum of the two banks sums of squared errors for each bank estimated from the regression applied to each bank (each ratio) separately:

2(q-1) = Numerator degrees of freedom

N-2q - Denominator degrees of freedom.

3. Results and Analysis

CAPITAL ADEQUACY

The various ratios measuring Capital Adequacy in case of NCTB, KDCUB and PCUB banks are depicted in Tables 1. It is obvious from the Tables that NCTB, KDCUB and PCUB have maintained the Average Capital Adequacy Ratio at 7.81%, 8.56% and14.43% respectively between 1998-99 and 2006-07. This shows that NCTB, KDCUB and PCUB banks have maintained higher CAR than the prescribed level during the last four years. According to the norms of RBI, each bank in India has to maintain 8% of their risk-weighted assets as capital with effect from March 2000. However, the growth of CAR is positive in case of all the three banks. The above also holds good with respect to Debt/Equity Ratio, wherein the compound growth rates are negative 17.59, 12.91 and 10% in case of NCTB, KDCUB and PCUB respectively. This indicates that the dependence on debt capital has decreased over the last ten years in case of all the three banks. The ratio of advances to assets to found higher in case of KDCUB. The same is also confirmed by F-test which indicates a significant difference in this rate of the three banks under reference. The NCTB has also outperformed KDCUB and PCUB in terms of the growth rate in this ratio (the percentage of advances to total assets). The positive annual growth of the ratio of advances to assets at 2.67% in NCTB indicates towards an improvement in the efficiency of the bank. The negative annual growth of the ratio of advances to assets at 2.04% in KDCUB and 2.23% in PCUB indicates towards a slow improvement in the efficiency of both the banks. As regards the ratio of Government Securities to Total Investments, the Tables under reference offer that while NCTB has maintained it always above 98% during last seven years, it ranges between 7.62 to 71.23% approximately in case of PCUB in the corresponding period and 2.32 to 89.61% approximately in case of KAR in the study period. The difference between these three banks on this count is found significant at 0.01 level of significance, which indicates the supremacy of NCTB over PCUB and KDCUB in terms of the ratio of Government Securities to Total Investments. Interestingly, this ratio (percentage of investment in government securities to total investment) indicates an increasing trend for NCTB & PCUB, but the compound growth rate is found insignificant in case of NCTB only. The negative compound growth rate is found on KDCUB. Hence the approach of all the banks is turning as conservative.

ASSETS QUALITY

Tables 2 present assets quality position of all the three banks under study in terms of three ratios: Gross NPAs to Net Advances, Net NPAs to Net Advances, and Net NPAs to Total Assets. The assets quality ratios have registered an increasing trend over the years. In so far as the absolute values of the above mentioned asset quality ratios are concerned, significant difference between all the three banks is revealed by the F-test applied for the purpose at 1% and 5% level of significance. The ratio of Total Investments to Total Assets is found at a low level in case of all the three banks. On an average, it is found 7.03% in case of NCTB, 7.46% in case of KDCUB and 4.50% in case of PCUB. There is no significant difference among all banks. Moreover, the ACGR regarding this ratio is found positive i.e. 109.5%, 67.33% and 47.97% in case of NCTB, KDCUB and PCUB respectively. The ACGR turns as significant at 1% level of significance.

MANAGEMENT EFFICIENCY

Table 3 exhibits the various ratios representing the level of management efficiency of the three banks under study. We might observe from these tables that almost each ratio indicates uptrend from the year 1998-99 irrespective of the bank concerned. Table 3 reveals that the ACGR concerning each of the management efficiency ratios is positive. The ratio of Total Advances to Total Deposits is an indicator of the management's efficiency is converting the deposits into high earning advances. Hence, the KDCUB and PCUB have turned more efficient than the NCTB in so far as the speed of converting deposits into advances concerned. The ratio of Business per Employee is found higher in case of NCTB, at 305.29% than PCUB and KDCUB where in the means of the ratio stand at 207.47% and 172.82% respectively, during 1998-99 to 2007-08. But the ratio of Profit per Employee is found higher in case of PCUB at 1.75% than NCTB and KDCUB wherein the means of the ratio stand at 1.39% and .72% respectively during the corresponding period. The same is also confirmed by F test, which indicates a significant difference in this ratio of the three banks under reference.

EARNINGS QUALITY

The position of NCTB, KDCUB and PCUB banks that has emerged on the basis of various ratios used as indicator of earning quality of a banks as per the CAMEL model is given is tables 4. It is evident from the former table that the ratio of Operating Profit to Average Working Funds has raised from 21.6% in 2004-05 to 35.78% in 2006-07 in case of PCUB. Contrarily, this ratio has declined to 1.72% from 3.29% in the year 2005-06 and 2006-07 respectively in case of NCTB and 1.95% from 5.43% in the corresponding period in case of KDCUB bank. The ACGR of this ratio is found 17.60% in case of PCUB, 12.57% in case of NCTB and 12% in case of KDCUB bank. The growth rate in the ratio of Operating Profit to Average Working Funds is found significant in case of NCTB but insignificant in case of KDCUB and PCUB bank. The table further offers that all the banks have registered an gradual increase in the ratio of Spread to Total Assets during the study period. However, the growth rate in the Spread is insignificant in case of PCUB and KDCUB bank. Regarding, profitability the Table reveals that PCUB bank has outperformed the KDCUB and NCTB as the mean of the ratio of Net Profit to Average Assets works out 1.31% (PCUB), 0.58% (KDCUB) and 0.55% (NCTB). While NCTB has outperformed KDCUB and PCUB in terms of Interest Income to Total Income and PCUB have outperformed KDCUB and NCTB in terms of Non-interest Income to Total Income. The significance of this difference is confirmed by the results of F-test in respect to all ratios. The differences in performance are found significant at 5% level of significance.

LIQUIDITY

Table 5 depicts the liquidity position of NCTB, KDCUB and PCUB banks. It is obvious from the tables that all the banks indicate negative trend in Liquid Assets to Total Assets ratio. On an average these banks are found maintaining this ratio at 38.76% (NCTB), 28.62% (KDCUB) and 35.79% (PCUB) during 1998-99 to 2006-07. This indicates that the liquidity position of NCTB and PCUB are sounder as compared to that of KDCUB. Same is the PCUB tern obtained about the ratio of Government Securities to Total Assets. It is, on an average, at 10.37%, 4.37% and 0.40% in NCTB, PCUB and KDCUB banks respectively. NCTB bank has outperformed PCUB and KDCUB so far as the ratio of Liquid Assets to Demand Deposits and Liquid Assets to Total Deposits are concerned. However, the trend is found negative in regard to both the ratios of liquid assets to demand deposits as well as liquid assets to total deposits. An attempt is also made to determine whether the liquidity ratios of NCTB, PCUB and KDCUB banks differ significantly. The result indicates significant difference between the liquidity positions of the three banks only in terms of one liquidity ratio (i.e., Government Securities to Total Assets) out of four ratios. Hence, there is no acknowledgeable difference in the liquidity position of the three banks under reference.

Overall Ranking

Exhibit 2: Ranking of NCTB, KDCUB and PCUB Co-operative bank According to Average of CAMEL Model Ratios for the period 1998-99 to 2006-07

	Ratios	NCTB	KDCUB	PCUB
Capital Adequacy	Capital Adequacy Ratio			√
	Debt-Equity Ratio (Times)			√
	Advances to Assets		√	
	G-Secs to Total Investment	√		
Assets Quality	Gross NPAs to Net Advances	√		
	Net NPAs to Net Advances	√		
	Total Investment to Total Assets		√	
	Net NPAs to Total Assets	√		
Management Efficiency	Total Advances to Total Deposits		√	
	Business Per Employee (Rs. Crore)	√		
	Profit Per Employee (Rs. Crore)			√
Earning Quality	Operating Profit to Average Working Funds			√
	Spread to Total Assets			√
	Net Profit to Average Assets			√
	Interest Income to Total Income	√		
	Non-Interest Income to Total Income			√

Liquidity	Liquid Assets to Total Assets	√		
	G-Secs. to Total Assets	√		
	Liquid Assets to Demand Deposits	√		
	Liquid Assets to Total Deposits	√		

Note: √ indicates the superiority of a bank over the other bank in terms of the concerning ratios.

CAMEL Model is used for rating banks according to their performance. Here, we have made an attempt to rank the three banks under consideration. Exhibit 2, prepared for the aforesaid purpose, reveals that, on the whole, NCTB has fared better than the other. NCTB has outperformed KDCUB & PCUB in respect of G-Secs. to Total Investment, Gross NPAs to Net Advances, Net NPAs to Net Advances, Net NPAs to Total Assets, Business per Employee, Interest Income to Total Income and Liquidity ratio. KDCUB has done better than NCTB & PCUB in respect of Advances to Assets, Total Investment to Total Assets and Total Advances to Total Deposits. PCUB has outperformed NCTB & KDCUB in accordance with Capital Adequacy Ratio, Debt-Equity Ratio, Profit per Employee, Operating Profit to Average Working Funds, Spread to Total Assets, Net Profit to Average Assets, Interest Income to Total Income and Non-Interest Income to Total Income. On the other, KDCUB performed in the ratio of Advances to Assets, Total Investment to Total Assets and Total Advances to Total Deposits

5. FINDINGS, SUGGESTIONS AND CONCLUSION

- PCUB has succeeded in maintaining CAR at a higher level than the prescribed level.
- The dependence on debt capital has decreased over the last nine years in case of all the three banks.

- The Asset Quality ratios have registered increasing trend. Thus is indicates poor asset quality position.
- All banks should take measures to reduce the Non-Performing Assets.
- Professionalism in the management should be improved.
- The earning quality, measured in terms of the ratios shows that PCUB has outperformed NTCB and KDCUB.
- NCTB has outperformed in terms of liquidity position than other co-operative bank.
- To ensure profits, UCBs will have to exercise caution in credit appraisal of new borrowers, effective follow-up of existing loan assets, arresting the leakage of income, improving recovery performance, etc.
- The UCBs management style has to be updated through proper training, the customer service has to be improved through computerization and ancillary services are to be introduced.
- On account of liberalization and financial sector reforms, it is now very much necessary for the management of the UCBs to impart a sense of discipline and work culture among its employees to face and meet challenges confidently by bringing about drastic change in their overall profitability through better customer service, improving business devising appropriate target and segment- oriented marketing strategies and last but not least, reducing Non Performing Assets (NPA) to an insignificant proportion.

The inherent weaknesses in the Indian Co-operative systems, viz: monitoring by multiple regulatory authorities, limited area of operation, weak co-ordination among the co-operative institutions / banks, lack of wide network, limited source of funds, weak capital structure, etc., stand as stumbling blocks on the path of progress of co-operative banks / UCBs. The UCB segment was considered as one of the robust and fast expanding segments of the banking systems. This paper clearly establishes the relationships among Capital Adequacy, Assets Quality, Management Efficiency, Earnings Quality and

Table 1: Capital Adequacy (in %)

Ratio	Bank	98-99	99-00	00-01	01-02	02-03	03-04	04-05	05-06	06-07	Mean	SD	F-Value	ACGR
Capital Adequacy Ratio (%)	**NCTB**	6.17	6.13	6.49	6.73	7.84	8.51	9.28	9.26	9.89	7.81	1.48	63.844***	7.027***
	KDCUB	8.42	7.83	7.59	7.40	8.19	8.77	9.37	10.00	9.43	8.56	0.90		3.008**
	PCUB	13.68	13.39	12.24	13.35	14.88	14.14	14.64	15.90	17.65	14.43	1.60		3.304***
Debt-Equity Ratio (times)	**NCTB**	19.51	19.43	15.63	15.17	10.54	7.50	6.39	5.46	5.18	11.65	5.88	9.73***	-17.587***
	KDCUB	9.59	9.07	7.92	6.90	6.48	5.14	4.41	3.33	3.69	6.28	2.29		-12.907***
	PCUB	4.49	6.14	5.84	4.70	4.14	3.55	3.16	2.68	2.50	4.13	1.30		-10.025***
Advances to Assets (%)	**NCTB**	43.61	38.63	40.64	37.78	39.71	40.81	43.20	48.97	51.58	42.77	4.70	35.92***	2.672**
	KDCUB	61.38	66.24	67.29	67.56	70.76	63.89	56.14	55.31	57.29	62.87	5.61		-2.037*
	PCUB	68.86	57.71	60.85	58.97	55.44	56.33	49.75	53.19	58.42	57.72	5.33		-2.226**
G-Secs to Total Invest-ments (%)	**NCTB**	-	-	-	97.84	98.84	98.84	98.84	98.84	98.96	98.69	0.42	7.24***	0.163
	KDCUB	71.75	83.40	89.61	7.16	4.17	4.17	2.32	-	-	37.51	41.58		-49.903***
	PCUB	7.62	-	-	-	68.00	65.34	70.85	71.20	71.23	59.04	25.30		32.366**

Note: *** 1% level of significance, ** 5% level of significance, * 10% level of significance

SD: Standard Deviation

Table 2: Assets Quality (in %)

Ratio	Bank	98-99	99-00	00-01	01-02	02-03	03-04	04-05	05-06	06-07	Mean	SD	F-Value	ACGR
Gross NPAs to Net Advances (%)	**NCTB**	0.63	0.99	14.33	16.57	14.56	11.08	12.14	9.65	10.59	10.06	5.68	12.83***	33.609*
	KDCUB	16.01	15.47	29.18	29.05	28.94	42.08	46.13	35.76	24.81	29.71	10.46		9.696**
	PCUB	11.72	10.92	31.11	36.64	27.75	24.60	25.31	33.55	22.60	24.91	8.90		9.022
Net NPAs to Net Advances (%)	**NCTB**	0.11	0.16	12.42	8.57	14.30	-	-	-	-	7.11	6.70	4.42**	294.162**
	KDCUB	12.91	11.33	23.34	22.57	20.56	26.40	21.47	-	-	19.80	5.57		11.672*
	PCUB	8.30	9.10	26.40	29.18	16.51	9.66	5.76	11.66	-	14.57	8.76		-4.073
Total Investments to Total Assets (%)	**NCTB**	0.06	0.10	0.15	6.05	11.52	11.77	11.37	10.96	11.32	7.03	5.48	0.93	109.496***
	KDCUB	0.35	0.45	0.61	6.73	10.28	10.36	12.84	13.24	12.24	7.46	5.58		67.332***
	PCUB	1.02	0.54	0.60	0.60	7.45	7.59	7.53	7.75	7.39	4.50	3.62		47.969***
Net NPAs to Total Assets (%)	**NCTB**	0.04	0.06	4.64	2.94	4.98	-	-	-	-	2.53	2.39	6.89***	287.305**
	KDCUB	7.07	6.72	13.62	12.91	11.98	12.58	8.19	-	-	10.44	2.98		5.756
	PCUB	5.24	4.68	13.85	15.34	8.23	4.92	2.60	5.64	-	7.56	4.62		-7.062

Note: *** 1% level of significance, ** 5% level of significance, * 10% level of significance

SD: Standard Deviation

Table 3: Management Efficiency

Ratio	Bank	98-99	99-00	00-01	01-02	02-03	03-04	04-05	05-06	06-07	Mean	SD	F-Value	ACGR
Total Advances to Total Deposit (%)	NCTB	55.58	50.69	54.78	51.86	54.72	54.2	58.62	66.35	70.62	57.49	6.7	37.00***	3.295***
	KDCUB	72.61	80.12	83.92	87.32	94.08	86.7	77.36	80.21	79.77	82.45	6.32		0.350
	PCUB	90.65	71.75	77.34	79.56	75.22	78.97	70.5	79.49	90.01	79.28	7.06		0.144
Business per Employee (Rs. in lakhs)	NCTB	162.25	215.64	235.12	311.53	308.82	335.16	349.2	380.61	449.25	305.29	88.52	10.02***	11.707***
	KDCUB	90.66	121.68	157.29	175.57	198.52	185.86	180.36	198.05	247.38	172.82	45.69		10.163***
	PCUB	103.51	156.03	180.75	207.12	223	225.16	256.81	247.95	266.86	207.47	52.82		10.450***
Profit Per Employee (Rs. in lakhs)	NCTB	0.63	0.85	0.87	1.14	1.39	1.59	1.67	2.05	2.28	1.39	0.56	4.61**	16.980***
	KDCUB	0.33	0.08	0.75	1.16	-	0.18	0.25	1.71	1.3	0.72	0.61		19.548
	PCUB	2.51	0.63	1.08	1.62	2.12	1.86	3.47	1.6	0.84	1.75	0.88		1.461

Note: *** 1% level of significance, ** 5% level of significance, * 10% level of significance

SD: Standard Deviation

Table 4: Earning Quality (in %)

Ratio	Bank	98-99	99-00	00-01	01-02	02-03	03-04	04-05	05-06	06-07	Mean	SD	F-Value	ACGR
Operating Profits to Avg. Working fund (%)	NCTB	1.05	1.17	1.80	1.70	3.27	3.75	3.34	3.29	1.72	2.34	1.05	29.74***	12.568**
	KDCUB	1.19	1.54	2.57	2.16	-0.10	3.58	3.37	5.43	1.95	2.41	1.59		12.007*
	PCUB	18.07	12.66	2.70	16.79	19.95	22.17	21.61	29.69	35.78	19.94	9.47		17.601*
Spread to Total Assets (%)	NCTB	2.22	2.42	2.53	2.49	3.44	3.66	3.45	3.65	3.11	3.00	0.58	6.14***	6.160***
	KDCUB	2.64	3.37	3.56	3.10	2.95	4.15	4.02	5.37	3.45	3.62	0.81		5.132*
	PCUB	4.53	3.19	2.92	4.21	4.99	4.10	4.29	4.22	5.15	4.18	0.73		3.554
Net Profit to Average Assets (%)	NCTB	0.62	0.52	0.44	0.43	0.50	0.55	0.57	0.67	0.66	0.55	0.09	3.84**	3.001
	KDCUB	0.63	0.11	0.77	1.02	-	0.14	0.18	1.04	0.71	0.58	0.38		3.951
	PCUB	3.90	0.69	0.89	1.08	1.29	1.07	1.67	0.76	0.40	1.31	1.04		-11.853
Interest Income to Total Income (%)	NCTB	97.91	98.28	98.52	98.57	98.19	95.73	96.89	97.36	98.07	97.72	0.92	14.09***	-0.140
	KDCUB	95.32	97.88	97.28	97.77	96.65	97.84	96.82	95.89	96.25	96.86	0.92		-0.053
	PCUB	87.86	95.52	91.84	96.54	96.97	91.43	91.87	92.57	95.19	93.31	2.96		0.288
Non-Interest Income to Total Income (%)	NCTB	2.09	1.72	1.48	1.43	1.81	4.27	3.11	2.64	1.93	2.28	0.92	14.09***	6.088
	KDCUB	4.68	2.12	2.72	2.23	3.35	2.16	3.18	4.11	3.75	3.14	0.92		2.327
	PCUB	12.14	4.48	8.16	3.46	3.03	8.57	8.13	7.43	4.81	6.69	2.96		-2.120

Note: *** 1% level of significance, ** 5% level of significance, * 10% level of significance

Table 5: Liquidity (in %)

Ratio	Bank	98-99	99-00	00-01	01-02	02-03	03-04	04-05	05-06	06-07	Mean	SD	F-Value	ACGR
Liquid Assets to Total Assets (%)	NCTB	43.91	47.88	45.40	42.29	36.87	37.66	35.86	31.60	27.34	38.76	6.72	7.95***	-6.027***
	KDCUB	37.42	32.41	31.16	24.64	18.00	24.78	29.99	30.16	29.01	28.62	5.55		-2.151
	PCUB	28.37	40.21	36.86	38.72	35.45	34.22	40.69	36.29	31.32	35.79	4.05		0.271
G-Secs to Total Assets (%)	NCTB	-	-	-	5.92	11.39	11.63	11.24	10.83	11.20	10.37	2.19	55.60***	8.957
	KDCUB	0.25	0.38	0.55	0.48	0.43	0.43	0.30	-	-	0.40	0.10		1.977
	PCUB	0.08	-	-	-	5.07	4.96	5.33	5.51	5.26	4.37	2.11		69.351**
Liquid Assets to Demand Deposits (%)	NCTB	884.34	919.20	741.05	606.82	459.80	429.30	359.46	308.61	256.99	551.73	247.72	6.23***	-15.367***
	KDCUB	382.50	367.64	301.91	271.48	195.61	274.34	305.59	282.49	247.98	292.17	57.28		-4.064
	PCUB	294.99	590.24	611.59	685.94	606.21	460.25	614.03	425.45	318.36	511.90	141.57		-1.765
Liquid Assets to Total Deposits (%)	NCTB	55.95	62.83	61.19	58.04	50.82	50.02	48.66	42.82	37.43	51.97	8.42	10.97***	-5.454***
	KDCUB	44.27	39.20	38.86	31.85	23.93	33.63	41.32	43.73	40.39	37.46	6.55		0.231
	PCUB	37.34	49.99	46.84	52.25	48.10	47.97	57.66	54.24	48.26	49.18	5.66		2.704*

Note: *** 1% level of significance, ** 5% level of significance, * 10% level of significance

Liquidity of selected UCBs. On the whole the Nicholson Cooperative Town Bank Ltd., (NCTB) is better than the Pattukkottai Co-operative Urban Bank Ltd., (PCUB) and the Karunthattangudi Dravidian Co-operative Urban Bank Ltd., (KDCUB).

REFERENCES

1. Barr R, L Seiford and T Siems (1996), "Forecasting Bank Failure: A Non-Parametric Frontier Estimation Approach", Recherches Economiques de Louvain, Vol.60, pp. 417-429.
2. Godse V T (1996), "CAMEL for Evaluating the Performance of Banks", IBA Bulletin, Vol.18, no.8, p. 8.
3. Subba Rao S R and Datta Lakshmikanta (1998), "Benchmarkding in Banking: A CAMEL Approach towards Sound and Strong Banking", BECON-98, Canara Bank, pp. 156-167.
4. Prasuna D G, "Performance Snapshot 2003-04", Chartered Financial Analyst, Vol. X, No.11, pp. 6-13.
5. Veni P (2004), "Capital Adequacy Requirement of Commercial Banks: A Study in Indian Context", GITAM Journal of Management, Vol. 2, No. 2, pp. 99-107.
6. Satish D, Juture sharath and Surender V (2005), "Indian Banking – Performance and Development 2004-05", Chartered Financial Analyst, Vol. 11, No. 10, pp. 6-15.
7. Bodla B S and Richa Verma (2006), "Evaluating Performance of Banks through CAMEL Model: A Case Study of SBI and ICICI", The ICFAI Journal of Bank Management, Vol. V, No. 3, pp. 49-63.

16

Recent Trends in Indian Banking

*P. Sridevi and R. Manjula,

The word 'Bank' comes to us from Italian. Bank of England was set up in 1694 which was later on followed by other central banks of different countries. In India, the first ever bank was established in 1786, called General Bank of India, which was followed by bank of Hindustan and Bengal bank the Reserve bank of India Act was passed in the year of 1934.

MONETARY AND BANKING TRENDS

The reserve Bank of India (RBI) has announced its annual monetary policy on April 29,2008, for 2008-09. The policy places complete focus on price stability and attempts at curbing inflationary expectations. With that end in view, the RBI has raised the cash reserve ratio (CRR) by 25 basis points to 8.25 per cent effective from May 24, 2008. This has come close on the heels of CRR increase of 0.50 percentage point to 8.00 per cent in two installments of 0.25percentage point each in April 26 and May 10. In view of the persistent monetary overhang,

*Lecturers of Commerce , Dhanalakshmi Srinivasan College of Arts & Science for Women, Perambalur.

the RBI has found it necessary to moderate monetary expansion and plan for reduced monetary growth. In the 2007-08 policy, the indicative target for M3 growth was 17.0 - 17.5 per cent and for the latest 2008-09 policy, it is 16.5-17.0 percent as against the average of over 21 per cent during 2005-08.

Indicative projections and Achievements of Key Monetary Variables (in per cent)

Year	M3 Growth		Aggregate Deposits		Non-Food Credit	
	Target	Achieve-ment	Target	Achieve-ment	Target	Achieve-ment
2008-09	16.5 - 17.0	-	17.0	-	20.0	-
2007-08	17.0 - 17.5	20.7	18.8	22.2	24.0-25.0	22.3
2006-07	15.0	21.5	15.6	23.8	20.0	28.4
2005-06	14.5	21.2	15.0	24.0	19.0	38.4

RECENT TRENDS IN MONETARY GROWTH

The trends in the month of April have kept up the tempo of accelerated monetary growth.M3 growth during the month ending April 25 has been 0.5 per cent as against 0.1 per cent during the corresponding month of the previous year. Almost all components of M3 as well as sources of M3 growth have experienced higher growth this year or have shown reduced rates of declines. A 3.7 per cent expansion in currency(Rs. 21,287 crore) appears very sizeable though fractionally lower than 3.8 per cent (or by Rs.18,576 crore) in April 2007. Time deposit growth at 2.0 per cent in April 2008 (Rs. 57,585 crore)has been higher than that in April 2007 (1.6 per cent or Rs. 38,093 crore). Net foreign exchange assets of the banking system have grown by 1.4 per cent (Rs. 17,145 crore) as against an absolute fall of Rs. 28,025 crore (or –3.1 per cent). The accelerations in the monetary growth and components are seen more sharply in the Year-on-year growth.

BANKING TRENDS

The behaviour of banking variables this year so far has followed a usual seasonal pattern. Generally after a year-end budge, there is considerable correction in the month of April each year, both in bank deposits and credit. This year too demand deposits have contracted by Rs. 56,524 crore in April 2008 as against a contraction of Rs. 52,059 crore in April 2007. This contraction is the result of year-end interest crediting by banks on term deposits, which augments the saving account balances towards March - end; such balances are withdrawn or deposited into other forms of time deposits in April. Accordingly, term deposits have expanded by Rs. 56,575 crore in April 2008 and by Rs. 33,290 crore in April 2007.Non-food bank credit has contracted by Rs. 16,052 crore in April 2008 as against a contraction of Rs. 46,718 crore in April 2008. Year-on-year basis, demand and time deposits have witnessed growth rates of 21.9 per cent and 23.3 per cent, respectively, as at end - April 25, 2008, compared with 1.6 per cent and 25.7 per cent, respectively, witnessed in the preceding 12-months period.

LOSSES ON CURRENCY DERIVATIVES

The huge mark-to-market (MTM) losses on currency derivatives incurred by businesses are due to the adverse movements in the exchange rates and partly due to improper understanding of the product, on the part of banks and corporate that signed such derivative contracts. Kotak Mahindra Bank has recorded a net profit of Rs 69 crore in the fourth quarter of 2007-08 has made a provision of Rs 86 crore towards MTM losses on derivative trading. Also, the bank's customers have negative MTM exposures of Rs 612 crore in forex derivative transactions.

ACQUISITIONS

Mumbai-based Abhyudaya Co-operative Bank is likely to acquire three co-operative banks; Udipi-based Janta Co-operative Bank, Baroda-based, Shree Krishna Co-operative Bank and Ahmedabad-based Manekchowk Co-operative Bank. The acquisitions will be completed by the end of June. Chennai-based Indian Overseas Bank (IOB) has plans to acquire Shree Suvarna Sahakari Bank (SSSB), a Pune-based co-operative bank. The acquisition would help IOB to establish its presence in the western parts of the country, as expansion through an acquisition is easier. Currently, SSSB has 12 branches in Mumbai and Pune.

HIGHLIGHTS

Corporation Bank has launched its reverse mortgage loan scheme for senior citizens, called 'Corp Shelter'. This scheme is available to borrowers of at least 60 years of age and married couples are also eligible as joint borrowers. South African private bank, FirstRand is opening its representative office in Mumbai. The bank has also sought permission from the RBI to open branches in Gurgaon, Chennai, Hyderabad, Bangalore and Coimbatore. The RBI is now looking at strengthening local institutions like co-operative, regional rural banks (RRBs), urban co-operative banks (UCBs), small banks and self-help groups (SHGs) in a bid to bring in more people into the financial fold.

The RBI has raised the aggregate ceiling for overseas investment by mutual funds registered with Securities and Exchanges Board of India (SEBI) from US$ 5 billion to US$ 7 billion with immediate effect. The RBI move will give more flexibility to mutual funds in their overseas investments. As per the guidelines, the mutual funds are allowed to invest in ADRs and GDRs, equity of overseas companies listed on recognised stock exchanges, public issues, foreign debt securities, government bonds, derivatives, etc.

BANK ACCOUNTS — CERTAIN RECENT TRENDS

Reserve Bank of India and the Institute of Chartered Accountants of India (ICAI) as members, many of the problems in the adoption of certain Accounting Standards in banking were sorted out last April.

FLOATING PROVISIONS

The RBI has this to say on 'floating provisions'. "Some of the banks make a 'floating provision' over and above the specific provisions made in respect of accounts identified as NPAs. The floating provisions, wherever applicable, could be set off against provisions required to be made as per the above stated provisioning guidelines. Considering that higher loan loss provisioning adds to the overall financial strengths of the banks and the stability of the financial sector, banks are urged to voluntarily set apart provisions much above the minimum levels as a desired practice".

GUIDANCE NOTES

The ICAI on its part needs to make it clear to its members as to the status of the guidance note issued by it on the audit of banks. In the material issued on Peer Review, members are asked to give a high priority to the guidance note. Having done so, the guidance note should provide clear cut pathways. Investments classified under 'Held for Trading' category are those which the banks expect to dispose of within 90 days from the date of such classification. Uncertainties referred to in AS-9 are cases where (i) It is unreasonable to expect ultimate collection; (ii) Uncertainty relating to collectability arises after the time of rendering the service; (iii) Consideration is not determinable; (iv) It is difficult to assess ultimate collection with reasonable certainty.

INTERNET OPENS NEW VISTAS FOR INDIAN BANKS

Indian banks have a chequered history. The British legacy left behind a host of large and small privately-held banks. As per IDC estimates, the total number of registered users for Internet banking in India is over two million. But this figure needs to be adjusted for dormant users and multiple accounts. India has a little less than a million active Internet banking users. And though this is just 0.096 percent of the total population, it represents 15 percent of the India's Internet user population.

ICICI Bank, "We had launched the Internet banking service even before the RBI had formulated its guidelines. Fortunately, as it was a comparatively new concept, the regulating authorities were extremely co-operative with us." After ICICI, Citibank, IndusInd Bank and HDFC Bank and Timesbank (now part of HDFC Bank), were the early ones to bite the technology bullet in 1999. Says C N Ram, head, information technology, HDFC Bank, "Our vision was very clear, we were not enamoured by the concept of Internet banking but looked at it more as an add-on service which our customers should gradually adopt."

INDIA'S RECENT MACROECONOMIC DEVELOPMENTS

Recent growth experience:

Although the balance-of-payments crisis of 1991 led to considerable liberalisation of the Indian economy, economists note that the transition from "Hindu Growth" to a higher growth era actually took place around 1980. Nevertheless, the annual average growth in GDP per capita of 3.8 per cent during 1980-2000 looks anemic compared to the 50 per cent increase (in PPP terms) over the current decade. The Government of India projects growth of 8.1 per cent for fiscal 2005/06, which follows growth rates of 8.5 per cent and 7.5 per cent during the past two years saving and investment:

	2000-01	2001-02	2002-03	2003-04	2004-05	2005-06
Agriculture & Allied	0.0	6.2	-6.9	10.0	0.7	2.3
Industry	6.3	2.7	7.0	7.6	8.6	9.0
Services	5.6	7.1	7.3	8.2	9.9	9.8
Total GDP	4.4	5.8	3.8	8.5	7.5	8.

Monetary Policy, Prices and the Banking Sector

The Preamble of the Reserve Bank of India states that the objective of the Mumbai-based central bank is to "regulate the issue of bank notes and keeping of reserves with a view to securing monetary stability in India and generally to operate the currency and credit system of the country to its advantage."

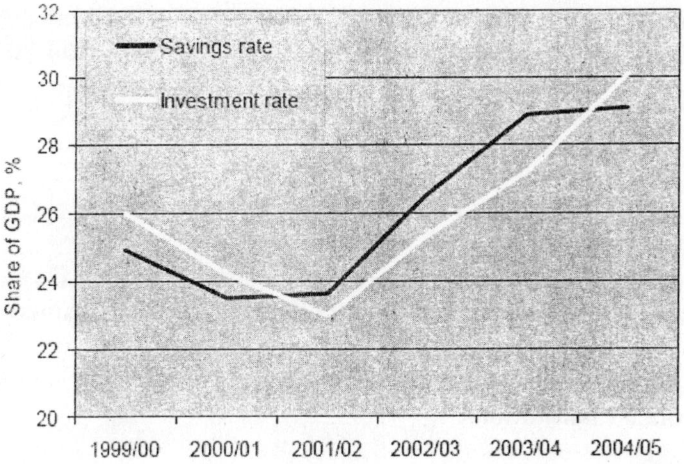

Figure 16.1

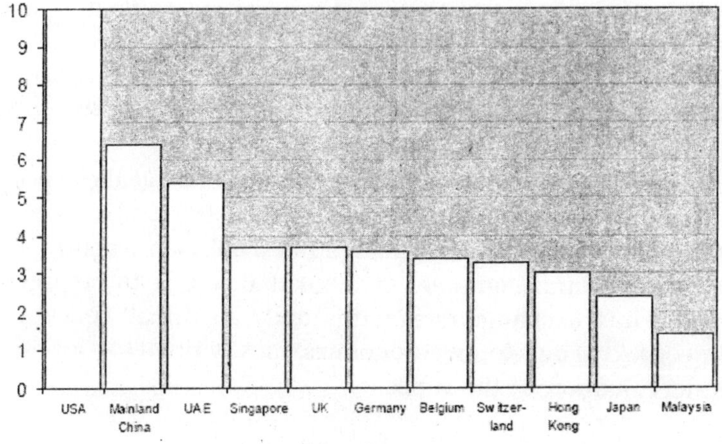

Figure 16.1

Major trading partners and their percentage shares in India's total trade, April-Oct 2005.

NON-PERFORMING ASSETS OF SCHEDULED COMMERCIAL BANKS, PERCENTAGE OF TOTAL ASSETS UP TO 2004-2005

	2002-03	2003-04	2004-05
Public Sector	4.2	3.5	2.8
Private Sector	4.0	2.8	2.1
Foreign Banks	2.4	2.1	1.4
All Groups	4.0	3.3	2.6

The amount of non-performing loans held by all financial institutions in India, at USD 30 billion in 2003, accounted for 2.3 per cent of non-performing loans globally that year. This contrasts with a global share of 23.6 per cent held by Chinese financial institutions.

EXCHANGE RATE POLICY AND CAPITAL FLOWS

Despite periodic interventions by the Reserve Bank, the Indian rupee has essentially been permitted to float against other currencies since March 1993. No fixed target or fluctuation band has been in place during this period, although the exchange rate has been subject to relatively close monitoring and management.

The Indian currency briefly touched its weakest point during this decade at 49 rupees against the dollar in mid-2002. The real effective exchange rate has risen recently, but estimates of misalignment of the actual rate with respect to equilibrium exchange rates (admittedly a difficult concept in the context of developing economies) mostly point to continued undervaluation of the rupee.

SOME FISCAL POLICY OBSERVATIONS

India's federal structure, 28 states and seven union territories, justifies a brief look at the fiscal balances at both the state and central government levels. Indian fiscal policy has increasingly focused on improving the country's infrastructure, including investment in health and education, while attempting to pursue fiscal consolidation. Indian authorities acknowledge that high deficits, unproductive expenditure and tax distortions prevented the economy from attaining its growth potential in the past. The Fiscal Responsibility and Management Act of 2003 emphasized revenue-based fiscal consolidation, the removal of distortions from the tax system and the attainment of better expenditure outcomes. Imbalances at the state level, in particular, necessitated the introduction of a restructuring scheme. The Twelfth Finance Commission (TFC), appointed in November 2002, contributed to this aim. The terms of reference of the TFC included reviewing the state of the finances of the federal government and the states, and suggesting a fiscal consolidation plan whereby macroeconomic stability, debt reduction and equitable growth would be achieved. Importantly, the TFC recommended that every state must eliminate its revenue deficit entirely by 2008/09.

CONCLUSIONS

The Indian government has recently signalled its intention to lift the economy to a higher growth path, whereby GDP would expand at an annual rate of 10 per cent. High growth, according to the government, provides the best antidote to poverty. The economic expansion that started in 2003/04 provides evidence that India's growth rates in favourable circumstances are comparable to Asia's powerhouse, China (although the growth experiences of the two countries differ in many respects). Whereas high domestic demand has increased inflationary pressures in the Indian economy and dragged the current account into deficit, China's economy has experienced deflationary tendencies that seem to reflect excess supply in the economy. In this regard, investment in infrastructure is imperative to increase the supply-side potential of the Indian economy.

17

Reforms of Indian Banking System

*K. Murali Selvam

There has been a considerable widening and deepening of the Indian financial system in the past few years. A range of structural and economic stabilization reforms emerged with the aim to promote efficient, competitive and diversified financial system. Banks play an important role in the development of a country's economy by financing the requirements of trade, industry and agriculture with high degree of contribution and responsibility. The recognition of banking system's potential to promote larger economic objectives, led to the nationalization of banks in 1969. It was considered a landmark decision as banks were made a tool in the growth and development of the economy. Later in 1991, the banking sector in India witnessed rapid changes with the Imitation of reforms. The Narasimham committee in the years 1991 and 1998 recommended may reforms on the aspects, like structure, organization, functions and supervisory arrangements of the financial system. The main objective of

*Lecturer in Commerce, Selvamm Arts & Science College, Namakka1

reforms was to increase the efficiency of financially sector and the range of financial service available within the economy.

The process of reforms necessitated the up gradation of operation standards and financial soundness of the banks to make them competitive in the international market. Thus, the first phase of reforms laid the basis for sound banking system. The RBI also made it clear that Indian banking has no option but to match international standards on income recognition, non-performing assets and structural regulations. Therefore, the public sector banks have to evolve strategies to successfully compete and improve their profitability. In tune with the global changes in Banking Industry, Indian Banking has to come out off its traditional way of functioning. Growing Information Technology and new Innovation in Banking led customers to expect more from Indian Banking Industry. To sell through competitive environment and to delight the customers, Indian Banking has to change its way of functioning. Hence the Reforms.

Narasiman committee recommendations have been adopted on the lines of Banks committee recommendation on international Banking. The reforms are in Accounting system, capital adequacy, liquidity in Bank, freedom to Banks through deregulation of interest rates, self recovery tribunals to help banks in recovery, training and development of personnel, computerization and customer orientation etc.

The Indian Banking system is in the midst of Structural reforms to improve their strength, competitiveness and resilience. The banking industry has currently been in the second generation reforms featuring consolidation and convergence. In the pre-reform scenario the banks have witnessed widespread expansion of branch network across the entire country to fulfil its social, commercial and development role.

NEED OF REFORME

Parlor to nationalization, banks were under private ownership of the maharajas or kings, of the princely states of

India. They mostly served the rich families and industrial houses aiming at economic considerations only, and thereby narrow down the scope of banking system. Soon, they started suffering from certain limitations of inadequate capital structure, unsound methods of operations and poor management. As a consequence, the Reserve Bank of India took up the task of consolidation by reconstruction and merger of weak units with sound ones in 1960s, leading to a sharp decline in the number of banks from 548 in 1947 to 89 in 1969.

Fourteen leading banks were nationalized during 1969 with the basic idea of ensuring economic growth, better regional balance of economic activities, wider spread of bank credit among the weaker and neglected sections of the society and the diffusion of economic power. Further six more banks were nationalized in 1980 to extend the reach of organized banking services to the rural and neglected sectors of the society and to align their goals with national objective of quickening the pace of economic progress in the country. To achieve the above said objective the policy makers imposed a strict credit rationing approach, formula-based lending and highly directed credit lending obligations. Post nationalization era witnessed a large spread of banking system to rural areas, thereby benefiting small scale, tiny and cottage industries. The gross domestic savings were raised from 15.7 per cent in 1970 to 24.20 percent in 1991. There was a Lipid expansion of branch network. The number of branches increased from 8,262 to 60,570 deposits rose from Rs.4,646 crore to 2,37,566 crore advances from Rs/3.599 crore to Rs.1.31.520 crore over the years 1969 to 1991 reflecting a rapid growth of banking activities.

But, the expansion of banking industry overshadowed may micro-level imbalances that crept into the system over the period. The government has an easy access and control over public funds and banks acted merely a tool in the hands of the government. There were no incentives to banks to make profit and improve their financial health. Trade unions became strong with political patronage and resisted any form of change in the banking. It was a highly regulated environment with administered interest rate structure, quantitative restrictions on credit flows, high reserve requirements which resulted in sub-optimal use of credit, decline in productivity and erosion of profitability. Thus, nationalization killed competition and stifled innovation in banking system.

By 1991, a number of these banks were plagued with poor profitability owing to poor lending strategy and lack of internal risk management. Most of the banks were undercapitalized with a high proportion of non-performing assets. i.e. bad loans. The quality of customer service was unsatisfactory. The banks significantly lagged behind international standards in terms of introducing computer technology. The poor financial condition of banks made it necessary to raise interest on commercial loans to cover a part of these costs. These had corresponding adverse effects on the investment climate of the country. Thus, the mismanagement of various factors led to define of earning in the banking sector. Knurs Committee (1989), too felt the rise in operational cost, lack of efforts in manpower planning, employee's welfare package, career plan, and training and performance appraisal system. These matadors of Indian banking system called for an urgent need of reforms in the banking sector.

REFORMS

The period of early 1990s was marked by the beginning of India's economic crisis with a precarious state of foreign exchange reserve and severe macroeconomic imbalances. The government, therefore, embarked upon a comprehensive structural adjustment programme which required the overhaul of existing policies in the financial, trade and industrial sectors. In November 1991, the government appointed a high level committee under the chairmanship of Mr.M.Narasimham to make recommendation on all relevant aspects, like structure, organization, functions and supervisory arrangements of the financial system. The committee submits its report in April 1992.

The recommendations of the committee were a fundamental departure from the then existing banking sector regulation. The major policy changes brought about emphasized deregulation and liberalization. The major objective of the recommendations was to create a viable and efficient banking system, which would thereby improve the productivity and efficiency of the financial sector. The first phase of the curative measures which included rationalization of the interest rate structure, progressive reduction of reserve requirements of both SLR and CRR maintained by the banks, strengthening prudential regulations, introduction of international settlement standards as regards capital adequacy in phased manner, lifting of entry barriers etc. The second phase aimed to strengthen the banking sector through rigorous operational, prudential and accounting norms, improvement in credit delivery system and gradually narrowing down the divergences in regulatory framework of different institutions.

*** Interest rate deregulation**

Prior to 1991, administered interest rate structure was the central feature of the Indian monetary and credit system. The rational behind it was to enable certain preferred or priority sectors to obtain funds at confessionals rate of interest. This resulted in higher lending rates for the non-confessional commercial sector, in 1991, Narasimham committee 'recommended that concessional interest rates should not be a vehicle for subvention and there should be real interest rates should not be a vehicle for subvention and there should be real interest rates. Therefore since 1992-93, the banks have been given complete autonomy for fixing the rates of interest on their deposits and loans. The only exception is the saving bank deposits for which the rate of interest is still decided by RBI. So far as loans are concerned any bank can set even on daily basis a number of prime lending rates (PLRs) corresponding to different tenures (Basu, 2005). The Reserve Bank publishes monthly PLRs based on the rates offered by five leading public sector banks.

*** Reduction in CRR and SLR**

The cash reserve ratio (CRR) refers to the cash that all scheduled commercial banks (except rational rural banks) have to maintain with the RBI as a certain percentage of their total demand and time liabilities. CRR serves as instruments to influence liquidity in the economy, as and when required. But, India's high reserve requirements based on CRR has been the main cause of yielding low profitability and high spreads in the banking system. Therefore, in line with the recommendations of the Narasimhan committee, the RBI reduced the CRR gradually from 15 percent in 1991 to 5 percent in 2006. The statutory liquidity ratio (SLR) is that reserve which is set aside by the banks for investment in cash, gold or unencumbered approved securities. It is taken as a buffer in case of run on a bank. Till 1991, the SLR was 38.5 percent and presently, it has come down to 25 percent in the year 2007.

*** Liquidity Adjustment Facility**

The Narasimham committee on banking sector reforms recommended that the Reserve Bank should provide support to the market through a liquidity adjustment facility (LAF). Initially it was introduced in April 1999 as an interim liquidity adjustment facility and later gradually converted into full fledged liquidity adjustment facility from June 2000. It operates through reports and reverses reports and provides a mechanism for injection and absorption of liquidity available to banks. The objective of LAF is to meet day to day liquidity mismatches in the system, restricting short term money market rates and steering these rates to be in consistence with monetary policy objectives.

*** Prudential Regulations**

The Narasimham committee recommended the introduction of prudential norms, to meet international standards Prudential norms are the controls and limits imposed by the central bank on the activities of the banks with the objective to ensure financial safety, soundness and solvency of banks and also to make sure that they do not indulge in excessive risk taking activities and violate regulations in pursuit of profit, Prudential norms are related to capital adequacy ratio, income recognition and asset classification based on their quality and provisioning against bad and doubtful debts.

(i) Capital adequacy ratio: RBI has stipulated that the banks have to comply with the capital adequacy requirements (CAR), whereby it must have capital of at least a certain percentage of its risk weighted assets and off-balance sheet exposures. Different types of assets have different risk weight ages. Loans to private sector customers normally have 100 per cent risk weightage, while loans guaranteed by other banks/ financial institutions have 20 percent risk weightage. CRR has Zero risk weightage, while SLR investments have a small risk Weightage on account of market risk. Housing and customer loans have risk weightage of 75 percent and 125 percent respectively. The Narasimham committee recommended the introduction of capital adequacy norm of 8 percent in tune with the norm set by the bank for international Settlement.

(ii) Off-balance sheet items: The off balance sheet items include letters of credit, confirmations and bank guarantees, in the form of advance payments, performance and deferred payments to enable their customers to participate in large value tenders floated on global basis or to raise big quantum of project finance. The off-balance sheet items are of great importance to any bank as these lead to non-interest or tee based income and help to boost its return on assets.

(iii) Income recognition and asset classification: The income recognition and asset classification (IRAC) norm set up by RBI deals with classification of assets according to its quality. An asset can be either performing or non performing. A performing asset is a standard asset yielding scheduled inflows/income at scheduled intervals. On the other hand, non performing assets(NPAs) are those assets on which payment of the principal or interest or both is overdue for a period of 90 days or more. Thus NPAs are impaired assets and their accumulation may spell doom for it. Therefore, according to the recommendations, banks should aim to reduce gross NPAs to 3 percent and net NPAs to zero percent.

Deregulation of Entry Barriers and Branching Restrictions

The entry of private sector banks both domestic and foreign has been allowed in 1992-93. The sole objective behind it was to generate competition for the incumbent public sector banks. The Reserve Bank of India ensured that the new entrants are professionally managed, financially viable and technologically strong. The capital norms for foreign banks have also been substantially liberalized. The joint ventures between foreign and Indian banks were permitted. The branch licensing policy was also liberalized and the banks were allowed more freedom to branch expansion in response to market needs provided that it meets the capital adequacy ration of 8 percent and has earned net profit for three consecutive years.

Restructuring of Public Sector banks

There is a need to restructure the banking industry as reforms have ushered in new changes and new competition. Restructuring and consolidation is one the routes through which the Indian banks could bring in competitiveness. The restructuring measures have generally been in the form of mergers, closing down of loss making branches, access to capital market etc.

i) Merger and Acquisitions: Banks mergers have increased globally, to improve the structure and efficiency of banking industry. A well planned merger can be a boon as it reduces cost of operation, expands the business profile, enhances growth, and increases the capital base which in turn increases the risk ability of the bank. New bank of India merged with Punjab national Bank in 1998. Century Bank merged with Centurion Bank in 1999, Sikkim Bank merged with Union Bank of India in 2000, Times Bank merged with HDFC Bank and bank of Madura merged with ICICI Bank in 2001. Bank of Punjab merged with Centurion Bank under the name of Centurion Bank of Punjab from the year 2004-05, Global Trust Bank has merged into Oriental Bank of Commerce in 2004. The Narasimhan committee too recommended formation of 3-4 large banks with international presence, 8-10 banks of national presence, local banks with regional presence and rural banks.

ii) Access to Capital market: The government of India decided to allow some stronger public sector banks to approach the capital market to directly mobilize the equity funds from the public. It was done in order to enable the public sector banks to take care of their additional needs of the capital. State Bank of India was the first public sector bank to tap the equity market in December 1993. The market responded favorably to public sector banks ventures to raise capital.

During the second phase of reforms, there have been indications of closing down the loss making and non-viable branches, reducing the number of regional and zonal offices and downsizing of staff through voluntary retirement scheme (VRS). In the first phase of VRS, around one lakh people opted for it, which had reduced the manpower of banks by 12-15 percent. Besides, retail banking has become the principal growth driver for banks. Banks need to restructure themselves to offer retail banking product at competitive rate

TECHNOLOGY IN BANKING

The Reserve Bank of India and the public sector banks have realized the importance of technology to survive and thrive with private and foreign banks. Technology has made the banking truly international and efficient. Banks have introduced innovative products such as, e-banking and e-payments. Electronic banking is mostly provided through automated teller machines (ATMs), telephone transactions and internet banking. Electronic payment are made effective through e-cheque, card based payments (credit card, debit card and smart card) and electronic fund transfer (EFT). The growth in banking technology and automation of banking processes has enabled the banks to expand their reach and low cost transactions with improved customer services. Customers are now demanding value-added services and hence, banks have to speed up their IT implementation.

IMPACT OF REFORMS

These reforms have made an impressive impact on the overall efficiency and stability of the banking system in India. The present capital adequacy has recorded a marked improvement and stood at 12.8 percent at the end of march 2005, comparable to 13.0 percent for US during the same period. The non-performing loans (NPLs) to total loans of commercial banks which were at a high of 15.7 percent on march 1997, declined to 5.2 percent on March 2005. These figures are broadly comparable to those prevailing in several leading European economies.

Net NPLs also witnessed a significant decline and stood at 2.0 percent of net advances on March 2005. The operating expenses of banks in India are much more aligned to those prevailing internationally, hovering around 2.21 percent and 2.16 percent during 2003-2004 and 2004-05. In developed countries banks' operating expenses were 3.5 percent in US. 2.8 percent in Canada and Italy and 2.6 percent in Australia, whereas the range falls between 1.1. to 2.0 percent in the countries such as, Japan, Switzerland, Germany and the UK. There has also been decline in the CRR from 7.25 percent in 1982 to 5 percent in 2006. SLR has also been decreased from 37.5 percent to 25 percent during the same period.

The financial liberalization has led to the emergence of some big bank's diversifying their activities into merchant banking, leasing, hire-purchase, factoring, insurance etc. Which has made them financial conglomerates (FC). Therefore, the financial entities now, have become increasingly conscious about risk management and thus have constituted risk management models based on product profile, business philosophy and customer orientation.

Bank computerization has been taking place at fast pace with significant improvement in the information infrastructure. The technological infrastructure has developed in tandem with modern day requirements in information technology and communication networking. Now, all the branches of banks are connected with each other through internet. ATMs have facilitated bank customers to withdraw money from anywhere in the India. credit cards, debit cards and smart cards have nullified the risk of carrying money. Challenges Ahead.

The reforms in the banking sector and financial sector as a whole are a continuous process that needs to be in tune with the emerging macroeconomic realities. In view of the rapid changes, that have taken place over the past few years and the growing integration of the Indian economy with the world economy, there has been a fierce competition from international banks. Here the size of the bank is likely to be more important which may force them for mergers and acquisitions. The Narasimham committee II also recommended formation of 3 to 4 large banks with international presence.

EFFECTS OF REFORMS

1. Banks have become more transparent in their accounting system. Focus has been shifted from mass Banking to performance Banking aiming at profitability.

Reforms made Indian Banks to think and act differently. Computerization with the help of IT took Indian Banking to newer heights. The business transactions have grown multifold.

2. Today almost all the banks have moved towards international benchmarks with regard to accounting standards, transparency, profitability, risk management and other regulatory standards.

3. The important aspect of the reform is that banks have to be partners for faster economic growth to achieve the international standard as per the BASIL committee accord. As a result banks have to adhere to stiff international norms, adopt new technologies to improve their operation and in diluting the government stake. International happenings have changed the role of the Indian banks from the traditional banking to fulfill their role in achieving the commercial as well as social banking.

4. Majority of the Indian bank are having their operations in the rural and semi-urban areas and their role has to be redefined to suit the commercial operation and to fulfill the social obligations. Agriculture is still the predominant occupation of the majority of people living in the villages and with the introduction of biotechnology the banks have to

redouble their efforts in tapping the vast manpower and thereby increasing their profitability.

5. Indian agriculture has its manifold complications as it predominantly depends on the monsoon. Agriculturists' requirements are to be fulfilled at the same time banks have to satisfy the prudential norms in case of any natural failure thereby affecting the recovery of loans advanced to the agriculture sector.

6. In the liberalized economy, the computers are occupying the center stage of the banking functions. Many nationalized banks are still lagging behind compared to the recent entry of private banks. With the introduction of computers the customer service has become very easy and efficient. Day to day housekeeping work of the banks has been improved and the delivery system has been improved. Information system has helped the banks in maintaining and improving the internal control systems for taking timely decisions. Risk management and asset/Liability management are some of the areas where information technology will be of immense use to the banks. Information technology also is useful in the areas of optimally using the ATMs and for quick transfer of funds within banks for optimizing the profits.

7. Banks have become customer-centric in their operations. Delivering what the customer requires is most important nowadays. New products to suit the customers have to be devised and delivered at the right moment. Product marketing is one of the key elements, which the banks have to concentrate. Customer attrition has to be arrested to stay ahead in the market. For that the banks have to effectively utilize the manpower to sustain them in the stiff competitive environment. Cross selling of products, strategic alliance with other banks/insurance companies/financial institutions will have to be done to capture and widen the customer base.

CONCLUSION

Bank reforms cannot be complete and whole without the total involvement of the workforce. In the liberalized economy, banks after adopting the new IT technologies have to necessarily tone up their work force. Without their active participation, success cannot be achieved. Hence banks have to redefine their human resource policies to suit the new emerging environment. Work force has to adopt the changes taking place in the whole industry. The banks have to be development Oriented. They are partners for economic development of the country. They have to guide the borrowers to grow and achieve prosperity of the nation.

REFERENCE

1. Banking and Financial system K.Nirmala Prasad & J. Chandradoss.
2. Indian Financial system, P.N. Varshney & D.K.Mittal.
3. The Indian Financial system, Vansant Desai
4. Business India 2006.
5. Business line 2007.

18

Reserve Bank of India's Monetary Policy: Are the weapons of Monetary Policy controlled Inflation?

*Dr. Palaniappan

The Reserve Bank of India (RBI) is the central bank of India, and was established on April 1, 1935 in accordance with the provisions of the Reserve Bank of India Act, 1934. The Central Office of the Reserve Bank was initially established in Calcutta but was permanently moved to Mumbai in 1937. Though originally privately owned, RBI has been fully owned by the Government of India since nationalization in 1949. The main functions of Reserve Bank of India are broadly same those of the Central banks of other countries. Though the primary functions of the Central Banks of all the countries are the same viz., note issuing, acting as banker's bank and banker to the government, the scope and content of policy objectives

*Head of the Department of Economics, Erode Arts College (Autonomous), Erode.

vary from country to country depending on the structure of the economy, the stage of development and the objectives of the government.

An important function of Reserve Bank of India in the capacity of the Central Bank of the country is to control and regulate the volume of currency and credit in the economy. It must take appropriate steps to control credit, when too much credit proves harmful, leading to inflationary situation or encouraging too much of speculative activities, so as to hinder the healthy growth of the national economy. These activities of the Reserve Bank to regulate the total volume of the purchasing power within the country in order to stabilize the level of prices, accentuate economic activity, create more employment and income, and are termed the monetary policy of the Reserve Bank. In other words, the monetary policy refers to monetary operations of the Reserve Bank, like the alteration of the bank rate, open market operations, variations of the cash reserves of the commercial banks, etc., to regulate the volume of credit with a specific objective of controlling inflationary or offsetting deflationary trends to achieve the ultimate objective of stabilizing the general level of prices and regulate the economic activity.

Inflation is the supply of excess money and credit relative to the goods and services produced, resulting in increased prices. Inflation results in the increase in the price of some set of goods and services in a given economy over a period of time. It is measured as the percentage rate of change of a price index. Inflation in India is also a grave issue of concern, given the vast disparity between the rich and the poor on the one hand or the Rural and the Urban on the other. Skyrocketing inflation robs the poor, and hurts others, though much less grievously. The fruits of the much-talked about economic growth have not reached large sections, especially in the rural areas.

Under extant conditions, the benefit of high prices paid by consumers does not flow back to primary producers, but is siphoned away by middlemen and speculators who enjoy a free run in an economy of shortages. If attention to agriculture has been limited to rendering lip service, inefficiencies in the physical market remain unattended. With production trailing demand in recent years, shortages of essential commodities have widened. Imports have become expensive because of high global market prices. It may be instructive to remember that inflation is not an overnight phenomenon in India, the onus to control and take control of the situation of inflation is upon the Reserve Bank of India (RBI). The Reserve Bank of India (Amendment) Act, 2006 gives discretion to the Reserve Bank to decide the percentage of scheduled banks' demand and time liabilities to be maintained as Cash Reserve Ratio (CRR) without any ceiling or floor. Consequent to the amendment, no interest will be paid on CRR balances so as to enhance the efficacy of the CRR, as payment of interest attenuates its effectiveness as an instrument of monetary policy.

Weapons taken by the Reserve bank of India to control inflation:

> *Since 1972, the Indian economy has been working with considerable inflationary potential. Because of continuous deficit financing by the government, there was considerable increase in money supply with the public and with banking system. There was expansion of bank credit to finance trade and industry. Finally a number of financial institutions had come up offering funds for investment. Expansion of credit was, therefore, no problem. But the real problem was the inflationary situation that was emerging because of these factors and also because of the global inflationary situation directly due to hike in oil prices. Hence, RBI was forced to abandon controlled expansion and adopt the policy of credit restraint.*

In mid 90s the thrust of monetary policy was to reduce the annual inflation rate and provide credit support for production. Money supply (M3) was reduced considerably, mainly because of a slow growth in bank deposits and a decline in the growth of reserve money. Another major factor in controlling this growth was the lower level of foreign exchange inflows. Slower monetary growth was accompanied by lower bank credit to the commercial sector. These trends were compounded by a decline in other sources of finance to industry, such as primary issues in the domestic stock market and GDR issues in Euro markets. Funds raised from capital markets declined and the amount rose through Euro issue

Table 18.1: *Major Monetary Measures Taken By RBI- Bank Rate, Cash Ratio And Statutory Liquidity Ratio*

Bank Rate(Per cent)		Cash Reserve Ratio(Per cent)		Statutory Liquidity Ratio(Per cent)	
Rate	Effective Date	Rate	Effective Date	Rate	Effective Date
11.0	17-01-1998	12.0	06-07-1996	38.50	22-09-1990
10.5	19-03-1998	11.5	26-10-1996		
10.0	03-04-1998	11.0	09-11-1996		
9.0	29-04-1998	10.5	04-01-1997		
		10.0	18-01-1997	38.50	29-02-1992
		9.75	25-10-1997		
		9.50	22-11-1997		
8.0	02-03-1999	10.00	06-12-1997		
		10.50	17-01-1998	38.25	09-01-1993
		10.25	28-03-1998	38.00	06-02-1993
		10.00	11-04-1998	37.75	06-02-1993
7.0	02-04-2000	11.0	29-08-1998	37.50	21-08-1993
8.0	22-07-2000	10.50	13-03-1999	37.25	18-09-1993
		10.00	08-05-1999	34.75	16-10-1993
		9.50	06-11-1999		
		9.00	20-11-1999		
7.5	17-02-2001	8.50	08-04-2000		
7.0	02-03-2001	8.00	22-04-2000	34.25	20-08-1994
6.5	23-10-2001	8.25	29-07-2000	33.75	17-09-1994
6.3		8.50	12-08-2000	31.50	29-10-1994
6.0		8.25	24-02-2001		

		8.00	10-03-2001		
		7.50	19-05-2001		
		5.75	03-11-2001		
	30-10-2002	5.50	29-12-2001	25.00	25-10-1995
	30-04-2003	5.00	01-06-2002		
		4.75	16-11-2002		
		4.50	14-06-2003		
		4.75	18-09-2004		
		5.00	02-10-2004		
		5.25	23-12-2006		
		5.50	06-01-2007		
		5.75	17-02-2007		
		6.00	03-03-2007		
		6.25	14-04-2007		
		6.50	28-04-2007		
		7.00	04-08-2007		
		7.50	10-11-2007		
		7.75	26-04-2008		
		8.00	10-05-2008		
		8.25	24-05-2008		
		8.50	05-07-2008		
		8.75	19-07-2008		
		9.00	30-08-2008		

Source: www.rbi.org.in/home.aspx

loans also fell down nearly 70 percent over the same period. Continued high levels of government borrowing associated with a large and over-budget fiscal deficit kept money markets tight throughout the period. This in turn put increasing pressure on interest rates.

In 1996-97 and 1997-98, RBI was concerned with heavy credit squeeze and serious industrial recession. Monetary policy of the RBI during these years was not so much concerned with control of inflationary pressure in the country but, rather, checks industrial recession and gives a big push to the economy. It was for this that RBI reduced the bank rate, the CRR and SLR and in general, influenced the banking and financial institutions to expand credit and lower the cost of their credit. The major policy measures taken by the RBI to tackle the inflation during the period from 1998 to 2008 are given in Table 18.1.

The steps generally taken by the RBI to tackle inflation include a rise in repo rates (the rates at which banks borrow from the RBI), a rise in Cash Reserve Ratio and a reduction in rate of interest on cash deposited by banks with RBI. The signals are intended to spur banks to raise lending rates and to reduce the amount of credit disbursed. The RBI's measures are expected to suck out a substantial sum from the banks. In effect, while the economy is booming and the credit needs grow, the central bank is tightening the availability of credit. The RBI also buys dollars from banks and exporters, partly to prevent the dollars from flooding the market and depressing the dollar – indirectly raising the rupee. In other words, the central bank's interactions have a desirable objective – to keep the rupee devalued – which will make India's exports more competitive, but they increase liquidity.

To combat this, the RBI does what it calls "sterilization" – it sucks out the rupees it pays out for dollars through sale of sterilization bonds. It then sells these bonds to banks. Economists point out that there has not been much success in such sterilization attempts in India. The central bank's attempt to offload Government bonds on banks has not been too successful inasmuch as the banks sell the bonds and get rupees instead. The state-owned banks strictly abide by the central bank's dictates and absorb the sterilization bonds. That discipline is lacking in India. The net effect is that the RBI has to resort to indirect methods of sterilization, such as raising interest rates and raising CRR to contract liquidity. This makes India more attractive for foreign capital flows that seek better returns and a vicious cycle follows. RBI has to buy more foreign currency and sterilize. The cycle becomes worse.

Consequences of RBI Policy

The credit policy for April-October 1998, aimed to accelerate industrial investment and output, keep inflation under control, continue financial sector reforms, reduce interest rates and improve credit availability to meet business requirements. Key reference rates were reduced by one percentage point each; sending a strong signal those commercial banks should lower interest rates for commercial borrowers. Banks responded by reducing prime lending rates to 13 percent. The Cash Reserve Ratio requirement was left unchanged at 10 percent. Under the new credit policy, FIIs were allowed to invest up to 30 percent of their assets in treasury bills, and banks were given freedom to fix penalties on premature withdrawal of deposits. In January 1998, the rupee hit a low of Rs. 40.45/ dollar, due in large part to concerns about the Asian currency crisis.

The RBI adopted a number of measures that stopped the rupee's slide and actually led to some appreciation. These measures included an increase in banks' cash reserve ratio and an increase in the RBI's bank rate. Once the rupee had stabilized, the RBI announced a two-phase rollback of the bank rate to 10 percent, and of the CRR to 10 percent. The interest rate on short-term domestic deposits was also deregulated and banks were allowed to set different prime lending rates. If the CRR and REPO rate are hiked frequently, the economy may take a U - turn, as most commercial banks religiously increase their lending rates, without actually studying the impact. The last time that the RBI had imposed its policy, the markets had signaled their resounding reaction by a sharp fall in the Sensex by nearly 500 points. The impact on economic growth is also likely to be sharp, judging by effects of similar therapy applied with disastrous effect in the mid-1990s.

This would reduce the level of investment activity in the economy, particularly in the infrastructure sector. Big corporate may ask for, and get, access to external commercial borrowing, but not so favoured are the bulk of small and medium entrepreneurs (SME). Housing activity will suffer an impact because most loaners are on floating rates and will face increased equated installments. These measures generally taken by the RBI do not effectively tackle inflation but on the other hand effectively stunts the growth pattern of the economy. The RBI seems to believe that by merely reducing the credit flow and money flow in the economy, inflation can be curtailed. Inflation is a consequence of increasing demand vis – a – vis the supply in the economy. The demand must be effectively curtailed or pushed down, which the present CRR policy is not managing to do effectively. The RBI, in an ideal world, would have also looked towards a mechanism to bolster the supply forces to meet the requirements of the consumers and thereby combat inflation. Our high interest rates are not only hurting business, but have become a magnet for foreign portfolio funds. Which, in turn is rapidly appreciating the domestic currency, and giving foreign institutional investors (FIIs) and their P-note beneficiaries a double bonus: first through returns on their investment and then on the appreciating exchange rate.

Between January and mid-October, 2007 the rupee has appreciated 12.5% over the US dollar. Only the Thai baht has raised more at 13.2%. As a result, we are creating a bizarre situation where portfolio investors have been enjoying the fruits of an equity-led bull run, while those who work their backs off to produce goods and services are getting badly hammered by high interest rates. Today, there is more than anecdotal evidence to suggest that 7,000 to 8,000 workers have been laid-off in Tiruppur. Garment and leather exporters are getting crippled. Brassware industry is also deep in the loss making zone. Those who can are switching to the domestic market. And pity the poor entrepreneurs who, seeing the large export demand growth in 2005 and 2006, invested in ramping up their manufacturing capacities. They are lambs to the slaughter. If this hard interest rate regime were to continue it will surely break the back of industry and with it, economic growth.

Conclusion

During 1950's and 1960's the monetary policy of RBI had twin aims: expansion of the economy and control of the inflationary pressure. Since 1970-71, however, the major objectives of monetary policy in India have been the control of inflationary pressure. No doubt, the RBI is the only authority which is empowered as well as capable to handle the situation. It is also not disputed that the monetary policy is important to fight inflation. The weapons and powers available to RBI are such that they cover only the commercial banks. RBI's general and selective controls will have some effect. But inflationary pressure is really brought about by deficit financing of the government and shortage of goods. The RBI seems to be concentrating only on the Demand end of inflation; as a result the entire perspective of supply is completely ignored. Inflation may also be curtailed if the supply is bolstered to meet the demands of the people. With the increase in supply, prices would inevitably come down and thus inflation may be controlled. The supply side would not be strengthened so easily, as it would require infrastructure development, planning, large scale investments etc. However, this is where the RBI could play an extremely important role. For the purpose of bolstering agricultural growth, development of infrastructure and all other avenues which the RBI may deem fit; it may lay down regulations to direct money either directly or indirectly with special importance to these sectors. To direct foreign capital in these fields and thus bolster infrastructure would not be a difficult task, as the RBI already does this function. Only this time it shall do it with the purpose of meeting the ever – rising demand.

This would serve a twin purpose. With the RBI increasing the CRR and other interest rates, it becomes difficult for the farmers to get their loans before their projects. It also becomes difficult for SME to obtain loans to fulfill their targets as well. Through this carefully routed capital, there may be an access to the required finance for these groups of people notwithstanding the high interest rate. Secondly and most importantly this would also enable the government to lay down measures to utilize this money to develop the infrastructure which would bolster supply and thus would be a huge boost in the fight against inflation in the long run. The government would also have to play an important role in controlling inflation without harming the economic growth by ensuring greater transparency in the RBI's sterilization operations. The Governments at the Centre and the States should take urgent action to make available adequate credit at competitive interest rates and offer other incentives. Inflation can be contained only if supply-side and demand issues are effectively addressed, apart from initiating appropriate fiscal and monetary measures.

REFERENCES

1. Dutt and Sundaram, "Indian Economy", S. Chand Publications, New Delhi.
2. Sankaran, S "Indian Economy", Margham Publications, Chennai-17.
3. Sundaram, K.P.M, "Money Banking Trade and Finance" Sultan Chand&Sons, New Delhi.
4. Vasant Desai, "Indian Banking", Himalaya Publishing House, Bombay.
5. Reserve Bank of India Bulletins, Various issues.
6. Web site: www.rbi.org.in
7. Web site: www.legalservice.com

19

Retail Banking – Opportunities and Challenges

*V. Gunasekaran

Retail banking is, however, quite broad in nature - it refers to the dealing of commercial banks with individual customers, both on liabilities and assets sides of the balance sheet. Fixed, current / savings accounts on the liabilities side; and mortgages, loans (e.g., personal, housing, auto, and educational) on the assets side, are the more important of the products offered by banks. Related ancillary services include credit cards, or depository services. Today's retail banking sector is characterized by three basic characteristics:

- Multiple products (deposits, credit cards, insurance, investments and securities);
- Multiple channels of distribution (call centre, branch, Internet and kiosk); and
- Multiple customer groups (consumer, small business, and corporate).

* Lecturer in Department of Commerce, The New College, Chennai)

In a recent book, retail banking has been described as "hotter than vindaloo". Considering the fact that vindaloo, the Indian-English innovative curry available in umpteen numbers of restaurants of London, is indeed very hot and spicy, it seems that retail banking is perceived to be the in-thing in today's world of banking.

Retail banking in India

Retail banking in India is not a new phenomenon. It has always been prevalent in India in various forms. For the last few years it has become synonymous with mainstream banking for many banks. The typical products offered in the Indian retail banking segment are housing loans, consumption loans for purchase of durables, auto loans, credit cards and educational loans. The loans are marketed under attractive brand names to differentiate the products offered by different banks. As the Report on Trend and Progress of India, 2003-04 has shown that the loan values of these retail lending typically range between Rs.20,000 to Rs.100 lakh. The loans are generally for duration of five to seven years with housing loans granted for a longer duration of 15 years. Credit card is another rapidly growing sub-segment of this product group.

In recent past retail lending has turned out to be a key profit driver for banks with retail portfolio constituting 21.5 per cent of total outstanding advances as on March 2004. The overall impairment of the retail loan portfolio worked out much less then the Gross NPA ratio for the entire loan portfolio. Within the retail segment, the housing loans had the least gross asset impairment. In fact, retailing make ample business sense in the banking sector.

While new generation private sector banks have been able to create a niche in this regard, the public sector banks have not lagged behind. Leveraging their vast branch network and outreach, public sector banks have aggressively forayed to garner a larger slice of the retail pie. By international standards, however, there is still much scope for retail banking in India. After all, retail loans constitute less than seven per cent of

GDP in India vis-à-vis about 35 per cent for other Asian economies – South Korea (55 per cent), Taiwan (52 per cent), Malaysia (33 per cent) and Thailand (18 per cent). As retail banking in India is still growing from modest base, there is a likelihood that the growth numbers seem to get somewhat exaggerated. One, thus, has to exercise caution is interpreting the growth of retail banking in India.

Drivers of Retail Business in India

What has contributed to this retail growth? Let me briefly highlight some of the basic reasons.

First, economic prosperity and the consequent increase in purchasing power have given a fillip to a consumer boom. Note that during the 10 years after 1992, India's economy grew at an average rate of 6.8 percent and continues to grow at the almost the same rate - not many countries in the world match this performance.

Second, changing consumer demographics indicate vast potential for growth in consumption both qualitatively and quantitatively. India is one of the countries having highest proportion (70%) of the population below 35 years of age (young population). The BRIC report of the Goldman-Sachs, which predicted a bright future for Brazil, Russia, India and China, mentioned Indian demographic advantage as an important positive factor for India.

Third, technological factors played a major role. Convenience banking in the form of debit cards, internet and phone-banking, anywhere and anytime banking has attracted many new customers into the banking field. Technological innovations relating to increasing use of credit / debit cards, ATMs, direct debits and phone banking has contributed to the growth of retail banking in India.

Fourth, the Treasury income of the banks, which had strengthened the bottom lines of banks for the past few years, has been on the decline during the last two years. In such a scenario, retail business provides a good vehicle of profit maximisation. Considering the fact that retail's share in impaired assets is far lower than the overall bank loans and advances, retail loans have put comparatively less provisioning burden on banks apart from diversifying their income streams.

Fifth, decline in interest rates have also contributed to the growth of retail credit by generating the demand for such credit.

In this backdrop let me now come two specific domains of retail lending in India, viz., (a) credit cards and (b) housing.

Credit Cards in India

The Credit Card holder is empowered to spend wherever and whenever he wants with his Credit Card within the limits fixed by his bank. Credit Card is a post paid card. Debit Card, on the other hand, is a prepaid card with some stored value. Every time a person uses this card, the Internet Banking house gets money transferred to its account from the bank of the buyer. The buyers account is debited with the exact amount of purchases. An individual has to open an account with the issuing bank which gives debit card with a Personal Identification Number (PIN). When he makes a purchase, he enters his PIN on shops PIN pad. When the card is slurped through the electronic terminal, it dials the acquiring bank system - either Master Card or VISA that validates the PIN and finds out from the issuing bank whether to accept or decline the transactions.

While usage of cards by customers of banks in India has been in vogue since the mid-1980s, it is only since the early 1990s that the market had witnessed a quantum jump. The total number of cards issued by 42 banks and outstanding, increased from 2.69 crore as on end December 2003 to 4.33 crore as on end December 2004. The actual usage too has registered increases both in terms of volume and value. Almost all the categories of banks issue credit cards. Credit cards have found greater acceptance in terms of usage in the major cities of the country, with the four major metropolitan cities accounting for the bulk of the transactions.

In view of this ever increasing role of credit cards a Working Group was set up for regulatory mechanism for cards.

The terms of reference of the Working Group were fairly broad and the Group was to look into the type of regulatory measures that are to be introduced for plastic cards (credit, debit and smart cards) for encouraging their growth in a safe, secure and efficient manner, as also to take care of the best customer practices and grievances redressal mechanism for the card users. The Reserve Bank has been receiving a number of complaints regarding various undesirable practices by credit card issuing institutions and their agents. Some of them are:

Unsolicited calls to members of the public by card issuing banks/ direct selling agents pressurizing them to apply for credit card.

Communicating misleading / wrong information regarding credit cards regarding conditions for issue, amount of service charges/ waiver of fees, gifts/prizes.

Sending credit cards to persons who have not applied for them / activating unsolicited cards without the approval of the recipient.

Charging very high interest rates /service charges.

Lack of transparency in disclosing fees/charges/penalties. Non-disclosure of detailed billing procedure.

The Working Group deliberated a number of major issues relating to: a) to customer grievances and rights: a) Transparency and Disclosure, b) Customer Rights Protection, and c) Code of Conduct. The Group recommended that the Most Important Terms and Conditions should be highlighted and advertised and sent separately to the prospective customer. These terms and conditions include various issues relating to: a) fees and charges, (b) drawal limits, (c) billing, (d) default, (e) termination / revocation of card membership, (f) loss / theft / misuse of card, and (g) disclosure.

These recommendations are being processed within the RBI and a set of guidelines would be issued which are going to pave the path of a healthy growth in the development of plastic money in India. The RBI is also considering bringing credit card disputes within the ambit of the Banking Ombudsman scheme. While building a regulatory oversight in this regard we need to ensure that neither does it reduce the efficiency of the system nor does it hamper the credit card usage.

Housing Credit in India

In view of its backward and forward linkages with other sectors of the economy, housing finance in developing countries is seen as a social good. In India, growth of housing finance segment has accelerated in recent years. Several supporting policy measures (like tax benefits) and the supervisory incentives instituted had played a major role in this market.

Housing credit has increased substantially over last few years, but from a very low base. During the period 1993-2004, outstanding housing loans by scheduled commercial banks and housing finance companies grew at a trend rate of 23 per cent. The share of housing loans in total non-food credit of scheduled commercial banks has increased from about 3 per cent in 1992-93 to about 7 per cent in 2003-04. Recent data reveal that non-priority sector housing loans outstanding as on February 18, 2005 were around Rs. 74 thousand crore, which is, however, only 8.0 per cent of the gross bank credit. As already pointed out, direct housing loans up to Rs. 15 lakh irrespective of the location now qualify as priority sector lending; housing loans are understood to form a large component of such lending. In addition, housing credit is also being provided by housing finance companies, which in turn are also receiving some bank finance.

Thus, from miniscule amounts, the exposure of the banking sector to housing loans has gone up. Unlike many other countries, asset impairment on account of housing finance constitutes a very small portion. However, with growing competition in the housing finance market, there has been a growing concern over its likely impact on the asset quality. While no immediate financial stability concerns exist, there is a need to put in place appropriate risk management systems, strengthen internal control procedures and also improve regulatory oversight in this area. Banks also need to monitor their exposure and the credit quality. In a fiercely competitive market, there may be some temptation to slacken the loan scrutiny procedures and this need to be severely checked.

Having delineated the broad contours of retail banking in India let me now come to its opportunities and challenges.

Opportunities and Challenges of Retail Banking in India

Retail banking has immense opportunities in a growing economy like India. As the growth story gets unfolded in India, retail banking is going to emerge a major driver. How does the world view us? I have already referred to the BRIC Report talking India as an economic superpower. A. T. Kearney, a global management consulting firm, recently identified India as the "second most attractive retail destination" of 30 emergent markets.

The rise of the Indian middle class is an important contributory factor in this regard. The percentage of middle to high income Indian households is expected to continue rising. The younger population not only wields increasing purchasing power, but as far as acquiring personal debt is concerned, they are perhaps more comfortable than previous generations. Improving consumer purchasing power, coupled with more liberal attitudes toward personal debt, is contributing to India's retail banking segment.

The combination of the above factors promises substantial growth in the retail sector, which at present is in the nascent stage. Due to bundling of services and delivery channels, the areas of potential conflicts of interest tend to increase in universal banks and financial conglomerates. Some of the key policy issues relevant to the retail banking sector are: financial inclusion, responsible lending, access to finance, long-term savings, financial capability, consumer protection, regulation and financial crime prevention. What are the challenges for the industry and its stakeholders?

First, retention of customers is going to be a major challenge. According to a research by Reichheld and Sasser in the Harvard Business Review, 5 per cent increase in customer retention can increase profitability by 35 per cent in banking business, 50 per cent in insurance and brokerage, and 125 per cent in the consumer credit card market. Thus, banks need to emphasise retaining customers and increasing market share.

Second, rising indebtedness could turn out to be a cause for concern in the future. India's position, of course, is not comparable to that of the developed world where household debt as a proportion of disposable income is much higher. Such a scenario creates high uncertainty. Expressing concerns about the high growth witnessed in the consumer credit segments the Reserve Bank has, as a temporary measure, put in place risk containment measures and increased the risk weight from 100 per cent to 125 per cent in the case of consumer credit including personal loans and credit cards (Mid-term Review of Annual Policy, 2004-05).

Third, information technology poses both opportunities and challenges. Even with ATM machines and Internet Banking, many consumers still prefer the personal touch of their neighborhood branch bank. Technology has made it possible to deliver services throughout the branch bank network, providing instant updates to checking accounts and rapid movement of money for stock transfers. However, this dependency on the network has brought IT department's additional responsibilities and challenges in managing, maintaining and optimizing the performance of retail banking networks. Illustratively, ensuring that all bank products and services are available, at all times, and across the entire organization is essential for today's retails banks to generate revenues and remain competitive. Besides, there are network management challenges, whereby keeping these complex, distributed networks and applications operating properly in support of business objectives becomes essential. Specific challenges include ensuring that account transaction applications run efficiently between the branch offices and data centers.

Fourth, KYC Issues and money laundering risks in retail banking is yet another important issue. Retail lending is often regarded as a low risk area for money laundering because of the perception of the sums involved. However, competition for clients may also lead to KYC procedures being waived in the bid for new business. Banks must also consider seriously the type of identification documents they will accept and other processes to be completed. The Reserve Bank has issued details guidelines on application of KYC norms in November 2004.

Some Random Thoughts

How do we see the future of retail banking? What are the major attributes of the shape of things to come in this sector? Let me share with you some of my random thoughts.

First, customer service should be the be-all and end-all of retail banking. The other day a document released by the British Bankers Association, entitled UK Retail Banking Manifesto: addressing the challenges that lie ahead for the industry and its stakeholders on September 29, 2004 came to my notice. This document analysed the key policy issues relevant to the retail banking sector and highlighted the role of financial inclusion, responsible lending, access to finance, and consumer protection. It is in this context that that one is reminded of the needs to develop the standards and codes for banking. The contribution of the Committee on Procedure & Performance Audit on Public Services (CPPAPS) (Chairman: Shri S.S. Tarapore) has been invaluable and has provided great insight. Based on the recommendation of the CPPAPS, the Annual Policy Statement for 2005-06 announced the decision to set up an independent Banking Codes & Standards Board of India on the model of the mechanism in the UK in order to ensure that comprehensive code of conduct for fair treatment of customers is evolved and adhered to. The codes and standards, together with the institutional mechanism to monitor them, are expected to enhance the quality of customer service, to the individual customer in particular. The codes will bring about greater transparency in the system and also tackle the issue of information asymmetry. The Board would function as an industry-wide watchdog of the banking code and ensure that the banks comply with the banking codes. The codes would establish the banking industry's key commitments and obligations to customers on standards of practice, disclosure and principles of conduct for their banking services. The Board will monitor compliance with the Codes by the affiliated banks.

Second, sharing of information about the credit history of households is extremely important as far retail banking is concerned. Perhaps due the confidential nature of banker-customer, banks have a traditional resistance to share credit information on the client, not only with one another, but also across sectors. Globally, Credit Information Bureaus have, therefore, been set up to function as a repository of credit information - both current and historical data on existing and potential borrowers. The database maintained by these institutions can be accessed by the lending institutions. Credit Bureaus have been established not only in countries with developed financial systems but also in countries with relatively less developed financial markets, such as, Sri Lanka, Mexico, Bangladesh and the Philippines. In Indian case, the Credit Information Bureau (India) Limited (CIBIL), incorporated in 2000, aims at fulfilling the need of credit granting institutions for comprehensive credit information by collecting, collating and disseminating credit information pertaining to both commercial and consumer borrowers. At the same time banks must exercise due diligence before declaring a borrower as defaulter.

Third, outsourcing has become an important issue in the recent past. With the increasing market orientation of the financial system and to cope with the competition as also to benefit from the technological innovations such as, e-banking, the banks are making increasing use of "outsourcing" as a means of both reducing costs and achieving better efficiency. While outsourcing does have various cost advantages, it has the potential to transfer risk, management and compliance to third parties who may not be regulated. A recent BIS Report on "Outsourcing in Financial Services" developed some high-level principles. A basic requirement in this context is that a regulated entity seeking to outsource activities should have in place a comprehensive policy on outsourcing including a comprehensive outsourcing risk management programme to address the outsourced activities and the relationship with the service provider. Application of these principles in the Indian context is under consideration.

Finally, retail banking does not refer to lending only. In the whole story of retailing one should not forget the role played by retail depositors. The homemaker, the retail shop keeper, the pensioners, self-employed and those employed in unorganised sector - all need to get a place in the banks. It is in this backdrop that the Annual Policy for 2005-06 pointed out issues relating to financial exclusion and had announced that the RBI would implement policies to encourage banks which provide extensive services while disincentivising those which are not responsive to the banking needs of the community, including the underprivileged. Furthermore, the nature, scope and cost of services need to be monitored to assess whether there is any denial, implicit or explicit, of basic banking services to the common person and banks have been urged to review their existing practices to align them with the objective of financial inclusion.

Conclusion

There is a need of constant innovation in retail banking. In bracing for tomorrow, a paradigm shift in bank financing through innovative products and mechanisms involving constant up gradation and revalidation of the banks' internal systems and processes is called for. Banks now need to use retail as a growth trigger. This requires product development and differentiation, innovation and business process reengineering, micro-planning, marketing, prudent pricing, customisation, technological up gradation, home / electronic / mobile banking, cost reduction and cross-selling.

While retail banking offers phenomenal opportunities for growth, the challenges are equally daunting. How far the retail banking is able to lead growth of the banking industry in future would depend upon the capacity building of the banks to meet the challenges and make use of the opportunities profitably. However, the kind of technology used and the efficiency of operations would provide the much needed competitive edge for success in retail banking business. Furthermore, in all these customers' interest is of paramount importance. The banking sector in India is demonstrating this and I do hope they would continue to chart in this traded path.

20

Security Issue in E-Banking

* Sangeetha. C & ** Latha. P

As use of the Internet continues to expand, more banks and thrifts are using the Web to offer products, services and communications with customers. Banking organizations have been delivering electronic services to consumers and businesses remotely for years. Electronic funds transfer, including small payments and corporate cash management systems, publicly accessible automated machines for currency withdrawal and retail account management, are global fixtures.

Continuing technological innovation and competition among existing banking organizations and new market entrants has allowed for a much wider array of electronic banking products and services for retail and wholesale banking customers. These include traditional activities such as accessing financial information, obtaining loans and opening deposit accounts, as well as relatively new products and services such as electronic bill payment services personalized financial "portals," account aggregation and business-to-business

* Lecturers, Department of Commerce with Computer Applications, Vellalar College For Women,, Thindal, Erode.

marketplaces and exchanges. It's evident from the document and from a general study of the business case of Internet banking, that security is perhaps the biggest concern. A connectivity issues to remote locations is also very important, but the need to be secure is far more pressing. The Internet offers the potential for safe, convenient new ways to shop for financial services and conduct banking business, any day, any time.

Internet Banking : Features & Services

Features of Internet banking are:

- It removes the traditional geographical barriers as it could reach out to customers of different countries/legal jurisdiction.
- Security of banking transactions, validity of electronic contract, customers' privacy, etc., which have all along been concerns of both bankers and supervisors have assumed different dimensions given that Internet is a public domain, not subject to control by any single authority or group of users.
- It poses a strategic risk of loss of business to those banks who do not respond in time to this new technology, being the efficient and cost effective delivery.

Internet banking services are classified into three types:

- The basic level service, in which the banks' websites disseminate information on different products and services to customers. It may receive and reply to customers' queries through e-mail.
- Simple transactional websites, which allow customers to submit their instructions, applications for different services, and queries on their account balances. They do not permit any fund-based transactions on their accounts.
- The third level of Internet banking services offered by fully-transactional websites, which allow customers to operate on their accounts for transfer of funds, payment of different bills, subscribing to other products of the bank, and to transact purchase and sale of securities.

Standards for Safeguarding Customer Information

- Each bank shall implement a comprehensive written information security program that includes administrative, technical, and physical safeguards appropriate to the size and complexity of the bank.
- A bank's information security program shall be designed to:
  - Ensure the security and confidentiality of customer information;
  - Protect against any anticipated threats or hazards to the security or integrity of such information.
- The Guidelines apply to customer information maintained by national banks, branches and agencies of foreign banks, and any subsidiaries of such entities.

Components of Security Controls

The key components of security concerns are,

1. Authentication: The assurance of identity of the person in a deal.

- Banks should use reliable methods for verifying the identity and authorization of new customers as well as authenticating the identity and authorization of established customers seeking to initiate electronic transactions.
- Customer verification during account origination is important in reducing the risk of identity theft, fraudulent account applications and money laundering. Failure on the part of the bank to adequately authenticate customers could result in unauthorized individuals gaining access to e-banking accounts and ultimately financial loss and reputational damage to the bank through fraud, disclosure of confidential information or inadvertent involvement in criminal activity. Establishing and authenticating an individual's identity and authorization to access banking

systems in a purely electronic open network environment can be a difficult task.

- The bank must determine which authentication methods to use based on management's assessment of the risk posed by the e-banking system as a whole or by the various subcomponents.
- As authentication methods continue to evolve, banks are encouraged to monitor and adopt industry sound practice in this area, such as ensuring that:
  - Authentication databases that provide access to e-banking customer accounts or sensitive systems are protected from tampering and corruption. Any such tampering should be detectable and audit trails should be in place to document such attempts.
  - Any addition, deletion or change of an individual, agent or system to an authentication database is duly authorized by an authenticated source.
  - Appropriate measures are in place to control the e-banking system connection such that unknown third parties cannot displace known customers.
  - Authenticated e-banking sessions remain secure throughout the full duration of the session or in the event of a security lapse, the session should require reauthentication.
- Banks can use a variety of methods to establish authentication, including PINs, passwords, smart cards, biometrics, and digital.

2. Non-Repudiation: Banks should use transaction authentication methods that promote non repudiation and establish accountability for e-banking transactions. Non-repudiation involves creating proof of the origin or delivery of electronic information to protect the sender against false denial by the recipient that the data has been received. A bank may issue digital certificates using public key infrastructure (PKI) to a customer in order to secure communications with the bank. Risk of transaction repudiation is already an issue with conventional transactions such as credit cards or securities transactions. However, e-banking heightens this risk because of the difficulties of positively authenticating the identities and authority of parties initiating transactions, the potential for altering or hijacking electronic transactions, and the potential for e-banking users to claim that transactions were fraudulently altered.

3. Data and Transaction Integrity: Data integrity refers to the assurance that information that is in-transit or in storage is not altered without authorization. Failure to maintain the data integrity of transactions, records and information can expose banks to financial losses as well as to substantial legal and reputational risk. As e-banking is transacted over public networks, transactions are exposed to the added threat of data corruption, fraud and the tampering of records. Accordingly, banks should ensure that appropriate measures are in place to ascertain the accuracy, completeness and reliability of e-banking transactions, records and information that is either transmitted over the Internet, resident on internal bank databases, or transmitted/stored by third-party service providers on behalf of the bank.

4. Segregation of Duties: Banks should ensure that appropriate measures are in place to promote adequate segregation of duties within e-banking systems, databases and applications. Segregation of duties is a basic internal control measure designed to reduce the risk of fraud in operational processes and systems and ensure that transactions and company assets are properly authorized, recorded and safeguarded. Segregation of duties is critical to ensure the accuracy and integrity of data and is used to prevent the perpetration of fraud by an individual. If duties are adequately separated, fraud can only be committed through collusion. E-banking services may necessitate modifying the ways in which segregation of duties are established and maintained because transactions take place over electronic systems where identities can be more readily masked or faked. In addition, operational and transaction based functions have in many cases become more compressed and integrated in e-banking applications.

Common practices used to establish and maintain segregation of duties within an e-banking environment includes the following:

- Transaction processes and systems should be designed to ensure that no single employee / outsourced service provider could enter, authorize and complete a transaction.
- Segregation should be maintained between those initiating static data (including web page content) and those responsible for verifying its integrity.
- E-banking systems should be tested to ensure that segregation of duties cannot be bypassed.
- Segregation should be maintained between those developing and those administrating e-banking systems.

5. Authorization Controls: Authorization refers to the procedures, techniques and processes used to determine that a customer or an employee has legitimate access to the bank account or the authority to conduct associated transactions on that account. Banks should ensure that proper authorization controls and access privileges are in place for e-banking systems, databases and applications.

In order to maintain segregation of duties, banks need to strictly control authorization and access privileges. Failure to provide adequate authorization control could allow individuals to alter their authority, circumvent segregation and gain access to e-banking systems, databases or applications to which they are not privileged. In e-banking system, the authorizations and access rights can be established in either a centralized or distributed manner within a bank and are generally stored in databases. The protection of those databases from tampering or corruption is therefore essential for effective authorization control.

Sound Authorization Practices for E-Banking Applications

1. Specific authorization and access privileges should be assigned to all individuals, agents or systems, which conduct e-banking activities.
2. All e-banking systems should be constructed to ensure that they interact with a valid authorization database.
3. No individual agent or system should have the authority to change his or her own authority or access privileges in an e-banking authorization database.
4. Controls should be in place to prevent changes to authorization levels during e-banking transaction sessions and any attempts to alter authorization should be logged and brought to the attention of management.

6. Maintenance of Audit Trails: Banks should ensure that clear audit trails exist for all e-banking transactions. Delivery of financial services over the Internet can make it more difficult for banks to apply and enforce internal controls and maintain clear audit trails, if these measures are not adapted to an e-banking environment. Banks are not only challenged to ensure that effective internal control can be provided in highly automated environments, but also that the controls can be independently audited, particularly for all critical e-banking events and applications. A bank's internal control environment may be weakened if it is unable to maintain clear audit trails for its e-banking activities. This is because much, if not all, of its records and evidences supporting e-banking transactions are in an electronic format. In making a determination as to where clear audit trails should be maintained, the following types of e-banking transactions should be considered:

- The opening, modifying or closing of a customer's account.
- Any transaction with financial consequences.
- Any authorization granted to a customer to exceed a limit.
- Any granting, modification or revocation of systems access rights or privileges.

7. Confidentiality of Key Bank Information: Confidentiality is the assurance that key information remains private to the bank and is not viewed or used by those unauthorized to do so. Misuse or unauthorized disclosure of data exposes a bank to both reputation and legal risk. The advent of e-banking presents additional security challenges for banks because it increases the exposure that information transmitted over the public network or stored in databases may be accessible by unauthorised or inappropriate parties or used in ways the customer providing the information did not intend. Additionally, increased use of service providers may expose key bank data to other parties.

To meet these challenges concerning the preservation of confidentiality of key e-banking information, banks need to ensure that:

- All confidential bank data and records are only accessible by duly authorized and authenticated individuals, agents or systems.
- All confidential bank data are maintained in a secured manner and protected from unauthorized viewing or modification during transmission over public, private or internal networks.
- The bank's standards and controls for data use and protection must be met when third parties have access to the data through outsourcing relationships.
- All access to restricted data is logged and appropriate efforts are made to ensure that access logs are resistant to tampering.

Banks should employ appropriate cryptographic techniques, specific protocols or other security controls to ensure the confidentiality of customer e-banking data. Banks should take appropriate steps to inform e-banking customers about the confidentiality and privacy of their information. These steps may include:

- Informing customers of the bank's privacy policy, possibly on the bank's website. Clear, concise language in such statements is essential to assure that the customer fully understands the privacy policy. Lengthy legal descriptions, while accurate, are likely to go unread by the majority of customers.

- Instructing customers on the need to protect their passwords, personal identification numbers (PINs) and other banking and/or personal data.
- Providing customers with information regarding the general security of their personal computer, including the benefits of using virus protection software, physical access controls and personal firewalls for static Internet connections.

Bank's Security Tools

128-bit Secured Socket layer (SSL)

Bank employs 128-bit Secure Socket Layer (SSL), which is one of the best encryption technologies commercially available and most commonly used by large-scale online merchants, banks, and brokerages worldwide. Encryption is a method of scrambling information to protect its transmission across the Internet. All online sessions between the customer and the bank are protected by upto 128-bit encryption.

Verisign Digital Certification

Verisign Digital Certificate provides the user with Third Party (Certification Authority) evidence of the server's authenticity. This safeguards users from trusting unauthorized sites and allows the session to be encrypted. Verisign is an internationally acclaimed Certification Authority and large-scale online merchants, banks and brokerages use their certificates worldwide.

Secured Login Page

The login page on which User ID and Password is entered by the Customers is also secured.

Locking of Password

Online access account is automatically locked if an incorrect password is entered for certain number of attempts.

Two Levels of Password for Financial Transactions

Fund Transfers and Bill Payment can be executed through Internet Banking only by the use of transaction password in addition to the password used for logging in. All main transactional facilities on the website cannot be done without entering transactional password. Such a password is machine generated and is known only to the Customer.

Firewalls: Servers that run banks site are protected by firewalls system that prevent unauthorised access to the network and which are constantly monitored to prevent security breaches.

Timed Logout: To protect customer accounts against unauthorized access, the systems are designed to terminate a secure online session automatically if extended inactivity is detected.

Expiry of User ID: Internet banking user ID expires if it is not used for a period of more than one year.

Biometric Technology is an automated view of physiological or behavioral characteristics used to identify and/or authenticate a person. Common forms of biometric technology include facial scans, finger scans, iris scans, retina scans, hand scans, signature scans, voice scans and keystroke dynamics. Biometric identification systems provide very strong authentication, but may pose greater implementation complexities than other identification/authentication methods.

Public key infrastructure (PKI), is where each party has a private/public key pair. The private key is secret so that only one person should use it. All parties use the public key. The private key generates an electronic signature on the document and the key pairs are designed so that a message encrypted with the private key can only be read by using the other key.

Digital Certificate. A bank may issue a digital certificate to a customer or counterparty to allow for their unique identification/authentication and reduce the risk of transaction repudiation. Although in some countries customers' rights to disclaim transactions are provided in specific legal provisions, legislation has been passed in certain national jurisdictions making digital signatures legally enforceable.

Types of Online Frauds

PHISHING: Phishing is an attempt by fraudsters to 'fish' for customer banking details. A phishing attempt usually is in the form of an e-mail that appears to be from the bank. The e-mail usually encourages customer to click a link in it that takes customer to a fraudulent log-on page designed to capture their details. E-mail addresses can be obtained from publicly available sources or through randomly generated lists.

To Protect From Phishing

Delete suspicious e-mails without opening them. If customer happens to open them, do not click any link or attachment they may contain.

SPOOFING: Website spoofing is the act of creating a website, as a hoax, with the intention of performing fraud. To make spoof sites seem legitimate, phishers use the names, logos, graphics and even code of the actual website Fraudsters send e-mails with a link to a spoofed website asking to update or confirm account related information. This is done with the intention of obtaining sensitive account related information like Internet Banking user ID, password, PIN, credit card / debit card / bank account number, card verification value (CVV) number, etc.

To Protect From Spoofed Websites

Users should not respond an e-mail requesting of Internet Banking security details like PIN, password or account number.

SKIMMING: Skimming is a method used by fraudsters to capture personal or account information from credit card. Card is swiped through the skimmer and the information contained in the magnetic strip on the card is then read into and stored on the skimmer or an attached computer. Skimming is a tactic used predominantly to perpetrate credit-card fraud - but it is also a tactic that is gaining in popularity among identity thieves.

To Protect From Skimming

- Sign on the reverse of credit card
- Collect receipts / charge slips
- Never allow a shopkeeper to take card to a different shop/room for swiping.

MONEY MULE: Once the fraudster has captured personal information using anyone of the ways explained above, they need an account to which they can transfer funds from the compromised account. A Money Mule is an unwitting participant in the frauds who is recruited by fraudsters to launder stolen money across the globe.

Be cautious about any unsolicited offers or opportunities offering the chance to make some easy money. Money mule adverts or offers can take a variety of different forms and they may even copy a genuine company's web site and register a similar web address to add authenticity to the scam.

VISHING: Vishing is an adaptation of Phishing attacks that uses telephone or VOIP (Voice over IP tools). Customer receive an email or SMS asking to call a free phone number to confirm details, or may receive a phone call with a recorded message asking to input account details. Once they have done, the attacker is free to use personal information to attack their account.

To protect from Vishing

Use only the published official call centre numbers for financial services company and be cautious in giving out personal information over the telephone.

Guidelines of RBI

The Reserve Bank of India (RBI) has created a comprehensive document which lays down number of security-related guidelines and strategies for banks to follow in order to offer Internet banking. The guidelines are about the types of risks associated with Internet banking, the technology and security standards, legal issues involved, and regulatory and supervisory concerns. Any bank that wants to offer Internet banking must follow these guidelines and adhere to them as a legal necessity. None of the Indian banks which offer Internet banking facilities have an IT security policy as stipulated by the RBI. While banks have been asked to file monthly reports to show compliance to the guidelines, most of them have sought time to satisfy the security policy criterion.

The RBI is insisting on a written document, signed by the Board of Directors to make the banks aware that IT security is not just an IT concern, but something that could affect overall business as well. The RBI is also empowered to audit the compliance to the policy.

Present Scenario of Indian Banks

Banks and financial institutions in India are in the process of Web-enabling their services in order to offer Internet banking to its customers. The RBI has drafted certain Internet banking guidelines that have to be followed by banks about to venture into online banking. It's the new generation of banking in India. Most private and MNC banks have already setup an elaborate Internet banking infrastructure.

They provide them numerous benefits like:

- Greater reach to customers
- Quicker time to market
- Ability to introduce new products and services quickly and successfully
- Ability to understand its customers needs
- Customers are given access to information easily across any location
- Greater customer loyalty

Multi-national and private sector banks in India have been very successful in setting up Internet banking services. This is mainly because these banks already had a robust automated banking environment on which they could build the Internet banking infrastructure. Most multi-national banks already have efficient Internet banking infrastructures running in other countries which could be emulated in India.

Challenges at Nationalized Bank

Challenges at nationalized bank are,

- A very large network of branches growing fastly nationwide.
- Lack of connectivity in remote locations
- A very large base of customers increasing fast
- 75-80 percent automation in main branches with less automation in remote cities and smaller branches.
- Large amount of legacy equipment which doesn't integrate well with other systems.
- Inefficient and outdated applications in some departments which are not flexible and don't integrate well with other applications.
- Slow-to-change mentality of an Indian customer who is used to dealing with a human teller.

Web-enabling banks with such infrastructure and number of branches nationwide at one go is a near-impossible task. However each of the challenges can be overcome with good planning phased implementation.

Banks Security Measures

Each bank must consider whether the following security measures are appropriate for the bank:

- Access controls on customer information systems, including controls to authenticate and permit access only to authorized individuals.
- Access restrictions at physical locations containing customer information.
- Encryption of electronic customer information, including while in transit or in storage on networks or systems to which unauthorized individuals may have access.

- Monitoring systems and procedures to detect actual and attempted attacks on or intrusions into customer information systems;
- Actions to be taken when the bank suspects or detects that unauthorized individuals have gained access to customer information systems and in Measures to protect against destruction, loss, or damage of customer information due to potential environmental hazards, such as fire and water damage or technological failures.
- Stop payment instructions received from account holders with regard to lost cheques can be put in computer so that a caution signal would be available whenever a lost cheque is presented for payment.
- The reconciliation of transactions relating to drafts issued and paid through computerised system would help early detection of fraudulent payments.
- Frauds relating to local clearing operations may be minimised through prompt reconciliation of number and amount of cheques through computerised system.

Customers' Safety Measures

The following are the safety measures fot the customers already using online banking systems.

- Confirm that an online bank is legitimate and deposits are insured.
- Keep personal information private and secure.
- Understand their rights as a consumer.
- Learn where to go for more assistance from banking regulators.
- Regularly monitoring account activity to safeguard against the fraud.
- Review account details regularly.
- Alerts on mobile and e-mail.

Computer Safety Measures

Always protect computer by using up-to-date anti-virus software that is capable of scanning files and e-mail messages for viruses. This will prevent the files getting corrupted or lost and also prevent computer from getting infected with the virus.

Any computer or device connected to the Internet that is not properly protected is vulnerable to a variety of malicious Internet intrusions and attacks. A personal firewall will help protect from intrusion. Firewalls create a barrier between to the computer and the rest of the Internet. A firewall can be a hardware device, a software application or a combination of the two.

It is very important to check the websites of operating system and web-browser vendors for software "patches" and "updates". Some operating systems and software can be configured to automatically check for new updates.

- Scan Computer for Spyware Regularly.
- When Not Using Computer, Shut it Down or Disconnect it from the Internet.
- Do not leave computer unattended for a long time.

CONCLUSION

Like any other product or service, Internet banking is not one-time activity. The advent of e-banking presents additional security challenges for banks. The banks should:

- Have a clear and widely disseminated strategy that is driven from the top and takes into account the effects of e-banking, together with an effective process for measuring performance against it.
- Ensure they have adequate management information in a clear and comprehensible format.
- Make active use of system based security management and monitoring tools.

However, safe banking online involves good choices and decisions.

21

Risk Management in E-Banking

*M. Mahalakshmi

E-Banking is defined as the automated delivery of new and traditional banking products and services directly to customers through electronic, interactive communication channels. Wireless E-Banking is a delivery channel, which enhances the convenience of E-Banking. Wireless E-Banking takes place when customer access a financial institution's network(s) using cellular phones, computers, or through different channels of communications.

Retail Services	Wholesale Services
Account Management	Account Management
Bill Payment and Presentation	Cash Management
Account Opening	Small Business Loan Applications, Approval & Advances
Consumer Wire Transfer	
Investment/ Brokerage	Commercial Wire Transfers
Loan Application	B2b Payment
Account Aggregation	Employee Benefits

*Lecturer, Department of Commerce, K.S.R. College of Arts and Science, Thiruchengode.

MAIN CONCERNS IN E-BANKING

Member institutions rate security as the most important issue of online banking. There is more need to protect customer's privacy and protect against fraud. Online banking via WWW provides an overview of Internet commerce and how one company handles secure banking for its financial institution clients and their customers.

E-BANKING COMPONENTS

Depending on various factors the system of E-Banking can vary. Financial institutions should choose their E-Banking system configuration, including outsourcing relationships, based on four factors—

- Strategic objective;
- Scope, scale and complexity of equipments, system and activities;
- Technology expertise;
- Security and internal control.

BANKING RISK

TRANSACTIONAL RISK

Transaction risk arises from fraud, processing errors, system disruptions, or other unanticipated events resulting in the institution's inability to deliver products or services. This risk mainly involves due to the institution's processing environment. In many cases, E-Banking will increase the work of the institution more complex. Since the customer expects availability of services 24X7 the institutions should ensure proper infrastructure containing sufficient capacity and redundancy.

CREDIT RISK

Generally, in any financial institution credit risk is not increased by the mere fact that a loan is originated through E-Banking channels. However, the company should consider additional precautions while approving loans over E-banking channels. The following aspects has to be considered while approving on-line credit

- Verifying the customers identity
- Monitoring and controlling growth in credit
- Monitoring the customers activities
- Collection of loans
- Monitoring any increased volume of lending

LIQUIDITY, INTEREST RATE, AND PRICE/MARKET RISKS

Funding and investment-related risks could increase with an institution's e-banking initiatives depending on the volatility and pricing of the acquired deposit. The Internet provides the ability of marketing once goods globally. But Internet originated deposit have the potential to attract customers who focuses mainly on loan rates.

LEGAL RISK

Compliances and legal issues arise out of the rapid growth in the usage of E-banking and the differences between electronic & paper based processes. E-Banking is a developing concept where the rules and regulations governing these services are still ambiguous or still an evolving concept. Because of the developing technology, institutions that offer both informational and transactional services have the higher level of compliance and risk.

FOREIGN EXCHANGE RISK

This arises when assets in one currency are funded by liabilities in another. Internet banking may encourage residents of other countries to transact in their domestic currencies. Due to the ease and lower cost of transacting, it may also lead customers to take speculative positions in various currencies. Higher holdings and transactions in non-domestic currencies increase foreign exchange risk.

COMPLIANCE RISK

This is the risk to earnings or capital arising from violations of, or nonconformance with, laws, regulations and ethical standards. Compliance risk may lead to diminished reputation, actual monetary losses and reduced business opportunities. Banks need to carefully understand and interpret existing laws as they apply to Internet banking and ensure consistency with other channels such as branch banking. This risk is amplified when the customer, the bank and the transaction are in more than one country. Conflicting laws, tax procedures and reporting requirements across different jurisdictions add to the risk. The need to keep customer data private and seek customers' consent before sharing the data also adds to compliance risk. Customers are very concerned about the privacy of their data and banks need to be seen as reliable guardians of such data. Finally, the need to consummate transactions immediately (straight-through processing) may lead to banks relaxing traditional controls, which aim to reduce compliance risk.

STRATEGIC RISK

A financial institution's board and management should understand the risks associated with E-Banking services and evaluate the resulting risk management costs against the potential return on investment prior to offering E-Banking services. Improper evaluation can cause strategic risk. Financial institution should give attention to the following:

- Adequacy of management
- Cost involved in monitoring activities of E-Banking
- Generate customers wants
- Competition
- New technology etc...

REPUTATION RISK

An institution's decision to offer E-services mainly increases the reputation risk. Some of the ways that influences an institution's reputation include:

- Loss of trust
- Disclosure of parties' secrets
- Failure to deliver marketing claims
- Failure to provide reliable services
- Customers' queries and

- Kayos and confusions.

RISK MANAGEMENT PRINCIPLES

E-banking has unique characteristics that may increase an institution's overall risk profile and the level of risks associated with traditional financial services, particularly strategic, operational, legal, and reputation risks. These unique e-banking characteristics include:

- Speed of technological change,
- Changing customer expectations,
- Increased visibility of publicly accessible networks (e.g., the Internet)
- Less face-to-face interaction with financial institution customers,
- Need to integrate e-banking with the institution's legacy computer systems,
- Dependence on third parties for necessary technical expertise, and
- Proliferation of threats and vulnerabilities in publicly accessible networks.

Management should review each of the processes discussed in this section to adapt and expand the institution's risk management practices as necessary to address the risks posed by e-banking activities.

Managing the risks and implementing controls for E-banking initiatives follows the same principles as other risk management processes. The most dangerous thing is to treat this as a technical problem and leave it to IT management to manage. As the previous enumeration of the risks has shown, this is a general management issue which needs attention from senior management. A general framework of risk management is set forth below.

Board and Management Oversight

The board and senior management should establish effective management control over the risks associated with e-banking activities, including specific accountability, policies and controls to manage these risks. Further, management should clearly understand the role of e-banking in meeting the institution's overall strategic objectives. The business should set specific objectives for e- banking, such as revenues, profits, transaction costs and service levels. An unambiguous objective sets the tone for a robust risk posture. E-banking projects may have a significant impact on the bank's risk profile and should be reviewed and approved by senior management. They should undergo appropriate strategic and cost/reward analysis. In addition, senior management should ensure that they do not engage in e-banking projects unless they have necessary technical and risk management oversight expertise at all levels.

Senior management should set the tone in managing risk by establishing key delegations and reporting mechanisms, separation of duties and escalation procedures. Management should set up a formal risk assessment process in the organization, so that line management is responsible for, and directly involved in risk identification and mitigation. Finally, management should ensure that ongoing due diligence and risk analyses are performed as the bank initiates or expands e-banking activities.

Security Controls

Security controls need special attention because of the open nature of the E-banking and the pace of technological change. Specific focus areas include:

- **Authentication–**This means ensuring customers are verified and their identities are established before conducting business over the Internet. Passwords, biometric methods, challenge-response systems, public key infrastructure are some of the ways of strengthening authentication. There is a growing trend towards single-sign-on applications, where the customer needs only a single ID to access his entire relationship. These increase the risk of compromise.

- **Nonrepudiation**–Banks should make certain that customers who transact on the Internet cannot later deny having originated the transactions. Using techniques like PKI (digital certificates), strong nonrepudiation can be achieved. However, legal enforceability in many countries is still suspect.
- **Segregation of duties** – As in any traditional process, segregation of duties is vital to prevent perpetration of fraud by any one individual.

Banks should ensure that there are appropriate measures to protect the data integrity of e-banking transactions, records and information. All e-banking transactions should generate clear audit trails, which should be archived. It is also vital to generate and protect records of customer instructions in a legally acceptable format.

Banks should strengthen information security controls to preserve the confidentiality and integrity of customer data. Firewalls, ethical hacking tests, physical and logical access controls are some of the methods available.

Legal and Reputational Risk Management

Legal and reputational risk management can be broken down into the following:

- **Privacy**–Banks should articulate a privacy policy and should communicate this to customers. Customers must be allowed opt-out options, and great care must be exercised before sharing customer information with outside entities. If customers are from a different jurisdiction, then the strongest privacy law may apply.
- **Availability**–Banks should have business continuity and contingency planning processes to help to ensure continuous availability of Internet banking services. This is challenging because of the potential for high transaction volume and the demand for 24-hour, seven-day-a-week availability.
- **Incident response**–Banks should formulate appropriate incident response plans to detect, manage, contain and

minimize problems arising from internal and external attacks. There should be clear escalation paths, a communication strategy for customers and the press and a documented chain of command. Finally, there should be a process for collecting and preserving forensic evidence after an adverse event.

The risks arising from e-banking are not restricted to information security areas, but span across all the traditional banking areas. Risk management for E-banking should be directed by senior management and incorporated within existing risk management disciplines in the organization. Control procedures need to keep pace with rapid changes in technology.

22

Self Help Groups and Bank Linkages – Empowering Rural Women

*G. Thamizh Chelvan

Nearly seventy percent of the population of India lives in its rural areas. That's over 70 crore Indians are living in 6,00,000 villages. Many of these villages are in desperate need of water, power, roads, sanitation, communication, livelihoods, health-care and education. India has witnessed a three-fold increase in population over the last half a century without corresponding growth in opportunities, especially in rural areas. The struggle for survival continues among the poor people, of which women are the worst sufferers. Indian women are often segregated. They are deprived of education, employment and awareness of their rights. This denies women access to a holistic understanding of their needs and expectations from the mainstream life necessities. Saddled

*Lecturer in Commerce, Dr. G.R. Damodaran College of Science, Coimbatore

with day-to-day responsibilities such as fetching water from a long distance, collecting fodder and fuel, grinding food grains, looking after the children and attending to the livestock and agricultural activities, the drudgery of rural women continues. In spite of their significant role in the family, they are suppressed and given an inferior status in rural society.

The importance of women to the economic development of India was first recognised during the country's struggle for independence. Jawaharlal Nehru, India's first Prime Minister, said, 'When we say a country is fully developed, it is not counting the heads of the men only. When the women and children are economically and socially developed, then we can say that country is fully developed.' For this reason the Mahila Mandal Scheme was launched throughout rural India as a means of developing women both socially and economically. Since independence, the government has implemented several development programmes for women. But these have not led to any remarkable improvement on a wider scale in the living conditions of women of the poorer and rural sections. The schemes failed due to low level of participation of people, lack of professional approach, poor communication and lack of financial support. Therefore building a down to the ground model became essential to eradicate poverty and trigger development. It was felt that the needed motivation to engage in enterprising activity in a sustained manner could be generated among rural and poor women if they functioned in groups rather than as individuals. This way the weaknesses of individual women could be filled up by the strengths of the others in the group and the group could provide the moral and other support and assistance for breaking out in a new path.

Genesis of Self Help Groups

This was the genesis of Self Help Groups (SHGs) to promote income generating activities and enterprise among women. SHGs lead to leadership development among women, enable the group to take up problems related to women, inculcate the saving habit, build their capacities to develop micro enterprises and generate income. Self-help groups are voluntary, small group structures for mutual aid and the accomplishment of collective goals. One of the important features is the homogeneity in the group in terms of social and economic status. The group has a membership between 10 and 20, and majority of the groups is of women. They are usually formed by peers who have come together for mutual assistance in satisfying a common need, overcoming common handi-caps or life-disrupting problems, and bringing about desired social and/or personal change. The initiators and members of such groups perceive that their needs are not, or cannot be, met by or through existing social institutions. Self-help groups emphasize face-to-face social interactions and the assumption of personal responsibility by members. They often provide material assistance, as well as emotional support; they are frequently "cause"-oriented, and promulgate an ideology or values through which members may attain an enhanced sense of personal identity.

In India, these Self-Help Groups are promoted by N.G.O.s, banks and co-operatives. The National Bank for Agriculture and Rural Development (NABARD) launched a pilot project for linking SHGs in February, 1992. The Reserve Bank of India advises the commercial banks actively to participate in the linkage programme. Normally, after six months of existence of SHGs and after collecting a sufficient thrift fund, the Groups approach the link banks (either commercial or co-operative) with its credit plan. The NABARD gives 100 per cent refinance to the Banks on their lending through the SHGs.

Focus on Women Empowerment

Women are an integral part of every economy. All round development and harmonious growth of a nation would be possible only when women are considered as equal partners in progress with men. However, in most developing countries, women have a low social and economic status. Empowerment of women is a holistic concept. It is multi-dimensional in its approach and covers social, political, economic and social aspects. Of all these facets of women's development, economic empowerment is of utmost significance in order to achieve a lasting and sustainable development of society.

Today, SHGs of women in India have been recognized as an effective strategy for the empowerment of women specifically in rural area, bringing women together from all spheres of life to fight for their rights or a cause. Since the overall empowerment of women is crucially dependent on economic empowerment, women through these SHGs work on a range of issues such as health, nutrition, education, agriculture, forestry, etc. besides income generation activities and seeking micro credit. In addition to economic empowerment, SHGs are extending the basic literacy skill, rights of women, group dynamics, leadership training, health training, legal training with special emphasis on legal rights, accounts training and vocational skill.

Of late, particularly in the decade of the 1990s it has become the official policy of the central government to promote SHGs by the provision of funds under various central schemes for skill training, technology transfer, provision of inputs, training in entrepreneurship and enterprise management, and micro credit. The Swarna Jayanti Rojgar Yojana (SJRG) for instance provides fund to the state governments for the SHGs. The NABARD, which initiated this policy, has now over 12 lakh such groups all over the country. Many of these SHGs have also helped women by giving opportunities to raise resources, credit an, there continue to be some limitations.

Features of Self Help Groups

- Self-help builds on the participant's own innate resources.
- The starting point for self-help is the participants' acknowledged common problems.
- The size of the SHG can vary from group to group depending on the context, though homogenous, democratic and accountable groups are better sustained.
- The goals of the SHG need to be clear and arise out of the aspirations of its members and should be known to all members.
- An external facilitator may facilitate the formation and

activation of the group, but the group is controlled by its members.

- Intra-group conflicts may reduce the cohesion of the group, resulting in its dissolution.
- The groups usually create a common fund by contributing their small savings on a regular basis.
- Most of the groups by them-selves, or with the help of NGOs, evolve flexible systems of working and managing their pooled resources in a democratic way, with participation of every member in decision-making.
- Request for loans are considered by the group in their periodic meetings and competing claims on limited resources are settled by consensus.

SHGs and Bank Linkages

As soon as the SHG is formed, a couple of group meetings will be held and SHG can open a Savings Bank account with the nearest Commercial or Regional Rural Bank or a Cooperative Bank. This is essential to keep the thrift and other monies of the SHG safely and also to improve the transparency levels of SHG's transactions. Opening of SB account, in fact, is the beginning of relationship between the bank and the SHG. The Reserve Bank of India has issued instructions to all banks permitting them to open SB accounts in the name of registered or unregistered SHGs. In order to promote and strengthen the SHG's financially, a linkage between banks and SHG's was initiated. Microfinance programs like the Self Help Bank Linkage Program in India have been increasingly promoted for their positive economic impact and the belief that they empower women.

NABARD initiated the concept of linking banks and SHG's with the objective of providing sustainable access to financial services to the rural poor, with a focus on those who had been considered unbankable. By using the existing rural financial infrastructure of 150,000 banking and cooperative retail outlets and linking them to savings and credit groups with joint liability, there are economies of scale and scope, resulting in substantially lower transaction costs. National implementation started in 1996, after four years of pilot-testing.

MODELS OF LINKAGE BETWEEN BANKS AND SELF-HELP GROUPS

Three distinct models can be observed in linkage programmes between banks and low-income groups. (*Source:* Y.C. Nanda, *Country Report - India.* APRACA-GTZ Regional Workshop on the Linkage Programme: Focus on Implementation Issues, 26-28 October 1994.)

MODEL I : Bank-SHG with active support of SHPI

The most common linkage model in India is where the banks deal directly with individual SHGs. In case of most of these SHGs, the SHPI (Self Help Promotion Institution) had provided the initial training, guidance to rural poor in organizing themselves into thrift and credit groups. In many cases, the SHPI had also provided some initial support to these SHGs to segment their resources. The SHPI also keeps a watch and ensures satisfactory functioning of the SHGs even after the linkage. While linkage of the banks is direct with the SHGs, the SHPI has an important role in pre-as Well as post-linkage stages.

MODEL II: BANK-SHG

A slight variant to Model 1 is where banks have provided financial support to SHGs which had grown almost spontaneously without any intervention of SHPI. The SHGs were initiated on the basis of a common activity, problem and took up thrift and credit activities. The cases of such linkages are of course not very common.

MODEL III: BANK-SHPI-SHG

In this model, the SHPI have taken the role of a financial intermediary between the banks and a number of SHGs. Again, the SHPIs take up such responsibilities only in respect of the groups promoted/ nurtured by them and not for other groups. The SHPI accepts the contractual responsibility for repayment of the loan to the bank. In this respect it is indirect linkage support to the SHGs. This model is quite common.

MODEL IV

Another model that has emerged is a combination of SHG linkage concept and credit programmes where loan assistance is given to the individual members of the group and not to the group. It is also not directly connected to the savings of the group. The loans in these cases were given only for income generating investment credit activities. The SHG and SHPI help the bank in identification, preparation of loan application, monitoring, supervision and recovery of loans.

Do's and Dont's in Linking Banks and Self Help Groups (SHGs)

The following list is taken from a pilot project initiated by India's National Bank for Agriculture and Rural Development (NABARD) on *Linking Banks with Self-Help Groups*. The project was started on the recommendation of Reserve Bank of India, the central bank for India. The list was part of a set of guidelines issued to all commercial banks soliciting their participation. While the list is aimed specifically at bank managers and other officials, there are a number of lessons to be learnt for people's groups, NGOs, and others involved in providing credit to low-income groups, not in the least a changing attitude apparent in the banking institutions in India.

Pilot Project for Linking Banks with self-help Groups (PPLBG)

- Treat the PPLBG as your own bank's programme or scheme
- Make use of the guidelines given by the National Bank but feel free to modify it to suit the local situation, type of target group, risks involved etc.
- Examine the guidelines carefully but don't disregard some of them without good reason (eg. guidelines regarding selection criteria of SHG, providing loans as a multiple of SHGs savings, providing loans of shorter maturity with on or very short grace period to begin with, etc.)
- Take your own initiative. Find your own NGO or SHG.

Prepare your Bank for PPLBG:

- Train the staff involved (branch managers, development manager for Agriculture etc) by deputing to training programmes conducted by the National Bank or to programmes specially designed by your own training colleges.

Selection of NGOs for collaboration

- Though the National Bank will select a few reputed NGOs for the PPLBG project, banks may also select NGOs which are capable of providing adequate guidance to SHGs.
- The NGO selected should meet the following criteria: (a) it should have a good track record; (b) a proper system of book-keeping and audited balance sheets for the last three years; (c) approach of promoting and working with groups of people belonging to weaker.

Selection of SHG for Linking

- The following criteria may be considered: (a) village government leader should not normally be the officer bearer or the leader of the SHG; (b) there should not be any interference from the local authority; (c) satisfactory internal savings and credit activity for at least six months; and (d) proper book keeping system and procedure for lending and savings.
- If any of these criteria are not met, steps should be taken to remedy the situation by training, by arranging visits to SHGs working well, etc., if necessary, with the assistance of an NGO.
- It would be prudent to select SHGs only from a smaller geographical area so as to provide effective guidance and exercise and exercise proper supervision.
- Banks may be required to provide training to members of SHGs in book keeping, financial management, income generating activities, etc. with the help of an NGO.
- No credit to SHG without training or before ensuring it has necessary capability to participate in the PPLBG.

Savings

- Internal savings mobilization is the core of Self-Help.
- External finance must not replace adequate self-financing and internal savings.
- Banks may provide proper guidance to stimulate savings of SHG.
- Savings First: All Credit must be preceded by savings

- Banks may consider covering members of the group under Group Insurance Scheme of an insurance company.

Use of loans for productive purposes

- Loans to SHGs for group enterprise are discouraged in the initial stages as they have generally failed. Exceptions should be very carefully examined and supervised.
- The purpose for which loans are to be given to the SHG should be determined by the SHG and its members.
- SHG should be strongly encouraged to use loans for productive purposes. Loans should normally not be used for non-productive purposes. However, internal savings of SHG may be used for meeting emergent needs of its members.

Loan ceilings

- There is no general recommendation concerning loan ceilings to SHGs
- In principle, loan ceilings should be based on estimated absorptive capacity which in turn is based on the capacity to save, invest and repay.

Ratio of savings and credit

- Banks may consider two alternatives. One, it provide loans to a SHG which is two times the savings of that SHG. This ratio can be increased to a maximum of 1:4 as the bank gains greater confidence on the SHG.
- Second, request a deposit of blocked savings before a loan is granted. To begin with, start with a conservative ratio of 1:1 or 1:2 of savings to credit depending upon the bank's assessment of risks involved. With satisfactory repayment, the ratio may be increased after each cycle, until the absorptive capacity of the group and its members have been reached.
- Under both the alternatives, it should be ensured that internal or blocked savings are genuine savings of the group and its members and it has not been borrowed from external sources.

Repayment Period

- Maturities should be differentiated and not uniform. Particularly, loans should not all be at the recommended maximum maturity.
- Shorter maturities have two advantages which should be strongly emphasized in consultation with NGOs, SHGs and members: (a) they are easier to handle and thus less risky, (b) they permit a more dynamic growth of the loan portfolio.
- First loans under PPLBG to NGOs, SHGs or members could have shorter maturities. Subsequent loans may have longer maturities if justified.

Lend first cycle of loans without a grace period

- First loans from banks or NGOs to SHGs and from SHGs to members should be without a grace period.
- Exceptions should be carefully examined. Even if a loan is used for agricultural purposes, borrowers usually have income from various sources which permit monthly repayments.
- If shorter grace periods (eg. one, two or three months) are given, the loan amount should be kept small.

Insist on timely repayment

- Banks, NGOs and SHGs must insist on timely repayments. This is to be strongly emphasized at the time of lending, during discussions prior to lending and in training programmes.
- Loans from banks or NGOs to SHGs and from SHGs to members must be repaid in regular installments.

Loan repayment installments

- Loans from banks to SHGs could be repaid normally in regular monthly installments or as determined at the time of floating loan based on local conditions, activities undertaken by members etc.
- Loans from SHGs to members should be repaid in appropriate installment which may be daily, weekly on market days, fortnightly, monthly etc.

Deliver credit publicly

- If possible, credit delivery to SHGs and members should be simultaneous and in public, i.e. during the regular meeting of the SHG.
- If this is not possible, credit delivery to a SHG should always be in the presence of several office bearers of the SHG and selected members, at least one or two of the major borrowers. A loan must never be handed over to a single representative of the group.

With the massive support from governmental and non-governmental agencies and the banking sector, the programme grew rapidly and, by March 2002, encompassed 4,61,000 SHG's, covering 40 million household members. Average loan sizes are Rs 22,240 per SHG and 1,300 per member. With its balanced emphasis on both savings and credit, it is the largest microfinance programme in the developing world. By the end of 2008, it is expected to cover a population of 100 million, which is one-third of India's rural poor. 209 commercial banks, 191 regional rural banks and 44 commercial banks are involved as SHG Banking partners, with 17,085 participating branches. According to the NABARD, at the end of March 2007, 2.92 million SHGs cumulatively received bank loans of Rs 180,410 million. There can be no doubt about the programme's outreach to the poor.

The Reserve Bank constituted four informal groups in October 2002 to examine various issues concerning micro-finance delivery. On the basis of the recommendations of the groups and as announced in the Governor's Statement on mid-term Review of the Monetary and Credit Policy for the year 2003-04, banks have been advised as under:

- Banks should provide adequate incentives to their branches in financing the Self Help Groups (SHGs) and establish linkages with them, making the procedures absolutely simple and easy while providing for total flexibility in such procedures to suit local conditions.
- The group dynamics of working of the SHGs may be left to themselves and need neither be regulated nor formal structures imposed or insisted upon.

- The approach to micro-financing of SHGs should be totally hassle-free and may include consumption expenditures.

Benefits of bank linkages:

The linkages between SHGs and banks have resulted in win-win situation for both. The following are the major benefits.

- Financing becomes cost effective According to a study conducted by NABARD, there has been a 40 per cent reduction in transaction cost for banks due to externalizing banks' responsibilities in identification of clients, assessment of risk profile, loan monitoring and recovery.
- Borrowing becomes cheaper. The borrowers' transaction cost declined by 85 per cent with doing away of complex documentation and procedures and opportunity cost of wage loss due to repeated visits to banks.
- Easy accessibility due to door step delivery of the credit.
- Credit is long-term and continuing in nature.
- Peer pressure and peer monitoring act as intangible collateral; consequently repayment rates are high.
- Avoidance of high cost intermediation between bankers and client by credit brokers.
- The sense of ownership of the programme due to community involvement. The people themselves take their credit decisions.
- Positive impact on the qualitative dimensions through empowerment.

Achievements:

Studies by different experts in the field of rural development have identified the major achievements stemming from the functioning of SHGs, some of which are:

- Augmentation in skills and abilities of women in various productive activities.
- Increase in participant's income, savings and consumption expenditure.

- Increased self-reliance and self-confidence have improved the ability of women to mobilize various public services for their benefit.
- Widening of the social horizons of the members.
- Sense of satisfaction and fulfillment as productive and important to the members of the family.
- Development of high self-esteem.
- Significant decline in gender-based problems such as domestic violence, dowry, polygamy etc.
- Promotion of women entrepreneurship.
- Extension of the reach of the government's welfare schemes among target groups. Women are emboldened to question the elected representatives and officials about developmental works, as a result of which rural areas are now developing at a faster pace.
- The high visibility of these benefits often and strongly motivates other women to form self help groups themselves.

Challenges

In spite of the obvious developments taking place, the working model needs attention on certain issues, which are challenging the fundamental objectives for which SHGs were identified. It is generally accepted that SHGs often do not include the poorest of the poor, for reasons such as: social factors, in which the existing caste system in rural areas restricts the collective action of people; economic factors, the poorest often do not have the financial resources to contribute to the savings and pay membership fees, they are often the one who migrate during the lean season, thus making group membership difficult. Efforts are being made to overcome this bias, e.g. through participatory wealth ranking at the community level, or by using indices to identify the poorest. But including them in SHGs is not enough. Programs need to be designed in such a way as to promote overall rural empowerment of a country. Many political parties and women's organisations have failed to recognise the potential of this power. While the multinational companies have more money power, these groups have within them the extensive market potential of their own families and communities. When organised effectively, this could prove to be a true challenge to counter the influx and influence of multinational companies in India.

Conclusion

SHGs today play a major role in poverty alleviation in rural India. Without empowerment there cannot be growth. However, a lesson learned from the experience is that even though SHGs can create many economic opportunities through micro credit, integrating their contributions with the social and economic infrastructure is imperative. SHGs must be market driven to sustain them in the long run. The SHGs should not become a numbers game and systems should ensure that they are viable. Today more than 12 lakhs SHGs are functioning. It is certain that the SHG movement is here to stay and it is going to grow stronger and stronger.

References

1. Prema Wilfred, The Power of Transformation: India's Self-Help Groups-Major
2. Y.S.Nanda, Significance of Establishing Linkages with Self-Help Groups and Banks, NABARD, India.
3. Hans Dieter Seibel & Harish Kumar R. Dave, Commercial aspects of SHG's and banking- Micro Credit Innovations Department, NABARD, Mumbai
4. Emerging Self-Help Groups–Instrument for Promoting Micro Credit System-Dilip Sarma Head, Resource Unit, Rashtriya Gramin Vikas Nigam Guwahati, Assam.
5. Role of self-help groups in empowerment of women , Rekha R. Gaonkar M.E.S.college of Arts & Commerce, Zuarinagar, Goa,-03726 , India
6. Do's and Dont's in Linking Banks and Self Help Groups (SHGs) Hari Srinivas,gdrc.org.

23

Managing Service Quality in Banks

* Dr. L. Lakshmi

INTRODUCTION

The banking sector in India has made remarkable progress since the economic reforms in 1991. New private sector banks have brought the necessary competition into the industry and spearheaded the changes towards higher utilization of technology, improved customer service and innovative products. In the present scenario of competitive banking, excellence in customer service is the most important tool for sustained business growth. Customer complaints are part of the business life of any corporate entity. This is more so for banks abuse banks are service organizations. As a service organization, customer service and customer satisfaction should be the prime concern of any bank. The bank believes that providing prompt and efficient service is essential only to attract new customers, but also to retain existing ones.

*Reader in Commerce, Sri Sarada College for Women (Autonomous) Salem 636016

Customers are now becoming increasingly conscious of their rights and are demanding more than ever before. The recent trends show that most banks are shifting from a product-centric model to a customer- centric model as customer satisfaction has become one of the major determinants of business growth. In this context, prioritization of preferences and close monitoring of customer satisfaction have become essential for banks. Because of the development of information technology and use of internet, every bank starts to setup its own homepage to provide internet service and gain the advantages of unlimited time, area, fewer cost and more customers from internet bank. The service quality is an important weapon for banks to compete. Service quality appears to emerge as the most significant and enduring strategy in ensuring the very survival of organizations. Hence, to manage service quality effectively, the test lies in how well the banking services handles, understands and knows the customers they served.

The complex nature of services coupled with the growing prominence of the services sector has also increased the need for better service quality. Customer satisfaction is another important aspect for service organizations and is highly related with service quality. As service quality improves, the probability of customer satisfaction increases, which in turn leads to customer retention, increased tolerance for service failures and positive word of mouth advertising about the organization. Currently banks are focusing their efforts on attracting new customers and stimulating economic spending by the introduction of credit cards, which allow customers to make a wide range of purchases on an installment basis. Bank customers also expect employees to be competent, courteous, to provide prompt service and to be always willing to help the customer.

SERVICE QUALITY (SERVQUAL)

Service quality is defined as the degree of alignment between customer expectations and their perceptions of the service received. It works as an antecedent of customer satisfaction. In past, quality was measured only for the tangible products because of less dominance of service sector in the economy. Due to the increasing importance of service sector in the economy, the meaning of service quality became important. Many possible comparison standards including predicted service, ideal service, excellent service, desired service, deserved service, needs and values, cultural norms, promises, adequate service, best brand norm, product type norm, favorite brand model, comparative expectations, equity and fairness are available. However, SERVQUAL only incorporates a rough aggregated mixture of a selection of these. As applicable to banking, quality may be defined as the ability to satisfy the customer's requirements and needs to the fullest and to be able to replicate this on an on-going basis.

DIMENSIONS OF SERVICE QUALITY

The quality of service is measured by the following dimensions:

1. **Tangibility**-The physical appearance of the facilities, staffs, buildings etc.

2. **Reliability**-The ability to reproduce the same level of service again and again.

3. **Responsiveness**-The speed with which queries etc. are dealt with.

4. **Communication**-The clarity and understandability of the information given to the client.

5. **Credibility**-The trustworthiness of the service provider.

6. **Security**-The physical safety of the customer or privacy of client information.

7. **Competence**-The actual technical expertise of the service provider.

8. **Courtesy**-The attitude of the service provider and manner adopted by the server.

9. **Understanding**-How well the provider of the service under stands the client's needs.

10. **Access**-How easy is it to reach the service provider, geographically or by phone.

SERVICE QUALITY IN BANKS

Five factors for assessing the services of a bank emerged, as follows.

- **Relationship with the customer**, that is, attributes of the relationship between the bank and the customer during service fulfillment;
- **Business and financial transactions**, that is, attributes of the ultimate purpose of the bank, that of collecting financial resources from customers, making investments and distributing financial benefits to customers and shareholders;
- **Information technology**, that is, how IT supports the customer in his/her needs in services;
- **Branch**, that is, attributes of the physical environment where services are performed, like comfort and easiness of access for the customer; and
- **Image**, that is, how the bank presents itself to the community responsiveness is the most critical dimension of service quality.

Parasuraman and Zeithaml's SERVQUAL includes five **dimensions** of service that are relevant for measuring the service quality of banks by its clients. The dimensions are **reliability** (ability to perform the promised service, dependably and accurately), **tangibility** (physical facilities, equipment and appearance of personnel), **responsiveness** (willingness to help customers and provide prompt service), **assurance** (knowledge and courtesy of employees and their ability to inspire trust and confidence) and **empathy** (caring individualized attention the service provider gives its customers).

QUALITY PLANNING

The art of setting a corporate vision and focusing resources and energy on quality goals will propel the bank toward its vision of customer-driven, quality service. Quality planning requires that corporate activities reflect customer needs that products and services are designed to meet those needs, and that systems are customer-friendly.

Business plans must include quality, customers' needs, and the importance of continuous improvement, or banks cannot build a solid foundation for total quality management. Total quality management must be incorporated and connected to the corporate battery. After asking key internal and external questions and developing assumptions on which banks can base action plans, management must move from strategic planning to business planning. Quality business plans help us develop and run our business. Quality of products and services planning helps develop specific products and services designed to satisfy customers' needs and obtain competitive advantage. Quality of products and services makes the difference to customers, including service, as they perceive it, before, during, and after the sale. Banks must research target customers and their needs. After determining features, the bank should decide how it will measure the successful application of those features and compare those features to the competition. After research is completed and the product or service is ready for implementation, bank management must reveal it to the entire organization, before entering the market.

Far too many banks organize for their own internal efficiency or effectiveness. The bank's structure benefits systems and procedures, not customers. Banks must focus on why customers visit a bank, and the customers' view of the organization must dictate how to structure the bank and how processes are designed. It should be a pleasurable experience dealing with the bank, not an unpleasant road trip with roadblocks, detours, and dead-ends.

THE QUALITY KEY

Quality is especially important in the banking sector because duplication of products and services is relatively easy. Further, differentiation of products is difficult of hazy. Thus, quality becomes the only differentiator and the key to continuing success.

With increasing competition, banks that survive and succeed will be the one that provide quality service. Research studies have repeatedly proved that customers are willing to pay for quality service. Banks that wish to succeed and stay ahead must, therefore, systematically build a structure that aims at providing Total Quality Service. As with the bank's financial goals, success can be achieved only with proper analysis and suitable goals.

TOP MANAGEMENT COMMITMENT

Quality is a primary responsibility of top management and quality measures can only succeed with top management's commitment. Without commitment from top management, quality will remain a peripheral and possibly non-productive activity. Besides lack of management commitment could lead to service gaps or cause service gaps to widen. Quality must be a management priority. Igniting the explosion of quality leadership in a company means repositioning quality from a secondary to a primary management role. Quality service comes from inspired leadership. Employees and managers at all levels look to top executives to set an example and a tone for the rest of an organization.

Top management must foster a general awareness that quality improvement will take its place as equal in importance to traditional cost, profit, growth, and sales goals. Hence, it may be emphasized that, for any quality culture to exist and quality consciousness to develop, top management support and commitment are absolutely essential. Once the top management is convinced that quality is essential for the success and continued growth of the organization, it can begin to help the bank develop suitable quality programmes. Commitment must be backed by planned action, all employees must be trained to develop quality consciousness and an organization must continually strive to improve the quality of services provided. Senior management should clearly communicate its commitment and detailed implementation plans to all employees. A core cross-functional group may be formed that would help top management implement the Quality Action Plan. Middle and junior level employees will only be committed to quality programmes if they believe that it is important and to ensure this communication should be regularly maintained through meetings internal newsletters, formal feedback, etc.

Merely appointing a Quality Manager and organizing a few random quality programmes can lead to little or no improvement. In fact, a poorly implemented quality programme can result in loss of faith in the utility of such measures and employees may begin to regard this as just another chore or management's latest fad which will soon pass. Top management must explain and communicate to all levels of employees that quality is not an one-time job and is not about fixing problems, say, an irate bank customer who has been waiting to be attended to. The management must communicate that these problems arise because of the absence of quality consciousness and will continue to arise if quality is not ingrained as an accepted business norm. Quality is, as the Quality gurus say, a journey. A journey that continues as the bank achieves higher and higher levels of success. Once top management can successfully communicate this to all employees and ensure their commitment, the bank can successfully implement and reap the benefits of achieving high service quality.

EMPLOYEE EMPOWERMENT

A bank's employees are inherent part of the service provided by the bank. It is not enough that they can be trained to prove quality service, that they must know what to do and how to do it. It is also essential that they have the requisite authority to do what it takes to satisfy, customers, and a corresponding responsibility towards ensuring customer satisfaction. Top management may be totally committed in providing total quality service, but ultimate it is the employees who will actually interact with customers and provide them with the various banking services on an on-going basis. It is therefore essential that

- The employees be committed foro providing total quality service
- Employees be suitably trained and motivated and
- Employees are empowered to deliver quality service to customers.

To do this, the bank must first ensure that it recruits people who are suited ino providing quality customer service. They must have good team skill and a strong customer service and this should be a part of the bank's culture. They must be given authority, commensurate with their experience, to deal with their customers in the way they consider most beneficial to the bank. This will also encourage employees to identify common customer problems and find new ways of dealing with the situation in the best possible way.

Though employee empowerment is necessary, by itself it can only work to a somewhat limited extent in the banking industry. Though financial decision making has to be organized along structured lines for most levels of a bank's employees, non-financial empowerment can help to provide job enrichment and motivate employees to give their best. For example, a group of employees who individually handle a product, say, issuance of drafts, cheques, etc. may be given the group responsibility of handling the product n totality. From each person having individual responsibility towards a part of the task, the whole group has the total responsibility of delivering the product to the satisfaction of the customer. Along with the responsibility, the group, which may have a group leader, has the power to sanction leave to group members, permit flexi time schedules to employees who wish avail to it and permit interchangeability of roles within the group's members to see the totality of their efforts and the totality of the products they offer. They can see their collective efforts fructifying into customer satisfaction.

Since they can see what they are delivering, how they are delivering and to what extent the customer is satisfied as a result of their efforts, they can also recognize shortcomings and directly improve their services without the need of external supervision. This result in several benefits to the employees and the bank job content is improved, the job is broadened and thereby enriched. Employees' sense of self-worth improves, their sense of belonging to the bank improves and they are motivated to deliver quality service. Working in a group also helps them to develop better team skills and learn to shoulder collective responsibility–if the group grants leave to an employee, the remaining members have to take up the work load of that member. In the process, the employees also see how their individual contributions matter, how their fragmented jobs add up to a whole product and how their best efforts can really make a difference. Thus, employee empowerment can be amongst the best motivation rather than an external one and can help the employees to deliver quality banking services to their customers.

Employee empowerment is necessary but it is not a sufficient one for providing quality banking services. A bank must, however, ensure that this does not hamper its employees from delivering quality service. Empowered employees will take pride in their work and will suggest solution to difficulties necessary for a bank to equal the performance standards set by the selected leader. A bank may for example, decide that it wishes to improve its process up to a certain pre-determined point, based on its own plans, or it may decide to improve in steps.

BANKING SERVICES-TECHINICAL QUALITY AND FUNCTIONAL QUALITY

Service Quality can be thought of as having two dimensions: Technical quality and Functional quality. Technical Quality refers to 'what' the bank gives the customer. Functional Quality refers to 'How' the bank's services are provided to the customer.

Technical Quality

- The bank must ensure that its products and services are closely aligned with Customer needs.
- Customers are adequately informed about the bank's products and services
- The bank's front-line staff, has thorough knowledge of the bank's products and services .
- The bank's staff has been adequately communicate with customer queries
- The bank's staff is able to provide professional advice to its customers
- The bank's front -line staff, has been adequately trained to deal with 'difficult' customers and with customer complaints.

QUALITY TRAINING PROGRAMMES

Once the bank has decided on achieving high service quality, suitable training programmes should be introduced and all members of staff should get an opportunity to participate in these programmes. Such programmes should preferably be tailor-made to suit the bank's needs and should be preferably administered by experts. The success of these programmers cannot be immediately gauged completely, but the progress on various quality parameters should be regularly monitored, perhaps by an internal coordinator.

Functional Quality

Functional quality is concerned with how the service is provided to the bank's customer. A few elements that affect a banking service's functional quality include:

- Attitude of the bank's staff members
- Importance given to the bank's customers over routine work.
- Perceived credibility of the bank's officials to customer queries
- Ambience at the bank

- Ability to hold discussions with senior officials with a suitable degree of privacy
- Image of the bank as a whole

A bank must be equipped to deliver both technical and functional quality thus ensuring that it provides its customers with total quality service. A bank could set up appropriate policies and procedures, for example recruitment policies, to create enabling conditions for providing technical and functional quality to its customers. The ultimate focus should firmly be on providing quick and cost-effective quality banking services.

ORGANISATIONAL STRUCTURE

At the core of any structure is the customer. The wants, needs, and expectations of the customer must be the focal point for the bank. The key to the "right" organizational structure and the delivery of quality service is the business process. An ineffective business process ignores the internal and external customer, and an inefficient business process wastes valuable resources. A business process is a series of work activities that produce a service. To improve the different business processes within the bank, emphasis should focus on the customer, and departments should mobilize to provide for service as required by the customer. In both business process and organizational structure, people are the keys to success. In reviewing both aspects of the process, banks must manage change and provide support and guidance. Organizational structure and business processes are critical elements in the total quality management strategy. People, with management support, must change the way they view the customer if the process is to succeed in exceeding customer expectations. People in the front line are most often aware of quality needs of customers and can offer valuable suggestions. Banks should actively encourage all level of staff to contribute actively towards building a learning bank.

BRANCH PREMISES AND CUSTOMER LOUNGES

Is the branch easy to reach? Are the branch premises pleasing and comfortable? Are the customer lounges well maintained? Are there sufficient sofas for waiting customers? Is drinking water available to customers? Is there adequate reading material? Is the reading materials stock regularly updated? Is there sufficient variety of reading matter available? Does the reading matter conform to the reading tastes of the bank's customers? Are the customer lounges being adequately used to highlight the bank's achievements etc? Do customers look lost on entering the branch of is help readily available? Are the security personnel courteous and watchful?

ATM - Is the ATM conveniently located? Is it easy to access? Is there adequate parking space available? Are the ATM premises well maintained? Are writing material, deposit envelopes, etc. easily available? Is the security person polite and helpful? Is the ATM frequently 'not working' on holidays etc? Are the ATM premises being suitable used for the bank's publicity? Is the ATM easy to use? Is there help available to customers who may need it? Are the facilities offered at the ATM on par with the facilities offered by other banks?

TECHNOLOGY

Has the bank adopted relevant technology best suited to its customers' needs? Are the staff members adequately trained to use the bank's technology systems to better serve customers? How does the bank compare with others in the industry? Does the bank continuously upgrade its IT systems? Is training available to employees who may need them? Is there a suitable Disaster Management system in place? Is the troubleshooting team equipped to handle minor problems?

SENSITISING OPERATING STAFF ON HANDLING COMPLAINTS

The role of employees is critical to the success of any quality process. Total quality management is a people intensive process for delighting customers. To make total quality management work, banks must select the right people, train them effectively, recognize and reward them, and provide them with strong leadership. Communication is critical-open and honest communication. Satisfied employees enhance customer satisfaction. "Employees are the key to customer satisfaction, and customer satisfaction is key. Staff should be properly trained for handling complaints. We are dealing with people and hence difference of opinion and areas of friction can arise. With an open mind and a smile on the face we should be able to win the customer's confidence. The bank should then evolve suitable training programmes to ensure that there is no effort lacking on the bank's part in equipping the selected candidates to perform their duties satisfactorily.

Before a bank can embark on a total quality strategy, it is crucial for top management to set the stage. Quality improvement takes on many forms, but it must start with support and resources committed by top management. Management pronouncements must be clear, significant, and visible; otherwise, everyone will perceive quality as "just another corporate program that will pass. Quality service comes from inspired leadership, a customer-driven corporate culture, employee involvement, and effective use of systems and technology; all of which develop slowly. Quality service starts with top management commitment, action, and involvement. Once top management commits to quality at the bank, the quality process can start and the percentage of success increases.

ENSURING CUSTOMER SATISFACTION

The best way to determine what satisfies the customer is to ask the customer. Several organizations regularly send out questionnaires and direct mailers to their customers (both internal and external), analyze the feedback received and initiate appropriate action. Customer', who is central to the banking service, is not a homogeneous class. They come from varying socio-economic and cultural backgrounds.

The perception of the Quality of Banking Services provided will differ from customer to customer and even for the same customer at different points of time, depending on the mood and mind-set of the same user at a particular point of time. A customer who needs money and comes to an ATM on a Sunday and find that it is not working, is likely to be much more dissatisfied than if she or he were to find the same ATM temporarily out of order on a day when they happen to have popped in to the ATM on their way to work. Some other factors that may influence perceptions of banking service quality are:

- Overall ambience at the bank
- Past experiences with the bank
- Familiarity with the services offered by the bank
- Knowledge of or experience with competitors products and services
- Banking with a particular bank which may be regarded as a status symbol
- Interaction with and or opinions of other customers' rights etc.

For example a bank's Customer Service Standards may stipulate that all incoming phone calls be answered within three rings, all queries be attended to within five minutes, no call be transferred more than twice, all messages be recorded and communicated to the concerned person/ department within thirty minutes, etc. Today, it is estimated that there are over 1500 banking websites, with the growing importance of the internet; banks will have to formulate standards for internet interface also. These could be, for example all queries to be answered on e-mail within 12 hours and to be followed up with written communication within 24 hours, etc. Where there is direct interface with the bank's employees, it must be ensured that all customers go back with a sense of satisfaction. Many banks have set standards- for example, not more than three people should be waiting in a queue at any counter, all in a queue should be deposed off in 3 minutes, all deposits should be accepted and receipt issued in 10 minutes, etc.

MEASURING SERVICE QUALITY

Measuring quality in the services sector and in particular in the Banking sector is more difficult than measuring the quality of manufactured goods. This is mainly due to the following reasons. The services sector as a whole is very heterogeneous and what is very heterogeneous and what may hold true for one service may not hold true for another service sector. For example, the nature of banking services is very different from, say, the nature of services provided by an airline or a hotel. Even within banking there are a variety of dissimilar services like retail banking, commercial banking, investment banking etc. This heterogeneity makes standardized service quality measurement very difficult. Services are intangible in nature and, unlike in the case of goods, there is no 'real' product that the customer takes home. This is true of banking services and most other financial services where the service offered is only what the customer experiences fleetingly. There is no scope for inspection before the service delivered. All services have a here-and-now attribute that makes standardized quality testing and control procedures followed by manufacturing sector difficult to adopt. Unlike a good manufacturer, a bank cannot inspect its services and products to weed out unsatisfactory ones before they are presented to the customer.

MONITORING

Quality control charts can be used to ensure tracked regularly and any significant deviations are reported to top management, analyzed and rectified. Thus, suitable quantitative measures and policies should be designed to sustain continuous quality improvement in all area of functioning. The Bank must then implement the benchmarking programme under the guidance of the cross functional benchmarking team. It must monitor progress, calibrate performance and ensure that it is as per the plans formulated by the bank. We now have an India Benchmarking Centre

(IBC) the first of its kind in the world. Many banks committed in providing quality services, are now members of the IBC.

QUALITY AWARD

A logical progression for a bank that has a service quality approach to business is to get an ISO 9001/2 certification. ISO 9001/2 signifies continued commitment to quality. A bank wishing to get ISO 9001/2 certification would have to document all systems procedures in details. This requires time, effort and commitment. All functional heads and branch heads at the bank must be convinced of the need benefit of an ISO 9000 series certification. Banks can also compete for various quality awards. Even if a bank does not win, this can help the bank measure where it stands and how far it needs to go. Quality awards encourage excellence and foster a competitive spirit.

QUALITY ASSURANCE

Banks must strive to assure quality, that is, be able to affirm with adequate certainty that their products and services will satisfy given requirements of quality. Banks cannot be content with quality control. They must go beyond that and should strive to strive to give quality assurance. Some banks in India have experimented with service guarantees on deposit products, etc. But these have met with only moderate success. Quality awareness is now on the rise, and in the future we may see more and more attention being paid to assuring quality in banking products and services. The SBI has already taken a progressive step by formulating certain customer bills of rights, etc. and increasingly focus organization.

GUIDELINES FOR QUALITY SERVICE

The following are the guidelines for quality service.

- Ensure that the branch premises are comfortable and pleasing

- Ensure that front-line staff is knowledgeable and can adequately handle customer queries
- Train staff to be courteous and polite
- Ensure that customers are treated as individuals and are given utmost priority-especially over routine work that staff may have.
- Ensure that staff is trained to handle all companies in a non- confrontation list manner
- Encourage front-line staffs, who is directly dealing with customers, to suggest various quality improvement measures
- Ensure that ATM sites are well maintained
- Ensure that ATM is working at all items
- Ensure that a helpline is available from the ATM centre
- Ensure that deposit envelopes and writing materials are available at the ATM center
- Ensure that feedback is regularly sought from customers and acted upon suitably
- Let the customers know at one time what documentation is required to process loans
- Ensure that all letters of credit, guarantees, etc. are issued on time
- Explain all rates, terms and condition , etc. in simple terms, especially in the case of retail loans
- Address all queries promptly
- Ensure that names of senior executives are known to customers who may want to write to them
- Attempt to ensure transparent procedures within the organisation itself. Ensure that all systems and procedures are scrupulously adhered to and all deviations are promptly brought to the notice of the top management.

THE FUTURE

As competition increases, quality will become the only true differentiator. Successful banks will be those that compete on quality. We must realize that competing on price means we are dependent on what the competition is doing for our success. Banks that wish to surge ahead successfully into the new millennium would need to ingrain a quality culture. Every aspect of the bank's functioning would have to be governed by the quality principles. As we head into the new millennium, technology will be the backbone of many aspects of our lives. In India, also, most of the banks with their state-of -the -art technology have been able to provide superior service. ATMs help customers reach the bank even after closing hours. In the future, too, banks that wish to provide quality service will have to make investments in technology. Technology can help banks deliver superior service and provide better Management Information Systems and Decision Support Systems. Technology can help banks better analyze and manage various risks, and this will become increasingly important in tomorrow's global market.

The customer is a customer of the Bank and not merely of a particular branch of the Bank. This pioneering service, anywhere banking, has now become almost a necessity for companies across the length and breadth of the country. This is true innovation and will be the hallmark of the banks that will lead. Therefore, all the banks remains committed for providing technology-backed quality service to its customers and in building a service quality approach to banking.

FACING CHALLENGES

Today's banking institutions face pressure from all sides. They wrestle their competition for razor-thin margins on increasingly commoditized products and strive to control operational costs, all while required to comply with a formidable number of regulations. Savvy banking institutions are learning that to compete and win in such a business environment, they must embrace new operating models, focus on business innovations and take advantage of the most recent developments in IT. Many are transforming their business and IT infrastructures in an effort to create flexible, easily deployed architectures that integrate data and business processes from across the enterprise, as well as from key partners and clients.

Unfortunately, decades of IT evolution, not to mention mergers and acquisitions, have left most banking services companies with IT infrastructures that are fragmented, widely distributed, and increasingly complex. Furthermore, efforts to improve and maintain older core banking solutions can lead to greater problems or even jeopardize the security of transactions and databases.

CONCLUSION

Many banking institutions still face significant obstacles when migrating their back-office operations into the 21st century, even as the business pain-points are significant and require immediate improved agility. The new IBM* Worldwide Banking Center of Excellence can help transform their back-office processes and databases to solutions that reduce risk, time to completion and project costs. The center engages with clients by providing initial technical design, application prototyping, and benchmarking activities for use cases aimed at providing unique value propositions in the areas of high performance, continuous availability, global banking, security, disaster recovery, virtualization and innovation.

Commercial banks need to employ a customer management solution that consolidates information from all customer interactions, whether they are in-person meetings with advisors or inquiries to the call center or the Internet. Moving forward, it will be imperative that every banking representative has the ability to access a 360-degree view of any customer in real time to enhance customer retention and competitive advantage.

REFERENCES

1. Asubonteg, P., McCleary, K.G., Swan, J.E. (1996), "SERVQUAL revisited: a critical review of service quality", Journal of Services Marketing, Vol. 10 No.6, pp.62-81.
2. Babakus, E., Boller, G.W. (1992), "An empirical assessment of the SERVQUAL scale", Journal of Business Research, Vol. 24 No.3, pp.253-68.
3. Berry, L.L., Parasuraman, A. (1991), Marketing Services – Competing through Quality, Free Press, Macmillan, New York, NY., .
4. Berry, L.L., Zeithaml, V.A., Parasuraman, A. (1985), "Quality counts in services too", Business Horizons, Vol. 31 No.5, pp.46.
5. Gilmore, A., Carson, D. (1992), "Research in service quality: have the horizons become too narrow?", Marketing Intelligence & Planning, Vol. 10 No.7, pp.5-7..
6. Kotler, P., Armstrong, G. (1991), Principles of Marketing, 5th ed., Prentice-Hall, Englewood Cliffs, NJ., .
7. Parasuraman, A., Zeithaml, V.A., Berry, L.L. (1985), "A conceptual model of service quality and its implications for future research", Journal of Marketing, Vol. 49 pp.41-50.
8. Rust, R.T., Zahoric, A.J., Keiningham, T.L. (1994), "Return on quality (ROQ), making service quality financially accountable", Journal of Marketing, Vol. 59 pp.58-70.

24

Self – Help Group and Bank Linkage

*S. Palaniammal

Self Help Group has been organized by the NGO's in the rural areas. Rural women not less than 10 in number become members and their savings are either circulated among themselves or deposited in a bank which is utilised by the members so as to solve their financial problems. Their services include creation of awareness about sanitation, protection of drinking water, wasteland development, etc. harvesting. A Self-Help –Group (SHG) may be a registered or unregistered group of micro entrepreneurs having homogenous social and economic background voluntarily, coming together to save small amount regularly, to mutually agree to contribute to a common fund and to meet their emergency needs on mutual help basis. The group members have collective wisdom and peer pressure to ensure end –use of credit and timely

*Lecturer in Commerce, Anbu Arts and Science College, Komarapalayam

repayment thereof. In fact, peer pressure has been recognized as an effective substitute for collaterals.

SHG - ORGIN

The concept of SHG serves to underline the principles "for the people, by the people and of the people." The SHG is the brain child of gramean bank & Bangladesh, which was founded by prof, Mohammed yunas of Chitlagung University in the year 1975. The SHG sheme was introduced in Tamil Nadu in 1989.

CONCEPT OF SHGS

- SHGs are a small group of rural poor, who have voluntarily come forward to form a group for improvement of the social and economic status of the members.
- It can be formal (registered) or informal.
- The concept underlines the principle of Thrift, credit and self. Help.
- Members of SHG agree to save regularly and contribute to a common fund.
- The members agree to this common found and such other found (like grant and loans form banks),which they may receive as a group, to give small loans to needy members as per the decision of the group

SHG BANK LINKAGE

Indian is notable for the self-help group (SHG) bank linkage movement which has helped to bring financial service to large numbers of poor people. SHGs are members-owned and controlled financial services enterprises, providing saving and credit services to their members. They usually distribute their profit to members and they facilitate member's access to education and training. Micro co-operatives are linked to bigger financial institutions to keep their saving and provide add ional capital for on lending to members, SHGs have increasingly been seen as good asbusiness for bank–they are a source of deposits and reliable at repaying loans.

Year	March03	March04	March05	March06
SHGs liked (financial)	1,02,553	1,74,666	3,43,691	5,40,481
No.of Beneficiaries	12,33,660	21,50,752	48,11,674	75,68,,842
Amount Disbursed	324.84cr.	614.87cr.	1311.45cr.	2262.95cr.
Amount Out standing	269.43cr.	462.77cr.	872.08cr.	1459.89cr.
No. of SHGs Maintaining Saring A/C in The Bank	2,76,466	3,69,568	5,08,0396	6,36,067
(Amount in Rs) Amountinsaring A/C	261.36cr.	348.31cr.	411.82cr.	434.07cr.

The most widespread financial service providers in rural are of India are co-operatives. There are over 93,000 primary socities,served by 367 district co-operative banks with 12000 branches and there is a further tier of state level apex co-operative banks. They co-operatives, however, have a relatively small share of SHG business. This paper examines why this is and argues many primary societies have extremely poor loan repayment records, often below 50% and this could be improved by taking on more reliable business which the SHGS represent.

STEADY GROWTH IN SHG – BANK CREDIT LINKAGE PROGRAMME

SBI has actively participated is SHG – Bank credit linkage programme since its inception in 1992 as a pilot project of NABARD. Since then, the Bank has made a steady progress financing SHGs. As on march 2006, SBI's branches spread through the length and breadth of the contery have opened 6,30,067 saving Bank account of SHGs out of which more than 5.41 lakhs SHGs have been provided with credit facilities thus benefiting more then 75 lakhs poor people. Majority of these SHGs are women SHGs. The year wise cumulative position of SHGs - Bank linkage programme for the last 4 years as under:

Latest Micro Credit Disbursement Indicators

With a view to facilitating smoother and more meaningful banking with the poor, A pilot project for purveying micro cried by liking self -help Group (SHGs) with bank was launched by NABARD In 1991-92 with a view to facilitating smoother and more meaningful banking with the poor. RBI had then advised commercial banks to actively participate in this linkages programme. The scheme has since been extended to RRBs and co-operative bank . The number of SHGs linked to banks aggregated 4,61,478 as on march 31,2002. This translates into an estimate of 7.87 million very poor families brought within the fold of formal banking services as on march 31,2002 more than 90 per cent of the group linked with banks are exclusive women group, cumulative disbursement of bank loans to these SHGs stood at Rs. 1026.34 crores as on march 31,2002 with an average loan of Rs. 22,240 per SHG and Rs.1316 per family. As regards model -wise linkage, while model I, viz, directly to SHGs without intervention / facilitation of any NGO now account for 16% model II viz, directly to SHGs with facilitation by NGOs and other formal agencies amount to 75% and model III,viz. through NGO as facilitator and financing agency represent 09% of the total linkage while 488 districts in all the states / UTs have been covered under this programme, 444 bank including 44 commercial banks (including 17 in the private sector), 191 RRBs and 209 co-operative banks along with 2,155 NGOs are now associated with the SHG-bank linkage programme.

REPAYMENT PERIOD

Loans are repayable in monthly installments from 24to60 months.

INTEREST RATE

The percent of interest rate structure is Rs 9.25% p.a

BANKING RATING SYSTEM "MAIN POCAB COVERD"

- Composition of group.
- Age of groups.
- No. of meeting per month.
- Attendance of meeting by members.
- Maintenance of minute's book
- Participation of members in discussion

SECURITY

SHGs might not be in a position to offer any collateral security and classified loans under the "Advances to weaker Security".

PROGRESS OF SHG - LINKAGE

Received Best performance Award from NABARD in 2004. Every year bank is financing to 30,000 groups. Foreign Investor started in Micro Credit Project Govt.of India Vidal their notification date August 29,2000 have included in the lite of perm fled non-banking financial company (NBFC) activates for being consiclered for foreign direct Investment (FDI/Over seas) rportate bodice (OCB)/NON Rercelent Idians ((NRO) Investment to encourage foreign putridly in milso credit facility at milso level for provider finance to small produced and small micro enterprises in rural and urban areas.

BANK LENDING TO SELF –HELP GROUPS ON THE RISE

Micro-financing is gaining in importance in banks' lending programmes, Financing through self-help groups (SHGs) receive an impetus last year with banks more than doubling loan disbursements through such groups. As on March 31,2002, banks had distributed Rs. 1,026.3 crore to more than 4.6 lakh SHGs at an average of Rs. 22,240 per group. On the corresponding date a year ago, the disbursement stood at Rs. 480 crore at an average of Rs. 18,227 per group to 2.6 lakh SHGs is that banks see in lending to SHGs is that the loans fetch market rates but chances of default are very low. The repayment rate has been consistently above 95per cent over the past decade of SHGs-Bank Linkage Programme started by the National Bank for agriculture and rural development (Nabard) in 1992.

Self-help groups are a group of about 20 people from a homogenous class, who come together for addressing their common problems. They use their pooled resources to make small interest bearing loans to members. Banks being to lend, without collateral, to the groups once they mature in their financial behavior. According to NABARD data, under the SHG-Bank Linkage programme, the decade-old initiative has reached 78-lakh poor families comprising nearly four crore very poor people. The average loan per family has increased to Rs 1,316 from Rs1,0,72 a year ago.

During the last fiscal year, 1.97 lakh SHGs were added to the growing list of beneficiaries. While the four southern states of Andhra Pradesh, Tamil Nadu, Karnataka and Kerala accounted for the bulk of them (1,29,429SHGs) individually, Andhra Pradesh led the pack with 75,939 new SHGs financed.

Rural employment scheme to get Rs. 14,300 crores:

With a view in combating rural unemployment and poverty, Union Finance Minister P.Chidambaram on Tuesday (28.02.2006 passed on g3eneral budget) announced Rs.14300 crores for rural employment, and Rs.11,300 crores (including the north eastern region component) will be utilized under the National Rural Employment Guarantee (NREG) scheme and Rs.3000 crores is to be spent on the Sampoorna Grameen Rozar Yojana (SGRY). A massive allocation of the funds – to the tune of Rs.3,825.73 crores – is proposed for the Panchajdi Raj ministry. The ministry Revised budget for 2005 - 06 was Rs.50.49 crores. A bulk of this allocation goes to the nearly created backward regions fund

Selp-Help Groups

According to NABARD, almost 3 million SHGs have linked to near 500 banks since the program started, reaching over 11 million households across.

SHG Federations

Some NGOS such s MYRADA and Dhan Foundation have promote federation. These apex institutions aggregate savings from SHGs are act as intermediaries between financial institutions and SHGs. SHG Federations were envisioned as an exit strategy for the promoting agencies and a means of ensuring SHG sustainability. However, ability to mobilize sustained financial resources and the institutional capacity to run without the promoting agency's support.

Estimating the Annual Microfinance Demand in India

Assuming the entire poor population of India is potential microfinance clientele, the market size for microfinance in India is in the range of 58 to 77 million client demand of USD5.7 to 19.1 (INR 230 to 773 billion) assuming loan size between USD 100 and 250. If we assume that the low-income but economically active population including small and marginal farmers, landless agricultural labourers, and micro-entrepreneurs, are also potential microfinance client, the annual credit demand goes further up to an estimated 245.7 million individuals and USD51.4 billion (INR 2.1 trillion) in annual on -lending requirements.

Financing Strategies

Commercial bank, regional rural bank (RRBs) and cooperative banks primarily fund the SHG-Bank Linkage Programme, and NABARD in turn them. Credit lines to SHGs are critical limited, as they are based on a certain multiple of SHG members' savings accounts within banks. While the cumulative saving of SHGs could serve as a low-cost source of funds for on lending, their potent in is limited by the lack of aggregate savings across SHGs. Commercial equity investments are not available to for SHGs due to their informal status.

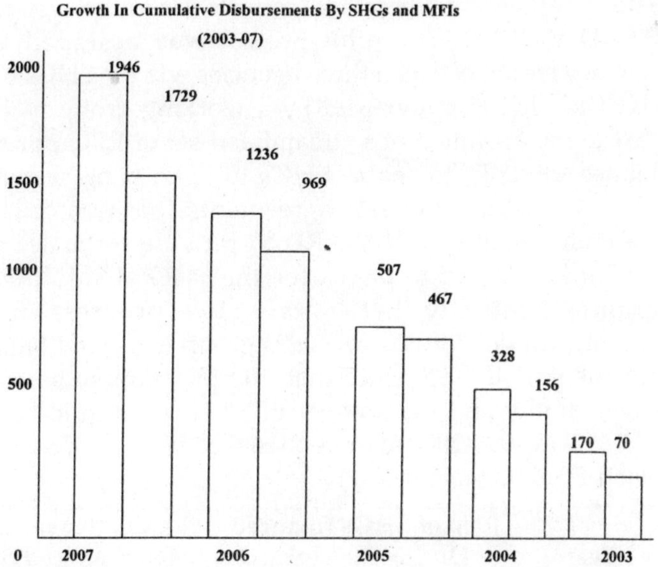

Figure 24.1: *Growth In Cumulative Disbursements By SHGs and MFIs*

Selp-Help GROUP – Bank Linkage Model

The SHG –Bank Linkage Programme is a major plank of the of the strategy for delivering financial services to the poor in a sustainable manner. The search for such alternative stared with internal introspection regarding the innovations which the poor had been traditionally making to meet their financial services needs. It was observed that the poor tended to come together in a Varity of informal way for pooling their savings and dispending small and unsecured loans at varying costs to group members on the basis of need. The SHG–Bank Linkage Progarmme was started as an Action research project in 1989 which was the offshoot of a NABARD initiative during 1987 through sanctioning Rs.10 lakh to MYRADA as seed money assistance for experimenting CRITID MANAGEMENT GROUPS. In the same year the ministry of rural development provided PRADAN with support to establish self -help group in Rajasthan.

The experiences of these early efforts led to the a pilot by NABARD IN 1992. The pilot project was designed as a partnership model between three agencies, viz the SHGs bank and NGOs. This was reviewed by a working group in 1995 that led to the evolution of a streamlined set of RBI approved guidelines to banks to enable SHGs to open bank accounts, based on a simple "interest" agreement. This was coupled with a commitment by NABARD to provide refinance and promotional support to banks for the SHG -Bank linkage programme. Initially there was a slow progress in the programme up to 1999 as only 32,995 group were credit linked during the period 1992. since then the programme has been growing rapidly and the number of SHGs finance increased from 81,780 in 1999-2000 to more than 6.20 lash in 2005-06 and 6.87 lash 2006-07(table below)

Year	No.of SHGs financed During the year (in lakh)	Cumulative no. of SHGs financed (in lakh)
2001-02	1.98	4.61
2002-03	2.56	7.17
2004-05	3.62	10.79
2005-06	5.39	16.18
2006-07	6.20	22.38
2007-08	6.87	29.25

NABARD, in association with GTZ, conducted a study, in 2005, on the comparative performance of SHG - Bank Linkage programme vis-à-vis other priority sector credit. The finding based on the data received from 27 commercial banks, 192 RRBs and 114 cooperative banks participated in the programme. One of the important observations of the study was that 1.44 million SHGs had saving accounts with the banks and the savings outstanding was Rs. 2,391 crore.

To cover all the 50 million odd poor households in India, the existing number of SHGs will have to be more than double and the extent of credit to the members of each SHG will have to be increased substantially.

Positive Features of the SHG – Bank Linkage Programme

The financial inclusion attained through SHGs is sustainable on account of it various positive features. The prgramme confronts many challenges and for further scaling up, these challenges need to be addressed.

Financial Inclusion of Poor Women

The committee noted that more than 90%of the members SHGs are women and most of them are poor and asset less. The SHG movement has been instrument in mainstreaming women by-passed the banking system.

Loan Repayments

One of the distinctive feature of the SHG – Bank Linkage programme has been very high on -time recovery. As on June 2005, the on-time recovery under SHG-Bank Linkage programme was 90% in commercial banks, 87%in RRBs and 86% in cooperative banks.

Programmme Impact

The major finding and recommendations of three studies on the impact of the SHG – Bank Likage Progrmme are summarized in Annexure III.

The main finding reveals that programme has:

Reduced the incidence of poverty through increase in income, and also enabled the poor to build assets and thereby reduce their vulnerability.

Enabled household that have access to it to spend more on education than non-client household. Families participating in the programme have reported betters school attendance and lower and drop out rates.

Empowered women by enhancing their contribution to household income, increasing the value of their assets and generally by giving them better control over decisions that affect their lives.

Reduced child mortality, improved maternal and the ability of the poor to combat disease through better nutrition and health - especially among women and children.

Contributed to reduced dependency on informal money lenders and other non – institutional sources.

Finally, it has space for different stakeholders to innovate, learn and replicate. As a result, some NGOs have added micro – insurance products to their portfolios, a couple and grain banks have successfully built into the SHG model in the Eastern Region. SHGs in some areas have employed local accountants explored by almost all for better management information system (MIS), accounting and internal controls.

Year	No.of SHGs financed		Bank loan (Rs.crore)		Per group loan (Rs.)	
	New	*Existing*	*New*	*Existing*	*New*	*Existing*
2003-04	361731	171669	1157.74	697.74	32005	40644
2004-05	539365	258092	1726.60	1267.60	32012	49114
2005-06	620109	344502	2330.45	2168.63	37581	62949

During the year 2005-06, the average loan provided to new SHGS was Rs. 37,581. On an average, per member loan work out to less than Rs. 4,000. Many believed that such loan amount are grossly inadequate fro pursuing any meaningful lived hood activity. Per capital loans in mature SHGs are increasing very gradually. It has also to be kept in view that members take short term loans of 3 to 6 month on many occasions and there can be more than one cycle of borrowing / repayment in one year.

Cost Recovery and Sustainability

It is important for banks to carefully work out their actual costs for SHG lending. While the SHG portfolio is often only small part of the total bank lending, and since the portfolio quality is good, it may be possible to reduce interest rates while ensuring recovery of costs. In the initial phase of the SHG movement, the group was formed by NGOs and hence start-up costs were low for banks. However, over the year banks have also evolved as SHGs. In the process, the start-up costs of group formation, etc. have devolved on the banks, impacting their pricing policies.

It is an accepted fact that banks will base their lending rate decisions on three important criteria – their cost of funds, transaction costs and the required spreads. While the sources of funds will determine the cost of funds is enabled. Banks need to recognize the cost elements involved in the decision-making process while approving credit linkage and in maintaining the accounts of the group, through the repayment period. Considering the small value of loans purveyed to groups, the rate of interest charged will also be in the lower slabs, thereby earning on thinly spread margins. The other major component of costs, viz., risk costs, is intrinsically low in SHG lending and, therefore, could play a limited role in pricing of credit products for SHGs. In this regard, the Committee perused the analysis made by the RBI on cost of transactions for small accounts. The same is indicated in Annexure IV.

Further, there is an element of indirect subsidy as presently NABARD supports the costs involved in formation and nurturing of SHGs up to the stage of credit linkage. This financial support is around Rs. 3,000 per SHG. The Ministry of rural Development (MoRD) has established a norm of Rs. 10,000 per group for the Swarnajayanti Gram swarojgar Yojana (SGSY) progrmme, Payable over four phases. If an additional one million SHGs have to be formed, the fund support would amount to nearly Rs. 1,000 crore, going by the MoRD norms. Accordingly, the Committee is of the view that the existing dispensation of subsidy in the form of a revolving fund initially and as capital subsidy for income generating activities in the second stage may not be sustainable with the exponential growth recently observed in the formation of groups under the programme.

At present, banks do not incur incremental costs for lending to SHGs, as it is done through the existing branch network. SHG lending to members has been reportedly at interest rate ranging between 15% and 24%. While this has been considered high, it is also reported that members borrow for short periods and do not feel the annualized burden of interest rates. Further, the interest income of SHGs is ploughed back into the corpus for lending and is beneficial to all members.

Regional Imbalances

The spread of the SHG - Bank linkage programme in different regions has been uneven on account of various factors like pro-active role of Governments, presence of well performing NGOs, socio -cultural factors, better performance of SHGs, etc. In March , 2001, 71% of the linked SHGs were from Southern Region Southern Region consisting of Andhra Pradesh, Karnataka, kerala and Tamil Nadu. The share of Southern Region has come down progressively over the year but it is still at 44% Many States such as Uttar Pradesh and Bihar with high incidence of poverty have shown poor performance under his programme. One of the major concerns was the slow progress of the SHG Bank linkage movement in the north-eastern and central parts of the country. It was even argued in some quarters that the SHG strategy was not suitable to the social configurations that prevailed in the north-east. As result of the special efforts made by NABARD, progress in the Regions / States where imbalances and low performance had been observed has picked up considerably, as detailed in following table.

Conclusion

The SHGs play a predominant role in transforming the rural economy. Microfinance fulfills their credit needs and helps the rural people their standard of living. Hence the SHGs are a new innovation in the field of economy by improving economic status in every household in the rural areas. SHGS

Development of cumulative nos. of SHGs financed

Region / State	**March 2001**	**March 2002**	**March 2003**	**March 2004**	**March 2005**	**March 2006**
NE Region	477	1,490	4,069	12,278	34,238	62,517
KBK Region	4,192	9,869	18,934	31,372	45,976	64,550
Orison	8,888	20,553	42,272	77,588	123,256	180,896
West Bengal	8,739	17,143	31,647	51,685	92,698	136,251
Bihar	4,592	3,957	8,161	16,246	28,015	48,138
Harahan	0*	4,198	7,765	12,647	21,531	28,902
Uttar Pradesh	23,152	33,114	53,696	79,210	119,648	163,439
Uttaranchal	0*	3,323	5,853	10, 908	14,043	16,060
Rajasthan	5,616	12,564	22,742	33,846	60,006	98,171
Himachal Pradesh	2,545	5,060	8,875	13,228	17,798	22,920
Madhya Pradesh	5,699	7,981	15,271	27,095	45,105	58,912
Chattisgarth	0*	3,763	6,763	9,769	18,569	29,504
Maharashtra	10,468	19,619	28,065	38, 535	71,146	131,470
Gujarat	4,929	9,496	13,875	15,974	24,712	34,160
All India	263,825	461,478	717,360	1,079,091	1,618,456	2,238,565

play a major role in women empowerment, micro-finance through bank linkages in collaboration with NGOs and contributes to the rural economy.

Reference

1. http://Megselhelp.go .in/fags.htm
2. http//egdif. Inc.in / shg.htm
3. http//www.rbi.org.in/scripts/FAQ.view.aspxinto?=7
4. http//www.state bank of India .com /view section.jsp?/ ang=osid=0,8,67
5. http//Andhra banks /scripts/ self help groups.aspx
6. http//negself help.gov.in/faqs.htm
7. http//www.thehindubusinesline.com /2002/10/22/stories/ 2002102202190500.htm
8. file://G:\2222\1111.htm

25

The Ethics of E-Banking

* M. N. Sivabalan and B. Narayanan.,

In this book we aim to open up the debate on the ethics of E-Banking by focusing on the activities of one case.

The aim to open up the debate on the ethics of E-Banking by focusing on the activities of one company in the wholesale banking sector. Press and academic attention to the subject of online banking tends to focus on consumer products (B2C) and the threat they pose to traditional branch operations if concerns about privacy and security can be adequately addressed. Writers have so far largely ignored ethical issues instigated by the enormous potential of the Internet in facilitating inter-bank transactions (B2B) in the wholesale market by reducing costs. Equally important is the development of the necessary management skills to ensure the sustained success of the new processes. Intertwined in the functional perspectives of marketing, human resource management and strategic planning are the ethical

*Head of the Department and Lecturer, Department of Commerce, Kurinji College of Arts and Science, Trichy

perspectives. One of the new management perspectives that will contribute to long-term success in electronic commerce is the associated moral responsibility of banking organisations and their stakeholders. Because electronic commerce is still developing and is rapidly changing, there is very little experience or agreement on its related ethical issues.

However, one of the few perspectives to emerge in the early stages of development is that of trust. In any transaction trust plays a key role. Face-to-face, transactions allow for the assessment of trust on the basis of physically observed information. This is not normally part of an electronic exchange. Trust may also be based on previous experience of successful transactions with predictable outcomes. This is not yet established in electronic commerce. Where there is no personal experience, the transaction partner might rely on reputation. Similarly, it is too early for electronic commercial activities to have built up a reputation in wholesale banking. The best the bank can hope for is to trade on its terrestrial reputation. High profile risks of electronic commerce such as security and privacy, the media and popular myths all act to confound the attempts of business to operate in cyberspace, not to mention the genuine imperfection of existing technology. Building high ethical standards and systems in which transaction partners can trust are imperative management requirements of the sustainable ethical enterprise.Beyond functional issues there are ethical ideals to which the responsible businessperson should aspire. New information and communication technologies have provided the structure for the new economy and a new economic order. Corporations often have more power and influence than public social institutions, their economic significance sometimes exceeding those of governments This level of power must bring with it responsibility. We can no longer look to governments or even religion to guide our activities – we must take responsibility ourselves, whether we are individuals, companies, non-governmental organisations or cyber- networks. There is a clear need for further serious efforts to raise ethical consciousness and ethical behaviour in the 'networked economy'.

FROM INITIAL TRADE TO E-BANKING

From Medieval Trade Fairs to eBanking

The development of money has been inextricably associated with the growth of trade and commerce. In Europe in the 1100s, rudimentary banking and foreign exchange institutions emerged as a direct product of the medieval trade fairs. Monetary exchange and banking systems then developed rapidly as foreign and domestic trade expanded exponentially following the onset of the industrial revolution. Although commodity-based money dates back to antiquity, money in its present primarily token form (i.e., money that does not exist in any physical form but takes the form of financial claims on banks and other financial institutions) has only assumed predominance during the past 100 years. International trade has grown significantly in the post-war period and with it the associated monetary flows. More recently, deregulation and globalization have led to a spectacular growth in the value of non-trade-related financial transactions. Every transaction whether trade- or non-trade-related gives rise to obligations that needs to be settled through a transfer of money between the parties involved. Settlement of non-trade-related and large value trade transactions is increasingly based on the electronic large value payment systems, which have been developed since the 1960s. Together this has led to a major expansion in payment and settlement systems which now handle payment volumes on a daily basis that collectively dwarf economic output in the main industrial countries. Electronic banking started with the use of proprietary software and private networks, but was not particularly popular until the emergence of the Web. The Internet and other global on-line networks have created new commercial opportunities for networked commerce. Development of an Internet electronic payment system provides opportunities for the creation of completely new sets of global and national trading relationships. The Internet offers the possibility of 'open systems' payment and settlement systems that operate in parallel to existing, more traditional bank-based networks. Electronic banking and electronic commerce are now seen as an inevitable aspect of financial services. The new global commercial market place permits goods to be ordered and paid for electronically irrespective of location. This requires new institutional structures as well as changes to existing outdated legal, commercial and ethical systems. The changes brought about by electronic commerce are similar in scope to those experienced when medieval trade fairs were established in Europe in the 11th century. The comparison is particularly apt, since that period saw the emergence of many of the banking institutional structures and payment instruments, which are now being reformed by the spread of E-Banking.

CASE STUDY (FOR EXAMPLE)

Case Study

The ABC Bank Group is active worldwide with around 1,500 branches and over 50,000 employees in more than 70 countries, including all the major financial centres. Ranked by total assets, market capitalisation and size of customer base, ABC Bank is one of Europe's leading banking groups. This case study focuses on Investment Banking, which is one of the bank's having four main divisions, and in particular the business area of foreign exchange trading run by the subsidiary XYZ. As noted earlier, press and scholarly attention to the subject of online banking has tended to focus on consumer products while the enormous potential of the Internet in facilitating inter-bank transactions by reducing costs has been largely ignored.There are increasing numbers of people in the world who are classified by banks as 'high net worth' meaning they have more than $300,000 in liquid assets. All banks are chasing this business, from which they can earn high fees for arranging and managing investments. It is estimated that XYZ earns some 40% of its profits from just 12% of capital usage in this area. There is absolutely no incentive for the bank to offer this group of customers web-based services that will cut out the banks intermediary and advisory role and hence reduce income by cannalising the existing lucrative business. Prospective electronic commerce projects in this business area therefore stand little chance of internal acceptance and the associated financial support. Projects which are likely to result in job losses within the bank through their automation of paper-based tasks also require support from sufficiently powerful factions if they are to go ahead, and tend to result in considerable tensions between areas of the bank reliant on traditional processing and the electronic commerce development teams. In order for an electronic commerce project to be financially supported it must demonstrate the potential to generate a positive return or be deemed necessary to keep up with competitor innovation in the area concerned, and 'not tread on too many toes internally'. One project that met these criteria was the development of a website which offered customers access to and information about the most important Internet applications concerned with investment banking. The service provides the latest news together with selected charts and useful links. Online trading in currencies is already possible, and additional transaction applications dealing with bonds, shares and derivatives will be online very shortly. Customers have their own personalised access to the world's capital markets online, and can see and respond to changes in global currency prices in real time. In this system customers are tapping into is the same as that used by XYZ for trading in the markets on its own account, in other words it is a multi-million pound investment in state of the art technology with the latest security protections. The bank has focused upon the foreign exchange transaction as its 'flagship' online product because such activity forms a natural starting point for capturing related business from customers. Very few international banking services do not involve the purchase or sale of currency, so from handling a customer's foreign exchange transactions it is relatively easy for XYZ to cross-sell other products or services. In many cases foreign exchange trading is offered to customers as a 'loss-leader' because of this potential. Although start-up costs are incurred in 'plumbing in' customers' systems to that of the bank, by settling transactions online the trading costs incurred by XYZ are more than halved. Fewer trading staff are required and the customer is 'locked in' through the system plumbing in process, so it is therefore more likely to use XYZ for subsequent related investment banking services. If the anticipated volume of trading is high enough, XYZ can offer to 'plumb in' a customer free of charge and still save money. However, the real potential of such online trading for XYZ does not lie merely in automation, but in the 'white-labelling' of the foreign exchange service. This means that the online trading facility is made available to the clients of XYZ's customers, branded as if the service actually belonged to the client. For example, if XYZ's customer is an Italian regional bank, then foreign exchange transactions can be made between XYZ and all the Italian bank's clients worldwide. From the end customer's perspective, the system they use for trading appears to belong to the Italian bank, because it will be 'badged' appropriately. The advantage to XYZ is the extension the facility affords to its customer base, as money laundering regulations prevent an investment bank from accepting transactions from individuals in this area, so the Italian bank performs a useful intermediary function. For the Italian bank the attraction is the ability to 'piggyback' access to an expensive and sophisticated online system, thereby incurring prestige but none of the set up costs.

A potential problem with this system lies in the allocation of credit limits Consequently, XYZ developed an 'add on' system which allows the Italian bank to set appropriate sub-limits for each of its customers that are using the system. The system was developed in consultation with XYZ's Credit Managers and designed to replicate both the qualitative and quantitative judgements that were previously made manually. The expensive Credit Manager role within investment banks is now threatened because of the success of the online system, which is now being applied to XYZ's own account trading.

ETHICAL OVERVIEW

Consideration of the ethics of E-Business has tended to focus on areas relating to the fragility of information of the ethics of eBusiness has tended to focus on areas relating to the fragility of information collected and held electronically and transferred via computer-mediated communication. These include privacy information about individuals, accuracy of information, ownership of information and intellectual property and accessibility of information held. These perspectives focus very much on the individual consumer and disregard the significant area of electronic commerce that is business to business. In theB2B case privacy based issues around information control are less critical at the personal level. By looking at a business to business case, we identify the moral precepts relevant to the case which may form a basis for further consideration of ethics in this area. These relate to: freedom of choice; transparency; facilitating fraud (ethical/illegal activities of others). There are likely to be other issues which would have risen from different sets of circumstances. Hence, while we think that these issues may have wider currency, we urge continued, systematic consideration of relevant ethical issues in this context. In this section we refer to some ethical theories to help identify rigorously observed notions of right and wrong. In particular, we identify discourse ethics as a potentially useful perspective to apply to electronic commerce. First though, on the positive side, the reduction of costs means that organisations can improve service and potentially generate more profits for shareholders and job security for employees. On the other hand, job losses are the means by which costs are cut and this has social implications for those in the firing line. The displacement of job opportunities away from face-to-face and back-office service roles to information system professionals is a common feature of the electronic commerce revolution. Employment issues aside, however, there are also positive aspects of online trading for business customers and in turn consumers. As the case study points out, access to expensive online systems is enabled by 'piggybacking'. From an ethical point of view, this means that high quality systems are not held by an exclusive group but made available to those other than the wealthiest, henceopening up fair access. Access to sophisticated systems comes with a catch. The need for 'plumbing in' of software and hardware, which means that business customers are locked into XYZ's facilities, is a form of restriction of free choice. When we buy one product from a certain supplier, we do not normally expect that this means our future choices of supplier are restricted in practice. The key ethical issue here is that the business customer should be quite clear that there are significant implications for future freedom of choice of suppliers of foreign exchange and related services. In much the same way that Microsoft has been criticised for implicit locking in of customers to its software, electronic commerce through reliance on customising computer access to the specific service encourages, even forces, the user to come back to a supplier once used. As a customer -whether a business customer or consumer - once time and energy has been put into setting up the electronic access, psychological choice for alternatives are removed. This is both a clever marketing play, and a somewhat devious capturing of business if the customer is not entirely clear about the extent of commitment which they are making. It is in this respect that transparency is so critical for ethical eBanking. Cyberspace offers fantastic opportunities for disguise. This can be used for overcoming prejudices but also for misleading either customer for supplier as to who you are and what you are offering. Clearly, outright fraudulent activities are to be condemned, but how far is it ethically acceptable for electronic commerce activities to convey ambiguously, by hint or absence of clarification, what it is they are offering? The white labelling aspect of our case study is illustrative here. Just like purchasing 'own label' products in a supermarket that are not actually made by the supermarket, there is an issue of misrepresentation. Branding theory demonstrates that we are drawn to products and producers that we recognise and trust. In the case of a packet of soap powder or cereal, there may be no real consequence other than discomfort at having been mislead. In cyberspace transactions, the consumer will be operating with significant capital as if they were dealing with the institution they know and trust when in fact it is a third party. Given the concerns about privacy and fragility of information mentioned above this could also have worrying consequences for the party whose details are gathered by XYZ in this case.

Five constraints for the use of this theory in practice:

1. Autonomous articulation of need-claims;
2. Bracketing of power differentials of the participants;
3. Transparency;
4. Participants should have empathetic ability in relation to different roles;
5. There should be comprehensive inclusion of all who will be affected.

How much responsibility do businesses have to prevent their products and services being used in the pursuit of illegal activity? In the US, for example, the selling and marketing of handguns emphasising the fact that the grip does not reveal fingerprints has been questioned in ethical terms. The Swiss banking system of confidentiality has repeatedly been challenged when criminal investigations are underway. XYZ is now enabling money laundering. While the bank itself can claim that it has not dirtied its hands, it is by implication responsible in some way perspectives that the business of business is to maximise profit, are no longer acceptable in the light of limited government power to deal with the global welfare issues of which business is an inherent part. Social contract perspectives on new roles and responsibilities of business organisations encourage responsibility for actions and consequences in the B2B and B2C contexts.

In the XYZ case the issues are not limited to the B2B perspectives because of the apparent direct link to, for example, the Italian bank's customers. Here we see the features of eBanking contributing to increasing depersonalisation, although corresponding standardisation of credit decisions. Ethically speaking, adding automatically applied rules to the allocation of credit limits can be viewed in two main ways. First, Kantian theory is concerned with the duty of the individual to act in a way that is universalisable, reversible and demonstrates respect for persons. In practice this means that rules of action can be identified which are absolute and independent of context or consequences. Furthermore, utilitarianism is concerned with following that course of action that maximises the greatest good for the greatest number: rule utilitarianism is where the rule applied results consistently in the maximisation of utility. Hence, according to both Kantianism and rule utilitarianism, rather than allowing favouritism, poor judgement, even corruption and bribery to determine credit limits between the banker and the customer, standard, automated procedures mean that everyone gets the same treatment. Whether this treatment is just depends on the quality of the rules applied.

Second, taking the personal relationship out of responses to credit limit applications has the effect of dehumanising transactions in the banking sector. A client's relationship with a bank or credit manager can be established over years of loyal customer commitment. Boiling this down to boxes ticked and computer-generated numbers would, according to an ethic of care, result in the loss of the development of individual relationships.

CONCLUSION

The issues raised in this article and the ethical perspectives which will emerge over the next few years in relation to electronic commerce require earnest responses by the eBanking and other sectors. We have proposed discourse ethics theory as a useful source of guidance for those seeking to act ethically in cyberspace. Legislation can only go some of the way to settling standards and guidelines, but the borderless nature of transactions is more acute still in electronic commerce than in the globalised marketplace generally. No law will reach all the electronic interfaces on which transactions will take place. More effective measures will be those that come from the pressures of professionalism and high technical and ethical standards. These take time to develop, and urgently require input from scholars to help identify and deal with ethical issues in electronic commerce.

26

Electronic Payment Systems in Bank an Overview

* Dr. T. Duraipandi

Introduction

In all segments of payment systems, electronic payments are growing rapidly. Electronic payment systems are proliferating in banking, healthcare and on-line markets. Electronic payment systems and e-commerce has intricately linked, given that online consumers must pay for product and services. Payment and settlement process is a potential bottleneck in the fast moving electronic commerce environment if we rely on conventional payment methods such as cash, cheque, and bank drafts or bills of exchange.[1] Customers are looking for efficient self-service modes of interacting with the bank. Therefore, instead of customers going the bank, the bank goes to the customers. Customers have the choice of interacting with the bank "anytime, anywhere, any way" (i.e. 24-hour banking).

* Dr. T. Duraipandi, Reader in Commerce, Kongu Arts and Science College, Erode.

Innovative Technological Developments

In this modern age of information revolution, many tasks can be achieved with better results by applying an appropriate technology. Computers are widely used in many business houses and almost all the key branches of leading banks make daily transaction daily through the computer. The Electronic fund transfer system facilitates the transfer of fund between individuals or organizations through the bank's "lock-box programme" or "Electronic mailbox" is used by the bank to ensure "Security" i.e. to maintain secrecy of the customer's account and information leading to him.

These days the financial industry is developing ways to transfer funds without creating a cheque or some other paper document for each payment. This reduces payment system operating cost. In many countries, customers can also get cash sitting at home through Electronic cash and other Banking services like Credit cards, Debit cards, ATM cards and smart cards etc.

Electronic Payment systems in the Global Banking Scenario

Over the past decade, the global financial system has been undergoing a tremendous change. It resulted in enhancement of cross border capital force in turn this has necessitated Financial Institutions to comply with international standards of accounting and coverage to common prudential norms. The implication of regulatory and monetary authority has become too difficult in India.

This phenomenon has resulted in greater competition between Banks and Non Banking Financial Institution (NBF). the growth of Banking and Non Banking Sectors have increased the complexity of International Banking and capital market operations. This in turn broadens the product range and emphasis a greater operational flexibility due to stringent capital adequacy norms. The capital market operations have become dominant part of banking reforms.

Changes in the Banking Scenario after Globalisation

As the activities of banks diversify, it is essential to offer new products such as factoring, leasing, hire purchase, term lending and investment banking etc. This will help the banks to make better use of funds and match the maturities with their assets and liabilities. Financial liberalization and bank investments must not be restricted to just government securities. Banks must also have allowed being more active in the capital market in terms of being able to raise its own capital. This need would arise as banks increase the level of activity and need to adhere to capital adequacy norms.

The Salient Features of Payment Systems in Bank

E-Commerce

E-Commerce is the name given to business process of selling your products, goods and services over the web in its simplest form. It allows your company's product catalogue have been hosted on a web server so that customers and potential customers can visit the web site to see what you have to sell and then place orders.

The Majority of e-commerce sites that sell to general consumers ask you to pay for the items through a credit card and so they present forms that can be safely and securely capture this information and performs automatic credit card authorization without human invention. India has taken longer period to recognize the need for adoption of Electronic Data Interchange (EDI) especially in the area of international trade. It was in 1991 that the Government of India started the economic liberalisation policy with the objective of opening up the economy and integrating it with global economy.

Some of the banks Electronic Data Interchange are specific to customhouse in different cities, should have connected for duty collection and draw back payments with appropriate linkage with customs.

E – Banking

The e-banking revolutions has fundamentally, changed the business of banking by scaling borders and bringing about new opportunities. In India also, it has strongly influenced the of strategies business considerations. It must be noted that E-banking provides many benefits to customers and banks it also aggravates traditional banking risks. Compared to developed countries, developing countries face many impediments that affect the successful implementation of e-banking initiatives.

Electronic Fund Transfer (EFT)

Electronic fund transfer is a scheme introduced by the RBI to help to banks after the customer money transfer from one account of a bank to any other account of any other bank. The number of benefits from the operations are:

- The money transfer takes place in just one day.
- There is no danger of instrument being lost in transfer
- The EFT charges are lower than Demand Draft charges

However, in India EFT scheme is not as successful as it should be because the customers are not fully aware of these schemes benefits and its significance.

Credit / Debit / Smart cards

In India, credit card operations of bank have been deregulated. Banks with minimum net worth less than the 100 crores need to take prior approval of Reserve Bank of India (RBI) for connecting this business except setting up of subsidiaries. The control of an issue of credit cards and recovery of dues, banks have been advised to adopt certain additional safeguards in the matter of recovery of over dues sharing the information on credit card product and profitable lines not only credit cards, but also Debit Cards in the globalization concept.

Automated Teller Machine (ATM)

ATM facility has been introduced through Indian Bank's Association shared network scheme and through by bank's own set up at strategic location. A number of benefits have been received after its establishment. Now a days, it is more popular because it provides 24 hours service. Due to success of ATM service, more Public sector banks have joined hands to share among themselves.

Internet

Internet is now established as the fastest growing communications medium in the world and becoming a primary source of development for various business organisations, particularly industries in the service sector. The World Wide Web is proving to be most cost effective way of advertising. There are currently well over 50 million internet user and growth exceeding predictions.

The internet is media of future and huge investments is currently being made by business organisations and individuals to be connected to the web.

Internet and e-commerce as being an integral part of their corporate strategic framework for this year internet survey conducted in 68 cities/town in India January 2001 (accounting for over 92 per cent of the total internet users in the country) by Nasscom on internet Usage Trends, indicates that more than 200 cities and town in India have internet connectivity. The capital cities (New Delhi and other state capitals) today account for 79 per cent internet connections across the country. Finally, they have estimated that India will have 35 million net users by the year 2004. The number of internet subscribers in India will record the sixth fastest rate of growth in the Asia Pacific region.

Banks Entry into Insurance Business

As part of the integration of financial services world over, new opportunities have emerged for banks enter into the area of Insurance. Insurance Regulatory and Development Authority (IRDA) Act 1999 has been set up with statutory powers to function as the sector regular for insurance in India.

Role of Private Banks

After Globalization, the role of banks changing very much in respect of deposits, loans and other services. Private Banks has more cutting edges over public sector banks in deposit mobilization and creation of more innovative schemes. Public sector banks cannot compete in this area because of its rigid regulations and procedures.

Standard Chartered Bank, HDFC, and ICICI bank etc., become more popular within a short span of time due to their effective functioning. Now a days new package schemes are being introduced constantly by private banks to attract the customers in all possible sources. It is made possible because of their large capital and flexibility in making decisions.

Retail banking system have been introduced in respect of consumer loans such as, Housing Finance, Educational loans etc. Special attention has been paid to customer care in the popular private banks to attract customers more easily in their network. The lists of customer services are extended day by day in the private banks depending upon the customer expectations.

Foreign Banks

The impact of Globalisation large number of foreign banks is making the entry in India to make use of their large resources in our wider market. They become very popular due to their technology and large resources. Because of these factors, competition has become very popular due to their technology and large resources.

Due to these factors competitions has become more severe for our private and public sector banks. Up gradation of technology and efficient operations are the key issues to be followed by our private and public sector banks to retain their existence in the market.

Factors Contributing to Improved Customer Satisfaction

In electronic cashless payments, the factors contributing to improved customer satisfaction include:

- Easy, Simple and less expensive systems are always better.
- One Common payment card system implemented.
- Sufficient disclosure of information on each payment system are introducing flexibility in the system.

Conclusion

Since payment systems can be seen as the circulatory systems for countries, there is the need for making payments system more sophisticated, so electronic payment systems are widely used in banks. The emerging area of cashless payments include, e-cash, electronic cheques, smart cards and credit cards. The Challenge for the future is to come to the right vision of how electronic payment systems will improve customer satisfaction.

References

Books

- Ravi Kalakota Andrew. B.Whinston, "Frontiers of Electroniic commerce" Addision Westley,1996,London.
- Pete Loghin, Paul A.Murphy, 'Electronic commerce, Jaice Publishin House,1999.

Journals:

- IBA Bulletin, January 2001.
- Advertising Marketing, May 1,1999.